ph
22.1.07

Health of Looked After Children and Young People

D0531417

Edited by
Kathy Dunnett
with
Sharon White, Janet Butterfield,
and Imelda Callowhill

'I warmly encourage you to buy, read and refer to this book. Following on from Kathy's success in establishing Champions for Children and Young People in Care she and her colleagues have now put together this most useful, comprehensive and well evidenced text on their health. The book will be invaluable in lobbying for the high quality health services looked after children and young people need and deserve.'

Earl of Listowel

RHP

Russell House Publishing

First published in 2006 by:
Russell House Publishing Ltd.
4 St. George's House
Uplyme Road
Lyme Regis
Dorset DT7 3LS

Tel: 01297-443948
Fax: 01297-442722
e-mail: help@russellhouse.co.uk

A catalogue record for this book is available from the British Library.

British Library Cataloguing-in-publication Data:

ISBN: 1-903855-83-7, 978-1-903855-83-6

Typeset by TW Typesetting, Plymouth, Devon
Printed by Cromwell Press, Trowbridge

About Russell House Publishing

RHP is a group of social work, probation, education and youth and community work practitioners and academics working in collaboration with a professional publishing team.

Our aim is to work closely with the field to produce innovative and valuable materials to help managers, trainers, practitioners and students.

We are keen to receive feedback on publications and new ideas for future projects.

For details of our other publications please visit our website or ask us for a catalogue. Contact details are on this page.

Contents

Section Four: Special Considerations

Preface

Kathy Dunnett

Health is everyone's responsibility, and there is an urgent need for us all to be working together to achieve robust and timely health advice and action when needed by looked after children and young people. This book is intended to cross the boundaries between the disciplines and to be read by all professionals who work with them.

It strives to:

- Help **designated health professionals** to consider different approaches to common problems. To be particularly supportive to designated professionals new in post.

- Help **social workers** to develop their skills, knowledge and understanding, particularly partnership working with health professionals.

- Help those health professionals, such as **school nurses**, **health visitors** and **general practitioners** who have wider areas of responsibility, to have a greater understanding of the difficulties that looked after young people face in accessing health care, and how their involvement can be essential in facilitating services for them.

- Provide background information and guidance to those **trainers** who are not specialists in this area but might be called on to work with carers and children's service professionals.

- Enable **policy makers** to understand better the dilemmas that frontline workers have to face on health and access of health care and the importance of partnership working and joint policies and protocols.

- Give **students** a convenient source of reference on the health issues for looked after children.

- Give support and guidance to **carers** and all **children's service professionals** when they are trying to develop their skills and improve the care or services they provide to looked after children.

The context of care

The health of looked after children can be challenging, as children and young people move placements, health histories become lost, young people refuse health care and carers and professionals become confused about issues such as consent and confidentiality. Hopefully, this book will prove helpful in clarifying some of these problems, and encourage local partnerships to consider ways forward to address them.

The document, *Promoting the Health of Looked After Children* (DoH, 2002) is perceived to be a helpful one in this regard, but needs urgent enactment across the country, as in some areas these issues are still largely unaddressed. Carers will need the support of multi-disciplinary negotiated health policies and protocols, mandatory training and a network of professionals to access support, advice and help for a range of issues.

Continuity of care

The aim of the book is to provide the reader with a deeper understanding of the difficulties of providing health care to this highly vulnerable group of children and young people. Health care should not, and must not, as it has been in the past, be a tick box exercise in an abundance of forms and papers that surround the child in the care system. The Health Assessment can be an important measure of the health of a child, but the most important issue to consider is continuity of health care. Achieving the Health Assessments is an important target, and figures are collected by all the local authorities, but if they are done in isolation on each occasion, with no reference to previous health plans, the reality is that issues identified from previous assessments will continually remain unmet, and the Health Assessment will essentially be worthless. Accessing and providing continuous care for children in care is a much more complex challenge than it is often perceived to be; Figure 1 on the next page illustrates how complex health and health care can be. Hopefully, this book will enable those studying and working in the field to better understand the complexities of health for children in care.

The structure of this book

This book has been divided into four sections:

- The Wider Context
- Health for Looked After Children: Everyone's Business
- Health Issues
- Special Considerations

Key references are highlighted in each chapter. Each chapter stands alone and can be read alone. It is not anticipated that the book will necessarily be read from cover to cover; the reader will find that they are able to 'dip in' and find the appropriate information as required, and thus this book will act as an easy reference guide. To enable each chapter to stand alone and be read alone there is a small amount of natural repetition within some chapters. Some of the health issues were picked out as areas of particular concern with children and young people generally, probably more problematic within care because of a number of difficulties – such as levels of engagement, relationships, confidentiality.

About the authors

All the authors have expertise in their chosen field and have between them a wealth of experience.

The chapters in this book have all been written in the authors' own words, in their own style and reflect their own opinions. The views expressed do not necessarily reflect that of the editors or the publisher, but it is hoped that the book will be a basis not only to enhance knowledge, but as a basis for future debate around the further development of the health services for looked after children.

The aspiration of this book

We wanted this book to come alive, and for the reader to truly consider the difficult plight of the children and young people involved. In many of the chapters you will find short case studies to illustrate or explain a situation. In all cases the names have been changed to protect these young people and to preserve confidentiality.

The completion of this book, I hope is not an end, but a beginning, a beginning of national agreements for health for looked after children, national standards and a genuine intention to facilitate excellent health care for looked after children wherever they may be placed in the country. Funding should not be an issue when it comes to addressing the health needs of children and young people, only common sense, timely and appropriate care given when it is needed, locally and effortlessly. Remember:

The healthiest choice must be the easiest choice.

(World Health Organisation, 1986)

References

Department of Health (2002) *Promoting the Health of Looked After Children*. London: The Stationery Office.

World Health Organisation (1986) *Ottawa Charter for Health Promotion*. Geneva: WHO.

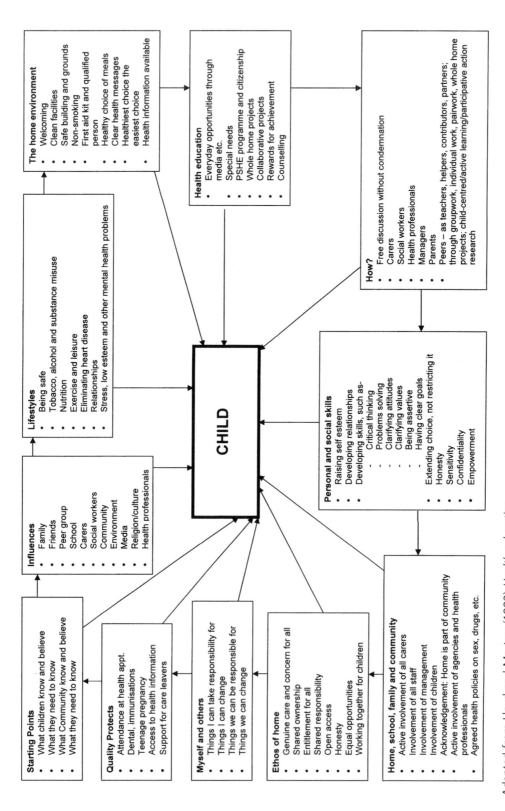

The home environment
- Welcoming
- Clean facilities
- Safe building and grounds
- Non-smoking
- First aid kit and qualified person
- Healthy choice of meals
- Clear health messages
- Healthiest choice the easiest choice
- Health information available

Health education
- Everyday opportunities through media etc.
- Special needs
- PSHE programme and citizenship
- Whole home projects
- Collaborative projects
- Rewards for achievement
- Counselling

How?
- Free discussion without condemnation
- Carers
- Social workers
- Health professionals
- Managers
- Parents
- Peers – as teachers, helpers, contributors, partners; through groupwork, individual work, pairwork, whole home projects; child-centred/active learning/participative action research

Lifestyles
- Being safe
- Tobacco, alcohol and substance misuse
- Nutrition
- Exercise and leisure
- Eliminating heart disease
- Relationships
- Stress, low esteem and other mental health problems

Personal and social skills
- Raising self esteem
- Developing relationships
- Developing skills, such as-
  - Critical thinking
  - Problems solving
  - Clarifying attitudes
  - Clarifying values
  - Being assertive
  - Having clear goals
- Extending choice, not restricting it
- Honesty
- Sensitivity
- Confidentiality
- Empowerment

CHILD

Influences
- Family
- Friends
- Peer group
- School
- Carers
- Social workers
- Community
- Environment
- Media
- Religion/culture
- Health professionals

Starting Points
- What children know and believe
- What they need to know
- What Community know and believe
- What they need to know

Quality Protects
- Attendance at health appt.
- Dental, immunisations
- Teenage pregnancy
- Access to health information
- Support for care leavers

Myself and others
- Things I can take responsibility for
- Things I can change
- Things we can be responsible for
- Things we can change

Ethos of home
- Genuine care and concern for all
- Shared ownership
- Entitlement for all
- Shared responsibility
- Open access
- Honesty
- Equal opportunities
- Working together for children

Home, school, family and community
- Active involvement of all carers
- Involvement of all staff
- Involvement of management
- Involvement of children
- Acknowledgement: Home is part of community
- Active involvement of agencies and health professionals
- Agreed health policies on sex, drugs, etc.

Adapted from Lloyd and Morton (1992) *Health education*

Foreword

Not overlooked any more

In the year of the millennium, a small group of optimists, committed to tackling health inequalities, were working in a London health authority (Caan, 2000a). We identified three groups of young people where the greatest inequalities were emerging, and where there was scope for interventions early in the lifecourse, before illness became entrenched (Caan, 2000b). The three groups chosen were *unaccompanied refugee children*, *children in the youth justice system* and *children in local authority care*. As soon as we began investigating their health needs, it became apparent that these three populations overlapped – the distinction was that we knew where to find the looked after children (Caan, 2002a).

This book will enable professionals from many backgrounds to engage effectively with children in care, across a range of ages and care settings. The editor Kathy Dunnett took a leading national role in setting up *Champions for Children and Young People in Care*, a group for all practitioners interested in looked after children, and a powerful advocate for improved services. The contributors deal with both practical and policy issues around delivering that health improvement.

Children who spend substantial periods in local authority care are likely to have had lacerating experiences such as prolonged abuse, severe neglect, early bereavement, incapacitating parental illness or desperate flight from danger as an unaccompanied refugee. During their time in care, the mental and physical health of young people often deteriorates further, and they are likely to enter adulthood with few educational qualifications or life skills (Caan, 2002b). Many children move frequently between different foster placements, or go on the run (which puts them at grave risk from living rough or from exploitation by adults). Residential care may be far from their home neighbourhood and in cultures of poor care the alienation of young people may be reinforced by low expectations among both staff and residents. Leaving care as teenagers they are at high risk of becoming jobless, friendless and homeless (Laming, 1997). We adult citizens are their 'corporate parents', even if we are unaware of what local social services are doing on our behalf.

In the United Kingdom, there have been a number of policy initiatives that included children in public care (in England: *Quality Protects*, 1998, in Scotland: *Scotland's Children*, 1995) especially the first attempt at an inter-agency strategy, *Promoting the Health of Looked After Children* (DoH, 2002). This book deals with frequent health concerns like mental health and sexual health, and the need for primary health care to engage fully with these young patients. The level of unrecognised or unmet need is high, for example one recent study found that 97 per cent of children in residential care had emotional or mental health problems (Jamieson, 2006). This book is likely to contribute to the current imperative, to improve the skills of the workforce in contact with socially excluded young people (DfES, 2006a). Ignorance and fear have led to much media and political demonisation of young people at the margins of our society (Caan, 2005). Thankfully, the

Children's Commissioner for England has taken a lead in opposing the scapegoating of 'adolescents as the problem', instead standing up for the human rights of all young people (Aynsley-Green, 2006).

The *Children's National Service Framework*, with its grounding in the National Health Service, and *Every Child Matters*, grounded in local government, have set good standards for all children's services, including children in 'special circumstances' (not with their birth family). In particular, the Children's Act 2004 demands a much higher level of co-operation ('integration') across all professions and agencies involved with a child, especially one that has needed 'safeguarding'. The Outcomes Framework for *Every Child Matters* will highlight where partnerships are making good progress and also where there are gaps in services. Planning care for vulnerable children benefits from a sense of 'purposeful foresight', seeing the child within the long-term context of their growth and potential (Caan, 2004). A fine example of foresight was the launch on 1 February 2006 of the Scottish Healthy Care Network. This included the vital voice of young people with first hand experience of the care system.

New types of service are already beginning to engage more effectively with children in public care (e.g. certain 'Pathfinder' Children's Trusts). Her Majesty's Government are now planning widespread re-design of all health care services in the community (DoH, 2006). Who can say how changes like 'GP Commissioning' will impact on looked after children? Nurses in the School Health Research Group (Caan, 2003) first chose research on the well being of children in care as a priority, and the Department of Health's wider Social Care Research Group also put a premium on gaining a better understanding of these children (Caan, 2006). Readers of this book may wish to contribute to the imminent *Consultation* on a national strategy for looked after children (DfES, 2006b). The new Green Paper on the care system (Smith, 2006) should benefit greatly from thoughtful, informed debate!

Woody Caan AcSS FRIPH
Professor of Public Health,
Anglia Ruskin University,
Chelmsford.
February 2006.

References

Aynsley-Green, A. interviewed by Owen, G. (2006) Child Tsar: Anti-Yob Crackdown is a Human Rights Abuse. *The Mail on Sunday*. January 29th: 9.

Caan, W. (2000a) Foreword. *Health Inequalities. Poverty and Policy*. London: Academy of Learned Societies for the Social Sciences. viii.

Caan, W. (2000b) Good for Mental Health: An Academy for the Social Sciences. *Journal of Mental Health*. 9: 117-9.

Caan, W. (2002a) Your Shout: *Mental Health Promotion Update*. DoH 3: 16-7.

Caan, W. (2002b) GP Involvement in Child Protection. *British Journal of General Practice*. 52: 678.

Caan, W. (2003) The Agenda For School Health Research. *On Target for Health* conference handbook. London: CPHVA.

Caan, W. (2004) Framework Shows a New Vision of Health, in Life. *BMJ*. 329: 1239.

Caan, W. (2005) Random Drug Testing in Schools. *British Journal of General Practice*. 55: 637.

Caan, W. (2006) Building Capacity for Social Care Research. *Social Care Research Capacity: 'A Wider Strategy' Revisited*. conference papers, London: DoH.

Department for Education and Skills (2006a) Options for Excellence: Review of the Social Care Workforce. *http://www.everychildmatters.gov.uk/* January 27th.

Department for Education and Skills (2006b) *Looked After Children Strategy Consultation* (in press).

Department of Health (2002) *Promoting the Health of Looked After Children*. London: DoH.

Department of Health (2006) *Our Health, Our Care, Our Say: A New Direction for Community Services*. London: DoH.

Jamieson, M. (2006) Launch of the Scottish Healthy Care Network. *Healthy Care Conference* circulated papers, Perth.

Laming, H. for the Social Services Inspectorate (1997) *When Leaving Home Is Also Leaving Care*. London: DoH.

Smith R. (2006) Looked-after Children: Debate on Care Green Paper Heats Up. *http://www.childrennow.co.uk/news/* February 1st.

About the Contributors

Paula Bell is a Registered Nurse and achieved a BSc (Hons.) in Community Health Care (Health Visiting) at South Bank University. She has spent over 20 years working with children and families in Brent, North West London. She spent 13 years as a qualified school nurse and six years as a health visitor before moving to work as the Designated Nurse for Looked After Children in Brent. She has just completed a Post Graduate Diploma to qualify as a Counsellor. She would like to thank her husband Phil and her colleagues for their invaluable support.

Andy Betts achieved an MA and a BA (Hons.) at De Montfort University (Bedford) and was previously employed as a homeless co-ordinator of a young people's information and counselling service, which he later went on to manage. For the past three years he has been employed as the County Drugs and Alcohol Co-ordinator for Hertfordshire Youth Service, with the prime objective to oversee the delivery of drug education to young people in an informal setting, across the spectrum of the service, whilst also acting as a support role to many voluntary organisations, he is a member of the Hertfordshire Drug Education Forum, with whom he is a registered trainer and educator.

Thanks to the Youth Service for their support, especially Lucy Bailey and Chris McNicol for proof reading, Steve Emmerson, Bernie Talbot for line-manager support and an extra special thanks to my wife Jacinthe and daughter Freya.

Deborah Bone RMN is a skilled mental health practitioner with a wealth of experience working with vulnerable adolescents. Deborah has completed training in neurolinguistic programming and human givens psychotherapy and uses a variety of these skills when working with young people and professionals. Deborah is currently working as an emotional and mental health advisor within a primary care trust in Hertfordshire.

John Brown has worked in Children's Social Care for over 25 years, mainly as a manager in children's services in Newcastle and Gateshead Councils. He was the North East's Regional Development Worker for DfES and was based at Social Services Inspectorate and Government Office North East. In that capacity, he led the regional support systems for Multi-Agency Looked After Partnerships (MALAPs) and supported the development of the North East's Regional Commissioning Unit for out of authority children.

Janet Butterfield qualified as a State Registered Nurse (RGN) in 1978 and for the past 18 years has predominantly been in community work with vulnerable children and young people in Leeds. During this time she obtained a BSc (Hons.) in Community Health Care Nursing (School Nursing). She has worked within the School Nursing Service for 14 years and latterly held the post of city-wide Clinical Development Facilitator for the service before moving into her current post as Designated Nurse for Looked After Children and Young

People, leading the city-wide Health Team. Janet is on the executive committee of Champions for Children and Young People in Care.

Woody Caan was appointed the first Professor of Public Health at Anglia Ruskin University in 2002. Improving the 'life chances' of young people with special needs, with problematic alcohol or drug use, with experiences of early adversity or social exclusion, and those with mental health needs, drives his work in public health. These concerns all come together, in promoting the health of looked after children. He was elected a Practitioner Academician of the Academy of Social Sciences for his work in the community sector, and is a Fellow of the Royal Institute of Public Health. Since finishing as chair of the interprofessional School Health Research Group, he has chaired the Social Care Research group for the NHS Research and Development Forum. He is a member of the editorial board of the Journal of Public Mental Health and of the national working group seeking to 'define' Academic Public Health. His latest collaborations involve an 'integrated' service for children with complex disabilities, an alcohol service for families affected by domestic violence, and a 'pathfinder' children's trust.

Imelda Callowhill MSc, Dip HE, RHV, RGN is an experienced nurse both in acute and primary care settings and has worked within primary care since 1994 primarily as a health visitor working with population groups from areas of deprivation. Moving on to a role as lead health visitor her main responsibility was to raise standards and to target services to those most in need in line with the government agenda. The role developed further to Lead Nurse for Children's Services again with the same brief but wider. Looked after children and young people delivered a greater challenge and in Jan 2001, Imelda took up responsibility for this client group as Lead Nurse for Looked after Children, developing services both locally and sharing her innovative projects on a national level with other nurse colleagues. Imelda is currently employed by Southend PCT, Interim Children's Services Manager, Nurse Member of the joint Board and Executive Committee at Southend PCT, Vice Chair of the National Forum 'Champions for Children and Young People in Care' and a co opted nurse member of BAAF.

Helen Chambers is a principal officer in the Children's Development Department at National Children's Bureau – Promoting Children's Health and Well Being. She is the lead officer for the Healthy Care Programme, and is responsible for the Healthy Care series of publications and the carers' magazine *Carers Can!* Helen has an MSc in Health Promotion and worked as a health promotion specialist in various areas in the South West of England centred on the health of vulnerable young people, particularly looked after children. Her previous experience includes work in higher education, youth service, the voluntary sector and media.

Mary Cooper R.D. has worked for the majority of her dietetic career in nutrition and health promotion across all age groups. Now she is heavily involved in school nutrition and the healthy schools programme, and working on care of children in looked after settings via improved service provision and staff training. She was previously involved with research on food provision in child care.

Dr Jeremy Cox MB, BS has been a GP in the home counties since 1988. He is a member of the Local Medical Committee, and a Lead in his Primary Care Trust for Children's Services as well as being the Named Doctor for Child Protection. Jeremy is particularly interested in services for vulnerable children and is keen to develop these locally. His family is important to him and he enjoys cooking and skiing.

Kathy Dunnett currently manages Hertfordshire's Pilot Children's Trust. Previous to this she was Looked After Children's Nurse in Hertfordshire for seven years. She has a BSc in Health and Social Care and a BSc (Hons.) in Nursing and qualified further with a post-graduate diploma in Child Studies from Kings College in London. She has been part of the DoH's NSF Children in Special Circumstances Group, a member of the national School Nurse Professional Committee with the CPHVA, a member of Young Minds Professional Committee, and their Management Committee. Kathy has just had a health chapter published in the *RHP Companion to Foster Care* (Russell House Publishing).

Wendy Gill has had a career in child care social work spanning 25 years. She has specialised in adoption and fostering, working both within the voluntary and public sector. Currently Wendy is a policy and development officer for Hertfordshire County Council.

Liam Hughes, MA, MSC (Econ), MBA, CQSW is the Chief Executive of East Leeds PCT, which hosts child health services for the City of Leeds. He was previously strategic director for early years, youth and community and social services for Bradford. He trained in psychiatric social work at the LSE and Maudsley Hospital, worked in community mental health in South London, and managed community care in Barnet. He joined Kirklees Council in 1985, becoming Chief Social Services Officer in 1990. He has been an adviser to the Department of Health, the Social Exclusion Unit and the DfES, and currently chairs the sub-regional managed clinical network for child health and maternity for West Yorkshire, North and East Yorkshire and North Lincolnshire.

With thanks to Sharon White and Janet Butterfield, designated nurses, Jean Baker Director of Children's Services, Dr Sharon Yellin, Consultant in Public Health for Children and Young People, Dr Mandy Thomas, Medical Director, and Professor David Cottrell Professor of Child and Adolescent Psychiatry, for their own support and the commitment of their teams.

Christine Jackson-Hayward BA, BSc Hons., is a registered nurse, health visitor and specialist community practitioner, who has worked with children and their families throughout her professional career. Recently she has focused on those children who are in need until her career pathway brought her into the working arena of children in local authority care.

Barbara Mary was a long time senior clinical medical officer in Child Health in Leeds, latterly half time consultant community paediatrician. She was the medical advisor to adoption and fostering and designated doctor for looked after children. She is totally indebted to the health team for looked after children and young people in Leeds.

Heather Miller currently works for Trent Strategic Health Authority as Policy Manager for children's services, CAMHS and learning disability. Heather has a broad ranging experience including work in both acute and primary care within health, Social Services, higher education and the private sector.

As a qualified Counsellor with experience and knowledge of the challenges faced by looked after children in an educational setting, Heather holds a particular interest in improving services for looked after children and has been involved in the national development of the Healthy Care Programme. She also acts as a mentor and advisor in the establishment of partnerships to implement Healthy Care.

Jane Scott is currently the Senior Nurse for Looked After Children and Young People in the North of County Durham. Jane has been working in the NHS for 30 years. During her nursing career she has worked as a school health advisor, midwife, district nurse and paediatric nurse. Her particular interests are in adolescent health, emotional well being, and mental health of looked after young people. She is a member of the Champions for Children special interest group and represents the Northern Region on the National Committee. She is currently undertaking work as an independent advocate for *Voice*.

Bernadette Shaddock has worked in advertising and publishing, and is now a freelance illustrator, designer and artist. She specialises in visually communicating to children/teens, parent's, carers and professionals. Bernie will take themes, texts or ideas and develop them into visual and meaningful concepts for print, web or character merchandising. Bernie lives in Hertfordshire and can be contacted on 01992 422505.

Jane Walton BSc (Hons.) SRN, RHV, School Nurse Cert, Family Planning Cert. Over a period of 10 years Jane worked locally as a school nurse and family planning nurse. She then qualified as a health visitor, subsequently working with a GP practice in North Hertfordshire and in a community development role with the Oughton Ward in Hitchin. Since 2001 Jane has been School Health Manager with North Hertfordshire and Stevenage PCT. Jane was part of the development of a recent CPHVA publication on partnership working.

Sharon White is a general nurse, midwife and Specialist Community Health Nurse (BSc (Hons.). School Nursing) whose key professional interests are focused on improving the health outcomes of the most vulnerable children in our society and driving forward the public health role of the School and Public Health nurses agenda.

For the past 17 years she has worked predominantly within school nursing in Leeds acting in the various roles of lecturer/practitioner, manager, project development, strategist and clinical development lead. She now works as Designated Nurse for Looked After Children and Young People.

Working at national level Sharon dutifully served as national chair of the CPHVA School Nursing Committee for three years, is currently on the Executive Committee of the national special interest group; *Champions for children and young people in care* and is currently national professional officer of the School and Public Health Nurses Association; SAPHNA UK.

Three special people

AC has been a foster carer for 10 years and has had approximately 15 placements. We think that carers like AC deserve a medal, and need all the support and help they can get to enable them to do the job that they do. We need to listen to the carers and act on their recommendations.

Donna Mapal is 17 and has been in the care system for several years. She uses writing and poetry for therapy to express her feelings. We are delighted to publish her poem.

Ishy (nick-name) is 19 and was in care from the age of two. Ishy has good and bad memories of being in care and we are very pleased to publish her thoughts and experiences of health whilst in care.

Acknowledgements

Our grateful thanks go to the following, who helped make this book possible.

Russell House Publishing, for their patience when things did not go according to plan.

Our critical readers; Christine Oker, Tink Palmer, Mel Wood and Peter James.

Our families and friends who have supported us generally when difficult times have interfered with this book's production.

All our authors, who have also been patient awaiting the final version, and individual acknowledgements from our authors are included in the 'About the Contributors' section.

Especially Ann Wheal, without whose constant encouragement it may never have happened.

And last, but not least, our greatest thanks go to the children and young people, whose lives and difficulties have given us thought, reflection and a deeper and greater understanding of human beings than we would have ever achieved had we not been given the opportunity. We are proud to have known you and perhaps been a small part of your lives. Thank you.

Reflections

Ishy's story

My name is Ishy. I am 19 years old. I have been in care since I was two years old. Most of it has been in foster care and the rest is in children's homes. In all the moves that I have had I wanted to call one of them 'home', but I was never in a placement long enough to call it home.

My health experiences are some good and some bad. The good is my community nurse. She has been there for me to help when social services couldn't help anymore. The bad is the fact that I was made to go for therapy for 2–3 years when I didn't want to go. I don't want to remember what had happened to me. I just wanted to forget it and move on, but you can't when you have people constantly reminding you. I lost a lot of my education because of attending therapy, and they only had appointments during school time. This definitely affected my education, and I kept missing my favourite lessons. I kept telling everyone that I didn't want it, I'd rather go to school with my friends, but social services and the therapists insisted that I kept going. It was embarrassing also, to have to keep missing lessons at school, and my friends keep asking me where I was going.

I have had two kids when I was in residential care, and with both of them there have been complications. With the first pregnancy, my placenta ruptured, and I needed lots of care. The baby was in hospital for two months. A worker at the community home stopped anyone from visiting me, and to this day I don't know why she did that, as it made me very sad. With the second pregnancy my community nurse told them that I might have similar problems, and to prepare for complications, but they weren't ready and I had to go into hospital by myself in the ambulance. The only person that was on the ball all the time was my community nurse. After the birth I had a major blood clot and nearly stopped breathing. I was at my ex-boyfriends house and he and his family helped me, I'd like to thank them for that. I went back to the community home after this, but had to go back again as I still wasn't well and my community nurse took me.

The only person that ever really helped me with sex education has been the community nurse, and no-one else really said anything else to me about it. I can take care of this now, but my community nurse is still my friend, and I know that I can talk to her about anything at all.

I think that the care staff in the homes should have more training on health and especially things like sex education, so we can talk to them about it, but if they don't like talking about embarrassing things like that, then we need lots and lots more community nurses!

Phoebe – My Fallen Angel

By Donna Mapals

I woke up one day and knew what I wanted,
a child,
to be able to bear the gift of life,
to be the mother I crave to have,
but I could not,
I am too young.
All through my life I have needed a friend, someone to comfort me and give me warmth.
Now as I begin to grow, I wish everyday that the warmth and comfort I possess can be
shared with the ones I desire to love.
I found someone, a fallen angel.
She was my only choice, one where I could receive my gift without the consequences.
I bought her as easy as an item of clothing but she is more than that especially to me.
She is my light when nothing but darkness clouds my vision.
She is my strength when I become too weak.
She comforts me in my darkest hours.
Her tears don't fall when she is hungry,
she does not need comfort,
she does not need love,
but no matter what she does need,
she will always be there.
She will not leave as others before her have,
she will not hurt me,
she will not try to destroy me,
she will love me as I do her.
Everything in my world is real
except for her,
but I can touch her,
I can feel her fingers beneath mine.
To me she is more than reality,
she is my angel,
my touchstone,
the one I lean on to keep me safe,
to protect me from the outside world,
she is more than my forbidden child,

         She is my doll!

Section One:
The Wider Context

Chapter 1

Historical Background: A Medical Advisor's Perspective

Barbara Mary

Over the last two decades it was usual for medical advisors to local authority adoption and fostering sections to be community paediatricians, though there were a minority of general practitioners who held the role. Most were senior clinical medical officers in child health, thrown in at the deep end with little or no training in this specialist field, and little coordination of services to the children in the care of local authorities.

Some authorities had traditionally had a collaborative agreement between social services and child health, and the then 'boarded out medicals' for children in the care system were undertaken by child health doctors rather than GPs (general practitioners). Other authorities used GPs, with the medical advisor commenting on their reports. These medical advisors had little influence over the quality of these medicals, unlike those done by child health doctors. The forms for these medicals were ancient social services medical forms and FFI forms (Freedom From Infection), which had been used for the screening medical undertaken before a child was moved into a foster placement. The ethos was very much that of an army type medical rather than a holistic assessment, and was a degrading process for the children and young people subjected to them, as well as for the professionals involved. Children's hearts, lungs and testes were checked repeatedly irrespective of previous examinations. Eventually these forms were replaced by BAAF (British Agencies for Adoption and Fostering) forms, giving a start to some consistency across the country.

The medicals were requested by social services to an administrator in child health and only children who were referred were seen. There was no method of identifying the children in care population, and no knowledge of whether issues raised at the medical were acted upon, unless a consultant community paediatrician was seeing them for another reason. It was seen very much as a statutory responsibility, but it soon became clear that at times the returned medical was filed in the child's social services file and that the social worker did not get to see it. It had become an administrative procedure, the medical sent by a clerical officer in child health and received and filed by a clerical officer in social services. It was obvious that not all the children in the care population were seen and that some children were seen by a doctor several times, and over 'medicalled'.

It was a daunting task for medical advisors, who were very isolated in their speciality. Joining local BAAF medical groups, where medical advisors met together to share expertise and experiences, helped enormously. The in care population for which each medical advisor had responsibility varied greatly in numbers, from one to two hundred to over a thousand. A representative from each region attended the central medical group of BAAF, which gave a national perspective on what was going on in other areas as well as the expertise of other medical colleagues, legal and social worker advisers, a direct route to the Department of Health, and an opportunity to influence change. Attendance was expected at the annual seminar for medical advisors, and attendance at any courses relevant to the work, although obtaining funding for these was difficult in some areas. At that time there had been virtually no research published on the health of the in care population for advisors to draw on.

The dawning of the Children Act in 1989 and the change in the naming of children in care, made it imperative to work more closely with social services. The act distinguished between those children who were 'accommodated', that is 'looked after' away from home with the full agreement of parents and without loss of parental responsibility, and those who were 'in care', that is 'looked after' away from home due to court orders and where there was shared parental responsibility between parents and the local authority, and those who were 'looked after' for respite or permanently, due to disability. Some were fortunate to have the privilege of a working relationship with a development officer in social services, but the majority did not. Such a relationship and the support of BAAF were essential in working effectively to improve the health of children in the care system. Those who had difficulty in identifying a person to work closely within social services were at a considerable disadvantage, especially as they were not involved in the interagency training around the Children Act, and cascading it to colleagues in child health.

It soon became clear that the status of senior clinical medical officer held no power and everything had to be passed through a consultant community paediatrician, in spite of the specialised nature of the work. This reflected the lack of status of the work with children in the care system and adoption. Some were included in the training of social workers in the use of the new Looked After Children (LAC) forms which had a large section devoted to medical information and the results of the boarded out medicals, the legislation and wording of which had not been changed in the Act. The medical information recorded on a child's social services record was incomplete and out of date, and only a small proportion of looked after children had a boarded out medical requested (around 25–30 per cent). There was little uniformity across an agency in the method of requesting boarded out medicals, and little importance was given to the content of the routine medical. Social workers used any contact with a health professional as an alternative to a boarded out medical whatever the content of the report. Immunisations were recorded as having been done using a simple tick box method, without recording the date given or verifying the accuracy of the information. Social workers reported that they found the LAC forms lengthy and time consuming to complete, and it became clear that they were not often being used.

Medical advisors, as the only paediatrician to have the welfare of looked after children as a specialty, were hampered in what they could do. They did not have a detailed job description around the specialty and there was no guideline on the number of hours dedicated to the different parts of the job. As a result BAAF produced a proforma job description and encouraged medical advisors to take this to management, with details of the time spent on each part of the role. The Department of Health were encouraged by the group to identify a role for a doctor in their forthcoming guidelines. Unfortunately, there was a delay in publicising the document, *Promoting the Health of Looked After Children* (DoH, 2002) and whilst in local areas, medical advisors were keen to implement the recommendations earlier, the delay in publication meant that many primary care trusts were reluctant to act in anticipation of the guidance.

Into the 21st century

The profile of the looked after population was raised by the launch of the government initiative, *The Quality Protects Programme: Transforming Children's Services* (1998). It had been produced in response to the Utting Report, *People Like Us* (1997). This was a critical and hard-hitting report, which included 147 recommendations. The initiative was to run over three years and to focus on looked after children and children in need. The key concepts included corporate parenting; joined up government; councillors' responsibilities and that children were to receive services '. . . you would wish for your child if they were in the care system . . .'. Social services had to produce a Management Action Plan (MAP) which set targets for the improvement of all aspects of the lives of children in need and the care system, over the three-year period. Government funding was dependant on the success in achieving these targets year on year. Child Health was now being asked to produce figures for immunisations, and health needs assessments for the looked after children, as well as visits to the dentist and unmet health needs. Due to inadequate IT equipment, skills and support, it was often difficult to identify the looked after population and record and produce the information easily.

The raised profile of looked after children and accountability of the corporate parents resulted in the development of new services in order to address these issues. The models used varied between different authorities nationally, ranging from introducing a specific health team for looked after children, to giving a single nurse a title and responsibility to identify and implement any changes in service provision required to meet their needs. As an example the remainder of this chapter will focus on the experience of a primary care trust in the North of England.

The health authority commissioned a senior nurse to undertake an audit of the current situation regarding the health needs of looked after children. This showed that only 27 per cent of LAC were identified as having had a health needs assessment according to the child health data base. It was acknowledged that others would have had assessments elsewhere e.g. at their GP or at child protection medicals. What was clear was that there was no central point for collecting data, including the recording of unmet needs, nor procedures and systems in place.

The foresight and enthusiasm of one of the consultants in public health medicine, obtained Health Action Zone (HAZ) money in the year 2000, to develop a health team for looked after children. The HAZ money obtained was £100K per year for two years, followed by a commitment by the health authority to continue funding thereafter. This transformed the service.

The team was made up of a designated doctor (Consultant Community Paediatrician) two sessions a week dedicated clerical time; a designated nurse, (H grade) three days per week; five named link nurses (H grade, one each for five primary care trusts) each working 1 to 1½ days per week; a whole time equivalent secretary; a grade four whole time equivalent clerical officer and a grade two whole time equivalent data input clerk. The current medical advisor was regraded to a consultant community paediatrician (five sessions) for the work in adoption and as designated doctor to the looked after population. The funding also supplied computers and most importantly IT training. The work of the medical advisor was transformed, after years of struggling alone and without recognition. This was to support a population of 1,500–1,600 looked after children and young people. (See sections on designated doctor, designated nurse).

The team were commissioned to achieve 100 per cent uptake of the statutory annual reviews of the children and young people's health needs. The 'medical' so hated by these young people was changed to a holistic 'health needs assessment', at which they would have the opportunity to discuss issues around their health in the broadest sense, and to receive information about their past history, so often unknown to them. Achieving the change was hard for every one involved, and in particular the young people themselves and their carers. Carers and social workers often tried to 'protect' the children and young people from being 'medicalled', and there was a continuous need for keeping all involved updated with the new approach. Health and family medical history needs to be gathered from diverse sources and recorded for their future reference. An innovative approach by one authority was a 'virtual clinic' at which all professionals and birth family involved with a child or young person coming into care, met and shared such information, which was recorded at the outset.

The first task as designated doctor was to produce an information sharing protocol, as sharing information between health, social services and education, had to meet Data Protection Act requirements and Caldicott guidelines. An information sharing protocol had been produced by social services to meet their children in need obligations, and it was adapted to meet the needs of the looked after health team. Advice from the trust solicitor was essential and after several drafts the protocol was signed off by the trust, social services, the acute trusts and primary care. Authorities produced an overarching information sharing protocol with smaller protocols that met particular needs, written on similar lines. When it came to sharing computerised information in the future, there were even more protocols to agree, which took time. These developments were way in advance of the current recommendations and guidance on information sharing and shared databases (DfES, 2005).

The next task was to develop a stand-alone database for the looked after population within child health, which identified also those receiving respite care due to disabilities. This was regularly updated with information from social services, and was designed by members of the team to meet particular needs and to have the ability to produce accurate information for statistical and research purposes.

The team agreed a proposed model of practice for the statutory health needs assessments based on the *Promoting the Health of Looked After Children* draft guidance document. Community paediatricians would complete the initial 'into care' assessments using the BAAF (British Agencies for Adoption and Fostering) IHA (Initial Health Assessment) form. This form is designed to collect information from the birth family and social services, as well as other health sources before the child is seen. Certain parts of the form need to be completed by the social worker, and the completed form brought to the assessment. This was new for social workers and became part of new procedures for social services, which involved training. It was helped by the fact that the new procedures including the IHA form were available on line, and so social workers with access to a computer were able to complete their part of the form electronically. It was possible to produce new information forms and request forms for health needs assessments, which correlated with the child health database and became part of the new social services procedures, and were able to be completed electronically by clerical and social work staff. An individual health plan for the child was produced following a comprehensive assessment of the child's health, developmental and emotional needs. Necessary referrals were made by the assessing paediatrician and actions initiated. The individual health plan was returned to the social worker and was used to inform the first independent child care review within three months of the child being accommodated.

Previously, these initial assessments were often completed at a child protection assessment at the hospital. This was not always thought to be the best time to complete them due to extra time being required and also the child and birth family were often unable to focus on health issues in amongst the child protection concerns.

It was agreed that the statutory review assessments, six monthly for children under the age of two, and yearly for those over two, would be completed by health visitors and school nurses, or where appropriate by a community paediatrician if they were already involved, in order to avoid unnecessary duplication. (See section on the role of the school nurse and the role of the health visitor.) The link nurses worked with the more difficult to reach young people. The team designed new health needs assessment tools, which moved away from the medical model to a holistic child/young person centred approach, which could be completed by or with the child or young person themselves. This often engaged them in discussion about their health and revealed concerns they had. All assessments included completion of a mental health tool. After discussion with CAMHS (Child and Adolescent Mental Health Service) colleagues the Strength and Difficulties Questionnaire was chosen (see chapter on Mental Health). This is cost free and easy to use and score. It was made clear that this was not to be used to trigger a referral to CAMHS but to allow an assessment of the mental health needs of the looked after population and to seek support as required using accurate information. It also proved helpful in identifying improvement or deterioration in the mental health needs of individual children, and for the older young people who completed their own questionnaire it was a useful way for them to identify their strengths and not just their weaknesses. Carers were also able to identify behaviours, with which they were struggling, and comparison of the carer's and the young person's questionnaires sometimes revealed a lack of communication and understanding between them. Where high needs were identified, these were highlighted to the social worker who was then able to put in support if necessary or to refer to the social work therapeutic team of CAMHS as appropriate.

In cooperation with the looked after children and young people, and the local Children's Rights Service, a leaflet to support the change in model and encourage attendance at the assessment, was designed and distributed to all school age children via the Social Service Information Pack, which is given to all looked after children and young people via their care review. The young people themselves also received an appointment letter to the assessment as well as their carer.

The assessments identified unmet health needs and generated actions, as well as the needs of carers e.g. training for certain health conditions such as epilepsy. In order to make sure that missed immunisations were completed, a protocol was produced, with pro forma letters to GPs, health visitors school nurses and carers. This identified any immunisations that had been given but where the information had not been received by the child health system, thus giving false statistics. The individual health plans feed into the care review system and the independent reviewers take responsibility for making sure that all actions are taken, and continue to be monitored.

Further protocols were produced for missed appointments at health needs assessments, and for the use of the Strength and Difficulties Questionnaire.

There is a need to liaise with primary care trusts (PCTs) about their responsibility set out in the guidance *Promoting the Health of Looked After Children* (DoH, 2002). Within this guidance it is the responsibility of social services to inform PCTs when a looked after child moves in, or out of their area. The new social services procedure included forms for this purpose, but the PCTs initially were uncertain what to do with the information, and there was a need for presentations at various levels within the PCTs, facilitated by the link nurses who had the closest relationship with them. In addition the new health and social services procedures involved a huge training programme for social workers, paediatricians, school nurses and health visitors.

References

DfES (2005) *Cross Government Guidance: Sharing Information on Children and Young People*. London: DfES.

DoH (1989) *The Children Act*. London: HMSO.

DoH (1998) *The Quality Protects Programme: Transforming Children's Services*. London: HMSO.

DoH (2002) *Promoting the Health of Looked After Children*. London: HMSO.

Utting, W. (1997) *People Like Us. The Report of the Review of the Safeguards for Children Living Away from Home*. London: The Stationery Office.

Chapter 2

Healthy Care: From National Policy to Local Implementation

Helen Chambers and Heather Miller

It should be somewhere you feel supported and encouraged both emotionally and physically. You shouldn't feel that you are responsible for everything as if you are alone.

This chapter outlines the development of the Healthy Care Programme for looked after children in the context of the national policy agenda of improving outcomes for all children and young people. It identifies emerging themes and challenges, including the part played by the creative participation of looked after children and young people, and the role of carers in the development of the work. A local and regional partnership perspective will be provided to identify key development issues, pointers for successful programme working and sources of future help and support. A case is built for a target to link health and education outcomes for looked after children with good care and promote positive well being.

They can support us by getting to know us, really knowing us. The things that we feel strongly about, that we believe in. Children in care just want someone to take an interest in them.

(NCB, 2005c)

Healthy Care Programme only applies to England because it supports the English policy agenda.

An introduction

The Healthy Care Programme developed by National Children's Bureau and funded by DfES aims to create an environment of care that provides the support and opportunities necessary for a looked after child to learn life-skills, and gain confidence and self-esteem that will lead to improved physical and emotional health and well being (see chapter on Mental Health). It has proved to be a highly successful way of ensuring that *Promoting the Health of Looked After Children* (DoH, 2002a) is implemented, and the five national outcomes for children are delivered for this population (DfES, 2003). The programme has benefits that go much wider than physical health and is intended to improve the health and well being of carers as well as children and young people. The multi-agency Healthy Care partnerships encourage the promotion and protection of health and well being and improve wider life chances through improved outcomes (see chapter on Multi-Agency Looked After Partnerships). It provides a national standard for improving the health and well being of looked after children, against which local Healthy Care partnerships can audit their work, with the participation of looked after children and their carers. The empowerment of individuals and communities to become actively involved in matters that affect their health is a key factor in promoting health (WHO, 1986). A significant element of Healthy Care Programme has been the Creative Participation of looked after children at a local level, leading to the development of the Well being Creativity and Play Project, at the request of young people, to improve their access to play, arts and leisure provision.

Healthy Care: developing a healthier environment of care

Children live in a healthy environment and their health needs are identified and services are provided to meet them, and their good health is promoted.

(DoH, 2002b)

The Healthy Care Programme developed over a four-year period. From pilot sites in five local authority areas and eight shadow pilots the programme has grown organically to a position where half the local authorities in England have adopted the programme and there is established support in Government Office regions, provided by partnerships that include regional staff. Early development of Healthy Care provided a research and practice evidence base for working in this field (Chambers et al., 2002) and contributed to the design of the national Standard to ensure a healthy care environment.

The *Healthy Care Programme Handbook* (NCB, 2005c) gives local areas and regions guidance on setting up a multi-agency partnership and on carrying out the service audit against the National Healthy Care Standard (Figure 2.1) including the views of children, young people and their carers, which is the starting point for healthy care.

Healthy Care Briefings (NCB, 2005a) identify research and best practice for looked after children and young people on public health issues including mental health, food and activity, sexual health, supporting young parents in care and substance misuse as well as on play and creative arts and leisure.

The role of carers in promoting health and well being is crucial to improving outcomes for looked after children's health and well being, and has developed as a distinct area of practice within many partnerships. NCB worked with Telford and Wrekin Healthy Care partnership to devise a *Carers Health Promotion Training Programme*, that was revised and piloted in North Tyneside, and is now available within the family of document resources from NCB. Experience shows that where carers are supported, trained and resourced to deliver the training, it enhances their care practice, improves self-confidence and demonstrates the relevance and benefit of the training for developing the looked after children's workforce:

Arguably the training, orientation and status of child care workers are key areas to address if services are to improve ... The emphasis on taking the 'whole child' into account is important, and addresses the need to take a holistic perspective on a young person's life. The emphasis on the development of a relationship between child and carer is also likely to be critical.

(Chambers et al., 2002)

The National Healthy Care Standard helps looked after children and young people achieve the five outcomes described in *Every Child Matters* (DfES, 2003).

- be healthy
- stay safe
- enjoy and achieve
- make a positive contribution
- achieve economic well-being.

Children and young people in a healthy care environment will:

- Experience a genuinely caring, consistent, stable and secure relationship with at least one committed, trained, experienced and supported carer.
- Live in an environment that promotes health and well-being within the wider community.
- Have opportunities to develop the personal and social skills to care for their health and well-being now and in the future.
- Receive effective healthcare, assessment, treatment and support.

A child or young person living in a healthy care environment is entitled to:

1. Feel safe, protected and valued in a strong, sustained and committed relationship with at least one carer.
2. Live in a caring, healthy and learning environment.
3. Feel respected and supported in their cultural beliefs and personal identity.
4. Have access to effective healthcare, assessment, treatment and support.
5. Have opportunities to develop personal and social skills, talents and abilities and to spend time in freely chosen play, cultural and leisure activities.
6. Be prepared for leaving care by being supported to care and provide for themselves in the future.

(NCB, 2005c)

Figure 2.1

It is clear that whilst all professionals play a vital role in promoting health and well being, it is the carer who can make the biggest impact on the child's experiences and environment; though all agencies and services contribute to the bigger picture. However, training programmes only affect the practice of the relatively small number of carers who attend courses. *Carers Can!* a magazine for carers has been produced and disseminated to carers in their homes to increase their understanding of the role of creative arts and play in promoting health and well being, as well as increasing their skills and confidence to work. For some children and young people this sort of creative work at home, school or in their wider community can provide a vital stepping stone to improved education outcomes, improved mental and emotional health, and self-confidence, as well as helping to build and sustain a supportive relationship with their carers.

Themes and challenges

Work at local level focuses on four key areas for action – policy, partnerships, participation, and improved practice, to ensure that the six entitlements of looked after children and young people are met. National development and evaluation of Healthy Care Programme has identified common themes and challenges – these include:

- Working with the policy agenda.
- Effective partnership working.

- Leadership.
- Carer development.
- Creative Participation.
- National and regional support.

Working with the national policy agenda

The National Healthy Care Standard developed a child centred standard, in advance of the *National Service Framework for Children, Young People and Maternity Services* (DoH, 2004) and *Every Child Matters* (DfES, 2003). It was therefore able to help inform their development, and now provides local authorities and their health partners with a means to deliver improved services for looked after children and evidence for Joint Area Revieew (JAR) (Figure 2.2).

Healthy Care Programme provides a targeted programme for improving the health and well being of looked after children and young people, helping local partnerships deliver the five outcomes for all children, as detailed:

National outcome	Healthy Care Programme provides the child/young person with
Being healthy	• Understanding of their needs and responsibility for maintaining their health and well-being. • Access to effective healthcare to enable a young person's health to be promoted, maintained and treated. • Healthy development supported by carers who are adequately trained, supported and resourced.
Staying safe	• Opportunity to make safe, protective, caring and continuing relationships with carers. • A sense of self-worth and positive self-direction in relation to the choices and challenges of everyday life. • A clear and positive understanding of their cultural beliefs and identity; that are respected and celebrated. • Skills, understanding and confidence to develop appropriate personal and social boundaries and respect for those of others.
Enjoying and achieving	• Knowledge and emotional resourcefulness, able to use their own emotions and thinking skills to guide and manage their positive behaviour, using a variety of strategies. • Achievement of their potential and pride in their achievements.
Making a positive contribution	• Knowledge skills values and attitudes to keep themselves safe, to prepare for adult life and to play a part in creating a healthy safe, community. • A range of sustained positive relationships with family, friends and community.
Economic well-being	• Support through childhood into adulthood.

Figure 2.2

The NSF states the importance of universal provision of services, and identifies the contribution of Healthy Care Programme to improving the mental and emotional health of looked after children, through their effective participation in multi-agency partnership working, on a child's entitlement/need focused agenda. It reinforces the view that services should be designed and delivered around the needs of the child:

> *Services are child centred and look at the whole child – not just the illness or the problem, but rather the best way to pick up any problems early, take preventative action and ensure children have the best possible chance to realise their full potential. And if and when these children grow up to be parents themselves they will be better equipped to bring up their own children.*
>
> (DoH, 2004)

Every Child Matters and the joint inspection of services present a tremendous opportunity to improve outcomes for all children and young people. They also provide significant challenges to agencies, tasked with a duty to cooperate, and to provide the corporate parenting for a transient population of children and young people. A population who are particularly vulnerable to poor health (Skuse et al., 2001), high rates of self-harm and high risk behaviour (Richardson and Joughin, 2000; Shaw, 1998), and for whom standards and indicators tend to focus on illness rather than health (Howell, 2001). Two thirds of looked after children were reported to have at least one physical health complaint (Meltzer et al., 2003).

The Children's Act 2004 contains the duty to cooperate between agencies. However there are still different organisational agenda, funding streams and targets that can impede service improvement. Schools and GPs are not included in this duty, yet it is they who are instrumental in developing and supporting children's health and well being. Healthy Care Programme does not form part of the Department of Health's *Standards for Better Healthcare*, and is not a requirement of the Healthcare Commission inspection; it is for local partnerships to decide how and whether to use the Standard to help them provide the culture of continuous improvement essential for improving outcomes for looked after children and young people. Engagement of Strategic Health Authorities, Care Services Improvement Partnerships (CSIP) and regional public health departments in the support of Healthy Care Programme strategic approach is proving extremely helpful for the improvement of outcomes for this vulnerable sector of the community . It is facilitating the effective engagement of primary care trusts (PCTs) to deliver their policy imperatives for Child and Adolescent Mental Health Services (CAMHS), teenage pregnancy and substance misuse.

The link between good health and education can be overlooked when the care setting is focused on targets for placement stability and educational attainment, without identifying the contribution played by good health and well being. Healthy Care Programme offers opportunity to affect a positive care environment where health and well being are the foundation for future achievement and life opportunities.

Effective partnership working

The Healthy Care partnerships comprise a range of local children's services including health, social care, education, leisure, the voluntary sector and other services who work together to fulfil their responsibilities to promote the health and well being of looked after children and young people, with their, and their carers' active involvement. *The Healthy Care Handbook* identifies over thirty agencies as potential partners with children and their carers. Good partnership working, led and monitored by a Healthy Care lead officer, with tasks allocated to task groups helps ensure effective outcomes, if adequately supported at senior management, children's trust and strategic partnership level. The meaningful involvement of children and young people within the partnership is crucial in providing the opportunity to check that changes in services are impacting favourably on them.

Looked after children's nurses are 'champions' for young people and provide effective, young people friendly services. They are frequently the vital link to good healthcare, providing consistent confidential support to children and young people in times of transition and change. The strategic role of the designated doctor and nurse is outlined in Guidance (DoH, 2002). However the implementation of this role is patchy, with emphasis often placed on safeguarding and child protection. The work of these key health professionals is vital to the promotion of health and well being and provision of a healthy care environment.

Cost efficiency and national targets drive developments in the main statutory organisations. Healthy Care Programme makes clear links between improvements in outcomes for looked after children and a range of national targets. This provides an opportunity to gather support from a variety of agencies and may also facilitate the development of joint interagency local targets. The table below highlights areas where Healthy Care Programme can contribute to the attainment of national targets across a range of agencies

The promotion of health and well being enables local authorities and health partners to achieve improved outcomes for looked after children and young people, which in turn can significantly impact on funding. It is well recognised that looked after children feature strongly in the target areas below, and that interventions for such issues as supported housing for young parents, or drugs services for young people are extremely expensive for services, and costly for the future well being of young people. A small improvement in incidence in such high cost intervention arenas would both reduce spend, contribute to targets and improve outcomes for children and young people.

Agency	Area of linkage for target attainment
Social Services	Placement stability, educational attainment, adoption and fostering, offending behaviour, child protection, substance misuse
Health	Teenage pregnancy, CAMHS, chronic disease/long-term condition management, child protection, effective patient participation, early intervention and prevention, quitting smoking, obesity, substance misuse, health inequities
Education	Educational attainment, bullying, exclusion rates, employment and training
Leisure housing	Social inclusion, access
Youth offending	Reduction in offending behaviour, substance misuse, mental health

Figure 2.3

Healthy Care leadership

Leadership at senior strategic level is essential to the success of Healthy Care partnerships. Heads of Children and Families Services, and Assistant Directors of Social Services have been vital advocates and champions for the Healthy Care Programme. They in turn have welcomed the partnership model to support Children's Trust development, commissioning of services and the meaningful engagement of children and young people.

At operational level the Healthy Care Programme lead officer is essential – this role takes forward much of the organisational development and administration of the Healthy Care partnership.

The role of the Healthy Care Programme lead officer usually includes:

- Supporting the development of the Healthy Care partnership including convening stakeholder meetings and ensuring relevant paperwork is available.
- Collating and analysing evidence for the Healthy Care audit.
- Coordinating the action plan.
- Monitoring and reviewing the action plan.
- Setting up a communication strategy.
- Reporting progress to the Healthy Care partnership.
- Linking with national Healthy Care Programme, attending regional and national seminars.
- Ensuring feedback to the children and young people's strategic partnership.
- Ensuring evidence is available to support inspection of services.
- Ensuring the action plan is implemented.

(Healthy Care Programme Handbook, NCB, 2005c)

The success of partnership working and effective programme development is often because of the drive and focus provided through the lead officer. This partnership development post is essential to the success of providing a multi-agency Healthy Care environment.

Carer development

The carers' role as advocate, with the support of careful care planning including for health and education, is crucial in ensuring a healthy environment of care that is based on the needs and entitlements of children and young people. Carers have much to contribute to Healthy Care partnerships, and need to be provided with opportunities to share their views and help shape service development. Carers have been involved in programme development, contributing to the writing and delivery of the Healthy Care Training Programme, and the development of the *Carers Can!* magazine, where ideas and tips for fun and creative activities with looked after children and young people are shared. This is not therapy; it is the everyday parental and care experience of meeting the needs of children and young people growing up.

Young people in a local partnership identified five issues as key in promoting their mental health and emotional well being (NCB, 2005c). These components are largely those of good parenting and good care, supported by effective healthcare and services, education and support.

1. A supportive and stable living environment with caring and consistent relationships

Children should have at least one secure attachment to an adult. They should feel safe with that person and be able to develop a trusting, loving relationship. A stable placement is crucial to allowing relationships to develop.

2. To be included and remembered

Isolation and loneliness was a key theme identified by children and young people. They want to be part of the communities they live in and to feel they belong and to have opportunities to meet with other looked after children. They also need help with feelings about the experiences and events, which led to separation from their family.

3. Opportunities to express themselves

Play and leisure activities including sport, art and drama promote emotional well being by developing confidence and self-esteem, give opportunities to develop supportive friendship networks, learn social skills and find positive role models.

4. Support and encouragement with education

Positive school experiences improve career options in later life, they also boost self-esteem and confidence, provide friendship networks and opportunities to develop and practice social skills.

5. Preparation for leaving care

Young people need to prepare for independence and the many challenges they will face. They will continue to need support and encouragement (see section on Leaving Care and After Care).

Good mental health and emotional well being requires a consistent, stable placement, supported by effective multi-agency staff and services – the carer's role is key to this. In Europe the training for children's workers and carers includes the theory of relevant methods of working, opportunities for practice placements, and a practical and creative skills dimension to ensure all professionals focus on the 'whole child'. Carers are skilled in building relationships with children in their care. In England there is currently a less consistent approach to carer training.

At local level, there remain the challenges of poor placement choice, inconsistency in approaches to mandatory training and payment for skills, low numbers of carers, and the poor uptake of training by carers. In the words of a young woman consulted in the early stages of Healthy Care Programme:

> . . . *things won't change for looked after children until things are better for carers.*

Creative Participation

> *Health is a base from which to develop, enabling people to do or choose to do as many things as possible to achieve their potential.*
>
> (Seedhouse, 1986)

Participation helps people to discover their potential, to realise their talents and raise their self-esteem. In turn this can help them to question their boundaries and explore issues, voice aspirations, identify needs and facilitate their learning and personal development. The participation of children and young people in all parts of the Healthy Care Programme is a key component of promoting the health of looked after children and young people:

> *Effective promotion of health and well being is about empowerment and the development of self esteem. If children and young people are part of the planning, the assessing of needs and the development of programmes and/or planned activities they are more able to participate and benefit.*
>
> (Chambers et al., 2002)

Children and young people taking part in local Healthy Care partnership meetings need to be part of a wider reference group that links to the larger community of looked after children and young people. Existing participation structures can be used to consult on Healthy Care issues. Some areas have a children's rights worker or equivalent who is a valuable link and can support children and young people to participate in and contribute their views to the Healthy Care partnership. At local levels young people participated creatively in music, poetry, drama, cookery, visual art and photography activities. These reflect the Programme's emphasis on the relationship between well being and creativity as part of a whole child approach to promote life chances and ensure the sustainable development of local services. This in turn provides opportunities to succeed and celebrate, and have fun with supportive adults and carers, all of which can be reflected in academic achievement and greater placement stability.

The process of involving children and young people includes:

- Informing children and young people of the issues.

- Encouraging them to form an opinion.

- Giving them opportunities to express their opinions to people who make decisions.

- Giving them feedback on how their opinions have shaped service developments.

- Making sure that appropriate and different ways are found to 'listen' to children of different ages, with different abilities, from diverse cultures and backgrounds.

A young person co-chaired the local Healthy Care Programme Conference at Telford and Wrekin and found the experience worthwhile. This is how she described it:

> *I was very nervous about doing this because I had never really done much speaking in front of large groups of people so co-chairing the conference was a little scary and a totally new experience. There were a few other people sitting at the table with Carol and me, which was nice because I felt that I had support from them. Looking at all of the people in front of us was very nerve wracking. The one thing that I was worried about was that the conference was going to be boring. I would hate to have seen people yawning and falling asleep right in front of me. Also, I have been to some very boring meetings and it is not very nice for the people who attend and the people who are holding them. Quite often the meetings are very valuable and the information given is important but because of the way that they are run people just don't listen. Luckily for us though, everyone seemed to be enjoying themselves!*

The conference set up some task groups to tackle different areas of the Standard. I was part of the task group that looked at foster care to see whether the young people were getting a fair deal according to the Standard.

Young people have participated in the Healthy Care Programme at all levels. Nationally, they were involved in helping to draft the Standard and in the feasibility studies, as well as the local auditing of work. Children and young people's active participation can enable meaningful assessment of whether these services are really making a difference.

National and regional support

The national Healthy Care Network offers support and links to other Healthy Care partnerships in the regions, sharing good practice, and facilitating cooperation and joint working. During the development stages of Healthy Care Programme, DfES Regional Development Workers, Public Health and Strategic Health Authority Children's Leads convened and developed regional groups, working with colleagues in CAMHS, Teenage Pregnancy, the Arts Council and others. In this time of change, with the newly developing children's workforce, Healthy Care partnerships still require support. National Children's Bureau will endeavour to continue to support Healthy Care Programme nationally by ensuring its further development across England. It will make strategic links with existing and emerging regional structures such as the new Field Force, Children's Services Advisers, Directors of Children and Learners, and staff in Children's Services Improvement Partnerships, strategic health authorities and public health departments to ensure effective co-ordination. During this time of policy and service reconfiguration and transition Healthy Care Programme provides a focus and set of tools for multi-agency work to achieve the five outcomes for looked after children and young people.

Key learning from early implementers

Earlier discussion identified the 'organic' development of Healthy Care Programme encouraged by enthusiastic innovators to develop regional and local programmes; common themes emerged and are shown below.

As with any programme a number of factors are essential to success. Early implementers of Healthy Care Programme have identified issues pivotal to the smooth delivery of the programme as given below:

- Local environment – it is important to assemble a clear profile of the local situation including number of looked after children, geography, demography of the area, stage of partnership development, existing services and any particular local difficulties. The multi-agency partnership can then be developed to take best advantage of any effective existing partnerships or can provide a useful opportunity to review groups and structures which require further development.

- Strategic and operational influence – ensure the multi-agency partnership has sufficient influence at a senior level to enable progression of the agenda. Strong links to planning, commissioning and decision-making structures within each of the participating organisations are essential. A link to operational groups is also required to enable decisions to be implemented. The most popular structure from early implementer sites places the multi-agency partnership as a subgroup of the Children and Young People's Local Strategic Partnership or Children's Trust Board, however, other models exist and consideration of each local situation must be taken into account throughout development. The identification of 'champions' in each agency has proved extremely effective in ensuring the influence and priority of the programme is maintained. Champions must hold the seniority to enable them to influence decision making.

• Communication – the involvement of children and young people, carers and staff has already been identified as essential within this programme. The challenges of communication within such a broad partnership, where participants have very different communication needs is substantial; consequently energy, effort and planning are required to ensure this is undertaken effectively.

Healthy Care Programme is a process of continual improvement with no end date in terms of achievement. The programme provides a mechanism for ensuring the well being of looked after children and young people is continually assessed and improved and contributes to national targets whilst making a real and measurable difference to the lives of one of our most vulnerable groups in society.

The five national pilots and early implementation sites in the North East have identified potential barriers to the effective implementation of Healthy Care Programme. These may vary, depending on local environment and the issues raised earlier in the chapter. However, Appendix 1 at the end of this chapter highlights some common issues and also provides possible solutions (solutions are taken from experiences of various programmes where issues have been successfully resolved).

Health and education: a joint target for well being

Health has an important influence on attainment throughout a child's life, and research points to the adverse effects of ill health on attainment, and the importance of the wider social context in improving health (Health Development Agency, 2003). The importance of measures which aim to have a positive impact on the health of individuals, and do so by addressing health needs holistically, are considered likely to promote school attainment (Health Development Agency, 2003). Education outcomes are strongly influenced by a child's emotional, mental and physical health; instability, bullying and trauma can all affect a child's emotional health (SEU, 2003).

Although some looked after children and young people need access to CAMHS, approximately 55 per cent do not have a diagnosable mental health disorder (Meltzer et al., 2003) but they may need help to build relationships, cope with loss and transition and overcome experiences of bullying or other trauma. Involvement in play, creative arts, sports and other leisure activities provide opportunities for children and young people to meet and interact with others and to develop friendships. This can counteract the exclusion that looked after children and young people may feel and provide valuable experience in developing social relationships and communication skills, and gives access to other adult positive role models. It has been argued that the development of these social skills can be

---

Play often stems from **curiosity**:

Curiosity leads to ....**exploration**

Exploration leads to ....**discovery**

Discovery leads to ....**pleasure**

Pleasure leads to ....**repetition**

Repetition leads to ....**mastery**

Mastery leads to ....**new skills**

New skills lead to ....**confidence**

Confidence leads to ....**increased self-esteem**

Self-esteem leads to a ....**sense of security**

Security leads to ....**more learning**

Figure 2.4

crucial in determining whether a child/young person flourishes socially and educationally (Goleman, 1996).

Safe, repetitive, patterned experiences help the brain to develop and the child to make sense of the world. Research (Perry, 2000) shows how children and young people taking pleasure in play drives learning.

Although play comes naturally to children and young people they need stimulation, resources and sometimes encouragement to develop their play. Looked after children and young people may not have had opportunity to play due to abuse or neglect in their past, difficult and damaging relationships with parents or carers, illness or disability. It is known that deprivation of opportunities to play and interact with others can have serious negative effects on a child/young person's social and emotional development (Brown, 2003; Bruner et al., 1985).

Well being Creativity and Play within Healthy Care Programme worked with seven local authorities, who demonstrated the importance of creative arts to ensure children's participation, improve education engagement and attainment, build relationships with carers and others, as well as provide expression for a variety of feelings and promote positive images of looked after children and young people. The work from this project provided a special exhibition at the National Gallery in Autumn, 2004, to which carers and young people were invited, and were proud to see the work shown.

Creative arts and play can:

- Enhance the self esteem and resilience of looked after children/young people.

- Promote social inclusion.

- Improve sensory awareness.

- Help to counteract the consequences of childhood abuse and neglect.

(Chambers, 2004)

Those who care for looked after children and young people will often identify the importance of mental health and emotional well being as a key factor in maintaining a stable placement, but this is not easily measured so target setting is difficult. For the five national outcomes to be achieved for looked after children and young people, there is a need to measure well being more effectively. Monitoring social functioning, which includes how children and young people engage and participate in social networks could provide a useful indicator, and the arts and play can provide one of the means of delivery; so assisting education attainment and placement stability. Whilst the national outcome approach to drive service development is welcomed, there is need for looked after children and young people's health and well being to be explicitly included in the DfES targets to improve education and placement stability.

In conclusion

Healthy Care Programme developed by NCB and funded by DfES provides a set of tools, information, support and experience for multi-agency partnerships and carers to help deliver improved outcomes for looked after children and young people, with their active involvement. The Programme's participation focus on well being through access to creative arts and leisure opportunities has highlighted the importance of this area of work in linking health and education to provide improved well being. There is, however, a need for a national target that supports positive health and well being to ensure that the health of looked after children and young people remains a concern on the joint policy agenda. In a fast changing, target driven culture with finite resources, it requires more than the good will of motivated enthusiasts to ensure that the corporate parent provides a healthy environment of care.

References

Brown, F. (Ed.) (2003) *Playwork: Theory and Practice*. Open University Press.

Bruce, T. and Meggitt, C. (1996) *Child Care and Education*. Hodder & Stoughton.

Bruner, J.S. et al. (1985) *Play: Its Role in Development and Evolution*. Penguin.

Chambers, H. et al. (2002) *Healthy Care*. London: National Children's Bureau.

Chambers, H. (2004) Creative Arts and Play for Looked After Children. *Highlight*, 212.

DoH (2002a) *Promoting the Health of Looked After Children*. The Stationery Office.

DoH (2002b) *Fostering Services. National Minimum Standards, Fostering Services Regulations*. The Stationery Office.

DoH (2004) *National Service Framework for Children, Young People and Maternity Services*. The Stationery Office.

DfES (2003) *Every Child Matters*. The Stationery Office.

DfES (2003) *National Outcome Indicators for Looked After Children*. London: HMSO.

Goleman, D. (1996) *Emotional Intelligence: Why it Can Matter More Than IQ*. Bloomsbury.

Health Development Agency (2003) *Emotional Health and Well-being Update. Promoting Young People's Health using the Health Behaviour in School-aged Children (HBSC) Study and the Health Development Agency's Evidence Base*. London: Health Development Agency.

Howell, S. (2001) The Health of Looked After Children. *Highlight*. 184.

Meltzer et al. (2003) *The Mental Health of Young People Looked After by Local Authorities in England*. The Stationery Office.

National Children's Bureau (2005a) *Healthy Care Briefings*. London: NCB.

National Children's Bureau (2005b) *Healthy Care: A Health Promotion Training Programme for Foster Carers and Residential Social Workers*. London: NCB.

National Children's Bureau (2005c) *Healthy Care Programme Handbook*. London: NCB.

Perry, B.D. et al. (2000) Curiosity, Pleasure and Play: A Neurodevelopmental Perspective. Haaeyc *Advocate*. Jun 15 at *http://www.childtrauma.org/ctamaterials/Curiosity.asp* (accessed 25 Nov 2004).

Richardson, J. and Joughin, C. (2000) *Mental Health Needs of Looked After Children*. London: Gaskell.

Seedhouse, D. (1986) *Health: The Foundations for Achievement*. London: Wiley.

Shaw, C. (1998) *Remember My Messages*. London: Who Cares? Trust.

Skuse, T. et al. (2001) *Looking After Children: Transforming Data into Management Information. Third Interim Report to the DoH of a Longitudinal Study at 30/9/99*. Loughborough: Loughborough University.

Social Exclusion Unit (2003) *A Better Education for Children in Care*. London: Office of the Deputy Prime Minister.

World Health Organisation (1986) *Ottawa Charter for Health Promotion WHO/HPR/HEP/ 95.1*. Geneva: WHO.

Wright, R. et al. (2004) *National Arts and Youth Development Programme Highlights*. McGill University. *http://www.mcgill.ca/naydp/symposium/* (accessed 1st December 2004).

Appendix I   Healthy Care multi-agency partnerships

Obstacle	Possible solutions/helpful tips	Comments
Geography	• Large geographical areas may require a small core group with a number of local Healthy Care multi-agency partnerships to prevent groups becoming too large and to address issues of distance.	The core group needs to take a coordinating role to ensure consistency.
Large numbers of children looked after/ capacity	• Implement Healthy Care Programme in specific service areas incrementally e.g. either by geographical area, type of provision (i.e. residential care) by age group etc. The whole process can be undertaken in one area and once completed another area be selected. • Share the workload between partners. • Network with other areas to share work. • Identify a mentor to assist and advise and to share work undertaken nationally. • Use existing groups, structures etc – link with existing groups for participation. • Attempt to mainstream work wherever possible and link with other initiatives in the local area.	Experience and learning will be gained and networked which will enabling the process to be more efficient. Examples of selected groups include: under 11s, girls aged 13 +, care leavers, children in foster care, residential homes etc. Choices of area selected have generally been due to awareness of particular challenges locally.
Low priority of looked after children's health issues – difficulty getting the issues onto agencies' agenda	• Ensure the Healthy Care partnership is placed in an influential position within the structure. • Ensure champions are identified within each agency/organisation and that issues are consistently raised. • Link to existing targets i.e. placement stability; educational attainment; youth offending; early intervention and prevention in CAMHS; chronic disease; teenage pregnancy; child protection; substance misuse; bullying, social inclusion; employment and training; adoption, inequalities targets, smoking, obesity etc.	Looked after children and young people record high incidence in many areas where national targets are in place. Improvement in the outcomes for looked after children and young people can have a significant impact on targets and resulting in high spend on high cost of interventions. Involvement of regional services can enable

	• Involve regional organisations e.g. Government Office, Strategic Health Authority. • Ensure commitment at a senior level is obtained and that accountability rests with the Children and Young Person's Strategic Partnership Childrens Trust or equivalent. • Undertake cost benefit analysis to exhibit possible long-term benefits of reduction in high cost interventions.	looked after children and young people's vulnerability to be identified in the performance management of these organisations providing a local drive to improve services.
Funding	• Consider alternative funding via leisure, teenage pregnancy, substance misuse etc. • Link with targets as above to access funding. • Undertake a cost benefit analysis. • Ensure the Healthy Care partnership is structurally linked with the planning and commissioning, strategic decision-making and operational groups. It is possible for the Healthy Care partnership to also act as a commissioning forum for looked after children and young people. This can assist with the development of Children's Trusts. • Develop a pooled budget.	This is linked with the previous point. Due to the very significant inequalities issues and the expensive nature of interventions, a small improvement in outcomes for looked after children and young people can prove highly cost effective. Links with commissioning, planning and strategy from the outset is essential, this will enable time for planning, and ensure change is factored into budget cycles.
Organisational complexity	• Use an existing group and amend membership to enable it to become the Healthy Care partnership. • Take the opportunity to reassess organisational structures, consider amalgamating groups to simplify the system. • Ensure champions for the Healthy Care Programme are aware of structures and can influence and increase awareness in appropriate arenas. Senior champions are vital.	Healthy Care Programme can act as a driver for organisational simplification, which can benefit many other areas of children's services.

Lack of a regional link	• Involve the Strategic Health Authority, CSIP Childrens Leads, Public Health Leads for Children, Government Office, Childrens Services Advisors and CAMHS Regional Development Workers and Teenage Pregnancy Coordinators to try to establish a regional group. Establish a network either within your region or make contact with one out of region that is already established. Link to the national programme lead in NCB.	
Information sharing	• Link with existing work for information sharing protocols and the national network in NCB.	Work is ongoing nationally on this issue.
Difficulties with partnerships	• Identify targets, aims, needs of each organisation and identify common ground. • Employ champions to approach their own organisations and to negotiate progress. • Identify areas of similar work where working together will be very beneficial. • Identify quick wins. • Use an external facilitator, mentor or regional lead to be involved in establishing the Healthy Care partnership. • Develop joint agency targets.	The simple establishment of the Healthy Care partnership can assist in partnership working. Learning from pilots has shown that agencies are often unaware of the work of other agencies even when in similar areas. The Healthy Care partnership provides an opportunity to discover new services and to link services.
Out of county placements/ placements in county from other authorities	• Undertake an individual audit on out of authority placements to identify the issues. • Link with appropriate authority if they are undertaking Healthy Care to negotiate an approach. • Feed identified issues to regional and national groups.	Work is being undertaken at national level on this matter. As Healthy Care Programme is rolled out across the country a consistent approach will be adopted.
Independent fostering agencies	• Involve providers in the Healthy Care partnership. • Use Healthy Care to demonstrate a healthy care environment.	Consortia of independent providers have found Healthy Care provides a focus for their joint development.

| CAMHS – lack of capacity, waiting times | <ul><li>Involve CAMHS representatives on the Healthy Care partnership.</li><li>Ensure links are made to discussions about NHS developmental funding and Mental Health Grant.</li><li>Link to targets e.g. youth offending.</li><li>Consider alternative options for the delivery of Tier 1 & 2 CAMHS (e.g. voluntary sector, expert parent/patient etc) to strengthen the preventative approach.</li></ul> | CAMHS development funding is available. Investment in services for looked after children; support for foster carers, support and advice for social workers and residential workers, engagement with arts and leisure staff can make significant impact on attainment of targets. |

Chapter 3

How Multi-Agency Looked After Partnerships (MALAPs) are Improving the Health of Looked After Children and Addressing Fragmented Corporate Parenting

John Brown

Introduction

All of the developments in the last eight years (since Sir William Utting completed his *People Like Us* Inquiry, and Frank Dobson announced the *Quality Protects* Programme) have been focused on creating dedicated and specialist looked after health services. This chapter will describe the rationale for specialist looked after health services alongside current successes and current barriers. It will also describe how new Multi-Agency Looked After Partnerships (MALAPs) are coordinating the improved delivery of looked after health.

Why do looked after children need a different system from other children in order to have their health needs met?

This is a key question. Unless we understand why looked after children need a different system from other children for addressing their health needs, the energy and commitment required to establish a different and better system will not be put into place. The answer to this question should also be led by research and evidence, rather than by opinion.

Why are looked after children different?

The main reason is that, once they have been removed from their family of origin looked after children become the responsibility of a well-endowed but deeply 'fragmented' corporate parent. The local authority as a corporate parent, is very much a 'fragmented corporate parent'. Looked after children also require the collaboration of two large bureaucratic institutions – The National Health Service and the local authority.

In a family living at home, there are a number of common parenting tasks that are coordinated by a (usually) consistent set of parents:

- Coordinating access to universal and specialist services.

- Coordinating access to health assessments and immunisations including dental check-ups.

- Supporting access to sports and leisure activities, including the provision of equipment and transport.

- Supporting health promotion and healthy eating as part of a healthy life-style.

- Offering sexual health advice when appropriate.

- Providing or coordinating access to mental health support.

- Offering substance misuse advice or coordinating access to support as necessary.

- Offering educational support or coordinating access to specialist education services.

- Assisting with employment preparation.

- Preparing for independence and offering post-independence support.

For children looked after, the above tasks are delegated to a wide number of (often transient) professionals: social workers, foster carers, residential staff, independent reviewing officers, paediatricians, specialist nurses, psychologists, DAT workers, teenage pregnancy staff, LAC teachers, personal advisers and leaving care staff. Coordinating this activity for all looked after children as well as specific individual children is a complex and often fragmented task.

Children looked after also need much more of the above support services than other children who are still living at home. This is primarily linked to poor parenting, and poor early life experiences. Children looked after are likely to have experienced abusive or neglectful parenting. Parental neglect, physical abuse, sexual abuse and emotional abuse all feature highly in reasons for children needing to be removed from their birth families. Although they are physically safe when placed in the care of their new corporate parent, looked after children will frequently bring with them the emotional and behavioural difficulties that arise from experiencing neglectful or abusive parenting.

The emotional health needs of looked after children far exceed those of other children (see Chapter 8 on The Mental Health Needs of Looked After Children).The research is overwhelmingly clear on this. A survey of the mental health of 1,039 looked after children carried out for the Department of Health (DoH, 2002) found that:

- 45 per cent had a mental disorder and of these, 37 per cent had conduct disorders, 12 per cent had emotional disorders and 7 per cent were hyperactive.

- Compared with other children living at home, looked after children were five times more likely to have a mental disorder.

- Of the looked after sample, 66 per cent of those who were Looked After in residential units had a mental disorder.

- The prevalence of mental disorders reduced according to the length of time spent in the current placement.

- 75 per cent of the children with a mental health problem had additional physical health problems (see Table 3.2 below).

- Children Looked After who had a mental disorder were twice as likely as those looked after children without any mental disorder to have visited an accident and emergency department of a hospital in the previous three months.

- 29 per cent had an accidental injury that required hospital assistance: a head injury, a broken bone in an accident, a burn or an accidental poisoning.

- Children with a mental disorder were twice as likely to have marked difficulties with reading (37 per cent compared with 19 per cent) mathematics (35 per cent compared with 20 per cent) and spelling (41 per cent compared with 24 per cent).

- 62 per cent of the looked after sample were at least a year behind in their intellectual development (38 per cent were two years behind and 24 per cent were three years behind).

- Among the looked after children with a mental disorder, 42 per cent had a Statement of Educational Needs (SEN). This was twice the rate of looked after children with no mental disorder and compares with a rate of about 3 per cent for other children not looked after and living at home.

- 39 per cent of the looked after sample had been missing from school for up to a week, and 25 per cent of children with emotional disorders played truant during the previous year.

- Looked after children with a mental disorder were four times as likely to say that they didn't spend time with friends (8 per cent and 2 per cent).

- 65 per cent of looked after children with emotional disorders were smokers compared with 19 per cent of looked after children without a mental disorder.

- 25 per cent of looked after children with a conduct disorder drank alcohol once or twice a week.

- 23 per cent of the looked after sample reported that they had been sexually abused or raped.

- 40 per cent of children with a conduct disorder had already had sexual intercourse in comparison with 26 per cent of looked after children without any mental disorder.

Additional information from DfES National Statistics (DfES, 2003) confirms these findings:

- 12.4 per cent of looked after children missed at least 25 days from school.

- 53 per cent gained 1 GCSE compared with 95 per cent of the general child population.

- 1.1 per cent of looked after children were permanently excluded compared with 0.1 per cent of the general child population.

- 9.5 percent of looked after children received a final warning or conviction compared with 3.6 per cent of the general child population.

A useful exercise for local authorities and PCTs is to examine national research information and apply it to the numbers of looked after children in their locality. Firstly, how many children should localities expect to have? In an average locality with a general population of 100,000, PCTs and local authorities can expect to have approximately 160 looked after children of whom 50 are new entrants. Some localities may be net importers of children, particularly if there are several independent agencies operating in the area. This will increase the demand for support services.

Table 3.1

Population	LAC	New Entrants
100,000	160	50
200,000	320	100
300,000	480	150
400,000	640	200
500,000	800	250

The same process can be applied to national research findings and the likely number of local looked after children who are affected. In Table 3.2 below 'a projection' is given for a 'hypothetical' locality with 300 children looked after:

Table 3.2

Condition	Research rate %	For 300 LAC locally no. children affected
Had a mental disorder	45	135
Conduct disorders	37	111
Emotional disorders	12	36
Hyperactive	7	21
1 year intellectual delay	62	186
2 year intellectual delay	38	114
3 year intellectual delay	24	72
Eye or sight problems	16	48
Speech or language problems	14	42
Bed wetting	13	39
Coordination difficulties	10	30
Asthma	10	30
Sexually abused or raped	24	72

The above list identifies that looked after children will frequently arrive into placements with multiple difficulties – physical health problems alongside educational problems and emotional difficulties. Their trust in adults may also have been abused or exploited and they may additionally move between placements too frequently. Subsequent loss of key health and education information has been common.

All of the above points to the need for a central information collection point, and the need for a range of designated professionals – a designated teacher, a designated nurse, and a designated doctor. This was clearly identified within the Looked After Health Guidance (DoH, 2002). These dedicated service arrangements for looked after children are being put into place in most localities, but at a very slow rate.

To date, the development of dedicated looked after support services has been a tale of three struggles. The first struggle has been for social services to commit the necessary funding for looked after children against their other competing priorities for vulnerable children and families and in child protection. The second struggle has been for local health services to similarly recognise the needs of looked after children against all their other competing priorities. The third struggle has been for other local council departments, as part of their corporate parenting responsibilities, to commit capacity and funding to social services in order to offer looked after children the wide range of support that they require.

Quality Protects and beyond

Until very recently, the history of looked after children's health has been littered with fragmentation, and poor coordination. Throughout the 1970s and the 1980s the main requirement was that children in care were 'free from infection' at their point of entry into care. Annual medicals were therefore cursory and lacked dignity for the children who endured them. Monitoring of take up was rare.

In 1997, The House of Commons Health Select Committee took representations on the then circumstances of children in care.

Professor David Berridge told the Committee that:

> *Most children looked after by local authorities have very, very severe problems. The level of deprivation, damage, injury, abuse, humiliation that those children have suffered, which we as researchers come into contact with on a regular basis is absolutely horrendous. Unless one realises the depth of damage that these children have experienced we cannot begin to conceive how to put a framework of services into place to deal with that. It is clear that Social Services on their own cannot begin to tackle the major problems that these children have got.*

The Committee heard a research summary from the Who Cares? Trust spanning the previous 20 years:

- *Education:* between 50 per cent and 75 per cent of care leavers complete their schooling with no formal qualifications compared with only 6 per cent of the general population (1992, 1995).

- *Further education:* between 12 per cent and 19 per cent of care leavers go on to further education compared with 68 per cent of the general population (1994, 1995).

- *Employment:* between 50 per cent and 80 per cent of care leavers are unemployed (1986).

- *Offending:* 23 per cent of adult prisoners and 38 per cent of young prisoners have been in care (1991).

- *Parenthood:* at least one in seven young women leaving care are pregnant or already mothers (1986).

- *Homelessness:* 30 per cent of young, single homeless people have been in care (1981).

- *Poverty:* one in ten 16–17-year-old claimants of DSS severe hardship payments have been in care (1993).

Other recent research suggests that up to 50 per cent of children looked after may be in need of some form of health intervention, that up to 30 per cent may have special educational needs, and that 67 per cent may experience psychiatric disorders compared with 15 per cent in the general population.

Among the 94 recommendations made to the government by the Health Select Committee in 1998 were:

Recommendation 70

Health education for looked-after children is at present regarded as a comparatively low priority. This is a very short-sighted attitude, given the problems caused for society as well as individuals by bad diet, obesity, drug abuse and under-age pregnancies. The statutory responsibility of local authorities to promote health education is clear, but as in so many other areas, there is currently no way of systematically monitoring the extent to which authorities carry out this duty, or of enforcing the duty on those authorities who neglect it. (paragraph 268.)

Recommendation 71

We recommend that the DoH should report to us with proposals for ensuring that appropriate health education is provided to young people in the care system. (paragraph 268.)

Recommendation 72

We believe that the current arrangements for providing psychiatric and other specialist services to children in care are grossly inadequate. It is a disgrace that children should have to wait as long as two years before even being assessed for treatment. We recommend that the DoH should investigate how more effective links can be created between SSDs and local health services, to ensure that the former can speedily access expert medical attention, including psychiatric care and guidance on sexual health, for the children in their care. (paragraph 269.)

In the previous year, on 13 June 1996, John Major the Conservative Prime Minister responded to a series of high-profile police investigations into long-standing abuse in specific children's homes in Wales, in the North West, and in the North East, by announcing a public inquiry. Sir William Utting, the recently retired Director of Social Services Inspectorate, led the inquiry. The inquiry into the circumstances of children's residential care was:

. . . as a result of continuing revelations of widespread sexual, physical and emotional abuse of children in children's homes over the preceding 25 years.

The review was entitled *People Like Us: The Report of the Review of the Safeguards for Children Living Away From Home* and was completed on 30 July 1997. This coincided with a change of government and the election of Tony Blair's New Labour Party. The inquiry was entitled *People Like Us*, due to the inability to caricature abusers of children as inadequate: they were often skilled and educated individuals, and, said Sir William, 'people like us'.

The New Labour Government therefore had two reports to respond to: a Commons Health Select Committee and a national review. Sir William's report wasn't responded to immediately while the New Labour Party conducted their first spending review. A key paragraph in the Utting Review stated:

*The Review believes that safety is a function of overall effectiveness and that **quality protects**. Improvements in both health and education services are needed for looked after children. Local authorities should take a corporate approach to deal with a situation in which over a third of children in residential care are not receiving education. They also have serious health needs which must be addressed in order to keep them safe.*

(p 27)

In November 1997 Frank Dobson the new Minister for Health announced the Quality Protects programme. This was a three year programme where new ring-fenced development funds were offered to local authorities (social services departments) in exchange for a written self-assessment and action plan, which was designed to remedy the specific local weaknesses of that department, including looked after health. There were also a small number of new performance indicators to complete for the self-assessment and action plan process. Assistant Directors at the time sent out their staff to find out *'how many looked after children do we have who have had their looked after health assessments completed on time?'* Administrative staff were sent around all their social work teams, to open all the filing cabinets and look through looked after children's files, in order to count the number and percentage of children who had their health assessments completed on time. This was because this important health information was usually buried deep in the individual files held by the social workers, and wasn't monitored or aggregated centrally.

There was usually no overall system for the social services department or the corporate parent to know how well the department was performing on this or other key indicators. Only a few foresightful Assistant Directors had established a database within which to hold this information.

Frank Dobson also addressed the need for elected councillors to accept their responsibilities within his now famous 'Corporate Parent' letter to elected members. The corporate parent was expected to behave towards their children in care as if they were their own children.

The Quality Protects years

Frank Dobson announced the Quality Protects programme in November 1997. It required councils to collect key performance data and to submit Management Action Plans to both the Department of Health and to Social Services Inspectorate. Information was also expected to be shared across multi-agency partners and to inform the Management Action Plans. In many places this information wasn't readily available.

In 1997 An American Psychologist called David Riley wrote an article in the *American Psychologist* journal describing the power of local data collection as a catalyst for driving local actions. Riley had been tasked with getting local communities within the State of Wisconsin to act upon state sponsored research findings on vulnerable children. Riley had struggled to gain any local commitment for this. Most localities suggested that the state-wide research wasn't applicable in their locality. Riley took the step of asking some localities to replicate the state-wide research but on a local basis. His 'discovery' was that each locality did indeed have the same issues that were identified in the state research. When the local communities discovered that they had the same difficulties, local steering groups were established much more readily, and local commitment to local actions was much more forthcoming. Local funding was made available to solve the problems that were being locally 'discovered' as if for the first time. Riley found that he was able to replicate this process in every small community. He subsequently delivered a state-wide change programme by 'changing 100 local communities'.

The Riley article is apocryphal because it mirrors the processes embarked upon within the Quality Protects programme. It also mirrors the current successes within the Healthy Care Programme: local partnerships of key people auditing local arrangements using pre-set templates to monitor for difficulties and areas for improvement, that lead onto local actions for improvement.

Between 1998 and 2003 Quality Protects Management Action Plans (MAPs) were the main vehicle for establishing joint-agency activities to support looked after children. Joint agency Quality Protects steering groups coordinated their action plan, the spending of the QP ring-fenced grant, and monitored performance. Participation officers were recruited to ensure that the voice of looked after children was heard. One of the early resentments expressed by looked after children was the annual looked after medical.

Jointly-funded posts were put into place in many councils. This led to increases in advocacy services, looked after nursing posts, looked after Child and Adolescent Mental Health Services (CAMHS), and looked after education services. New formats emerged for Personal Health Plans and Personal Education Plans. These were usually created in consultation with young people, who would normally be involved in the wording and the design of the documentation.

At the same time, pressures on council budgets and services led to:

- A reduction in the level of residential care provision.

- An increased reliance on foster care placements.

- Recruitment difficulties in foster care and in social worker posts.

Social services were generally able to use their new QP monies to improve the services for which they were solely responsible: fostering services, assessment services, participation and involvement services, and independent reviewing services. It was less easy to replicate this new commitment with other council departments (leisure, education, housing) or with health partners (CAMHS support, dedicated health assessments, and dentistry services). This ongoing struggle to obtain the resources, the capacity and the priority commitment for looked after children is what underpins the concept of 'fragmented Corporate Parenting'.

Currently the Quality Protects programme has ended and the ring-fenced monies and developments have been passported into mainstream services. Despite large-scale improvements in services for looked after children, progress has been uneven. Good practice models are emerging in a number of areas and the better councils have attempted to address the potential fragmentation in the coordination of services for looked after children. They have:

- Pursued a whole-system approach with coordinated multi-agency development initiatives in residential homes, with foster carers, social workers, designated teachers, designated health staff, school governors, and designated elected councillors.

- Linked health assessments with other screening tools for substance misuse, sexual health and mental health where necessary.

- Co-located multi-agency LAC specialists with dedicated LAC health capacity into single looked after health teams.

- Made closer connections between the designated services for looked after health, education, leisure and employment support.

Alongside our ability to specify better practice and improved performance, there is emergent key learning from the Healthy Care Programme (see Chapter 2 on Healthy Care). The Healthy Care Programme has been beneficial on a number of key issues. It has:

- Adopted a positive 'well being' model of health rather than a 'ill-health' model.

- Taken a four strand delivery model that includes: policy, practice, participation and partnership.

- Provided councils with a hands-on toolkit of materials that should be used locally and consistently within a multi-agency partnership.

- Recognised the requirement for looked after children's issues to be specifically and separately managed within a formally constituted multi-agency strategic process and thereby address 'fragmented corporate parenting'.

Although the Healthy Care Programme was commissioned as a pilot process with only seven original pilot sites, currently over 50 councils have implemented the Healthy Care Programme within a specific multi-agency partnership.

The Healthy Care Programme is implemented through a Multi-Agency Looked After Partnership (MALAP), which functions (for looked after children) along similar lines as those envisaged for Local Safeguarding Children's Boards. The Multi-Agency Looked After Partnerships (MALAPs) are in effect the ACPCs for Looked after children.

Successful pilots have fully involved children and carers in the partnership and its planning processes. Healthy Care partnerships have been successful where they are made up from a wide range of officers and agencies, and successful partnerships have received top-level support for their activity from directors and chief executives in councils and PCTs. Key partners include a core commitment from health, social services education and leisure departments.

Unsuccessful pilot partnerships did not devote the time and capacity to partnership working and often viewed 'health' as outside the core business of a social care organisation.

In several areas the Healthy Care partnerships have been re-named as Multi-Agency Looked After Partnerships or 'MALAPs' in order to escape any confusion over their purpose. These are configured as sub-groups of the council's Children and Young People's Strategic Partnership (CYPSP's) or the Children's Trust Board. They also have direct reporting links to the Corporate Parenting Committee or its equivalent.

This structural support and linkages to the senior planning groups is necessary and also emphasises the importance and complexity of the range of issues for looked after children.

The MALAPs have usually been re-configured from existing narrowly defined officer groups, e.g. the Quality Protects Steering Group or equivalent. The new MALAPs have

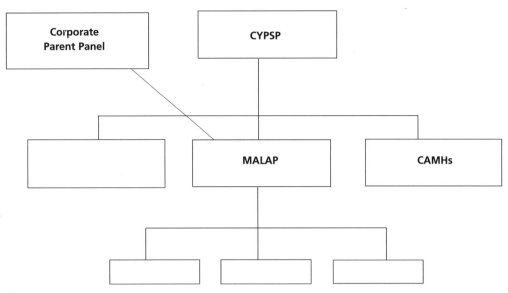

Figure 3.1

taken the opportunity to review progress against performance and good practice by using the Healthy Care Toolkit.

In other words, the MALAP is the formal infrastructure for multi-agency initiatives for looked after children, and the Healthy Care Programme is a toolkit of materials that the MALAP partnership can use to improve outcomes for looked after children. Because the Healthy Care Programme addresses most of the looked after children's agenda, the MALAP is in effect delivering the five outcomes for *Every Child Matters*.

In several Government Office regions there are MALAP Regional Support Groups in existence. In these Regional Support Groups, the Chairs of the MALAPs come together within a regional support forum led by key staff in Government Offices. In these groups, the Chairs of the MALAPs can share action plans, compare progress and share good practice. In several of these supported networks the MALAPs received:

- £1,000 to support the creative participation of children.

- 2 days of experienced consultancy support.

- The Healthy Care Standard.

- Healthy Care Evidence Grid.

- Healthy Care Audit Tool.

- The publication *Healthy Care: Building the Evidence Base*.

- Healthy Care Feasibility and Evaluation Reports.

- Access to a regional network of support, plus progress and feedback events.

The emerging MALAP infrastructure is therefore strategically well placed to take forward additional partnership tasks. The new MALAPs are not only delivering the Healthy Care Programme, they are also co-ordinating all the dedicated LAC services, e.g. increasing looked after CAMHs capacity and promoting resilience-building, improving the wraparound support to foster carers and residential staff, developing increased access to looked after leisure services, improving health promotion for looked after children, training foster carers using a multi-agency training model, increasing access to employability and helping looked after children to access education support services.

The MALAPs are also well placed to take forward other tasks, e.g. coordinating Joint Area Review tasks for LAC, the Choice Protects multi-agency service mapping tasks, and key commissioning activities (needs analysis, service-mapping, gap-analysis, local commissioning, with linkages to regional commissioning).

In some localities (e.g. South Tyneside Council) the MALAPs are also formal commissioning groups. They have formal commissioning plans which feed-into the Council's Commissioning Strategy for Children's services.

The MALAP therefore functions as a:

- Co-ordination group for delivering Looked After Improvement Programme (Life Chances of LAC).

- Coordination group delivering the government's *Every Child Matters* agenda for looked after children.

- Multi-agency group that monitors performance and outcomes for looked after children's life chances.

- Delivery mechanism for LAC performance indicators in the delivery and improvement statements, the annual performance assessment, the joint area review and the local delivery plans.

The MALAPs are therefore addressing the 'fragmented Corporate Parenting' as previously described.

One of the major benefits from adopting a MALAP model is in its wide membership and constitution. MALAP membership is usually made up from representatives of the following people:

- Young people and carers.

- Looked After Children's Participation Officer.

- LAC Leisure Services Officer.

- Children and Families Lead within social services.

- ConneXions Service Manager.

- Looked After Psychologists – clinical psychologist or ed. psychologist.

- LAC nurse or designated doctor for looked after children.

- Primary Care Trust's Children's Lead Commissioner.

- Teenage Pregnancy Coordinator.

- National Healthy School Standard Coordinator.

- Drugs Action Team Lead.

- Youth Offending Service Manager.

- Looked After Education Lead.

- Sure Start/Children's Fund Manager.
- Leaving Care Service Lead.

While it would be uncommon for all the above members to be part of the MALAP Steering Group they are all likely to be members of the various MALAP sub-groups. In several places the MALAP sub-groups are formed along the *Every Children Matters* five outcomes infrastructure (e.g. Durham County Council's MALAP). Successful MALAPs have begun by:

- Ensuring the MALAP is as widely constituted as possible, especially including young people's participation.
- Obtaining the formal sign-up and endorsement of the key minimum agencies (health, social services, education and leisure services).
- Identifying a communications strategy lead.
- Planning the multi-agency use of the Healthy Care Audit Tool and the Healthy Care Action Plan.
- Involving children, carers and young people in setting up the partnership.
- Clarifying reporting links with Children and Young People Strategic Partnership or Children's Trust Board.
- Formalising the reporting link to the Corporate Parent Panel.

Participation of children and carers has been a central theme for all the MALAPs. Children are active members of the partnerships – either by direct membership or by comprehensive representation.

In South Tyneside, a comprehensive review of the arrangements for Looked After Health Assessments uncovered substantial resentment that led to a major review of the processes for conducting Looked After Health Assessments. In Northumberland, the MALAP Action Plan was critiqued by their looked after children's participation group. The children were critical of several weak areas in the implementation of the plan that were subsequently addressed by the council. In Torbay Council, looked after children have been encouraged to 'inspect' the multi-agency service arrangements and to formally report back to the council on how well the services are being delivered. Gateshead Council, for example, has a children's Shadow MALAP (the young people wanted it titled 'ShMALAP'). It meets on the same basis as the MALAP and discusses the same documents that are considered by the MALAP. The children's comments on the council's looked after policies and Action Plans are formally presented to the MALAP and thereby onwards to the CYPSP.

Gateshead Young People's Shadow MALAP

In Gateshead there was a strong commitment from the outset for the formation of a MALAP and that young people would have a central role in influencing its decision-making.

The MALAP ensured young people participated in one of its first tasks in completing the Healthy Care Audit. Subsequently the MALAP ensured young people's wider participation throughout all MALAP activity.

The initial aim of this involvement activity was to:

- Ensure young people had formal access to decision-making at this level.

- Create transparency in the decision-making structures.

- Enable greater access to decision makers.

- Create mechanisms that would enable LAC's views to be heard through the MALAP.

- Create innovative projects based on young people's enhanced involvement.

Young people came together from across Gateshead in April 2004 to look at how they could create their own mechanisms to achieve these aims.

The young people were from a range of backgrounds. They lived in foster care, residential care and accessed services for children with disabilities. The group identified the need to 'shadow' the decision-making of the MALAP and created a dedicated group to do this. They named this group the 'ShMALAP' – (Shadow MALAP).

Over the first few weeks of the group coming together they achieved actions including:

- Feeding their views into the Healthy Care Audit through individual interviews based on questions generated by the MALAP.

- Creating a draft 'Who's Who' guide where young people interviewed members of the MALAP in their workplaces and asked them the following questions:
  – What is your job title?
  – Who do you work for?
  – Tell us what your job is in one sentence (not allowed to use words like *strategic*, *responsibility*, *policy* and other similar phrases)
  – What do you want to do on the MALAP?
  – How will this help young people?

Their answers along with their photos were placed into a guide to create transparency in decision-making and to generate relationships between the MALAP and ShMALAP that would encourage future debate.

Young people requested the creation of an email inbox at *shmalap@gateshead.gov.uk* to enhance young people's access and enable them to raise issues to the MALAP. Young people have formal space on the MALAP agenda dedicated to them.

The ShMALAP identified three main health priorities that they wanted action on for the year:

- Drugs and alcohol.

- Sexual health.

- Emotional well being.

The nature of the ShMALAP through the identification of these priorities changed from a regular meeting group to a more active development group with young people led activities and actions being facilitated under the banner of ShMALAP.

These development activities have included young people participating in projects relating to their priorities including:

Young Peoples Outreach Project

Young people participating in a six week drug education programme where they 'tested' the elements of the programme to be rolled out across the borough and changed them accordingly. A huge element of this project was around planning activities including a residential programme. The residential was devised, planned and organised by young people and included outdoor activities including caving and high ropes as well as drug education.

Sexual health

Young people came together and influenced the writing of the new Sexual Health Policy and Guidelines for Gateshead. An introductory session led to young people wanting to create an information resource for other young people. The content of these workshops will be placed on the One Voice Youth Network Site. *www.ovyn.org.uk*

Mystery shopping

Young people have participated in training and are developing standards to conduct a mystery shopping project to be carried out in all sexual health services across Gateshead.

Changemakers

ShMALAP members have been successful in securing their own funds from Changemakers and have planned, developed and facilitated a taster event to promote good health for care leavers and other young people who may be marginalised. The taster event included a Question Time with high level decision makers from Gateshead Council and Health and included councillors; penalty pool shoot out where young people played the Director for Learning and Children; to gather pledges and sign up activities for future projects.

Future projects

Young people have initiated interest in doing the Three Peaks Challenge and are currently looking at funding and support for this project.

Young people are also working on an allotment project. They have identified a community health site and are working with Parks to build up their experience and expertise.

Examples such as these are being repeated around the country as the MALAP infrastructure genuinely engages with children and carers.

How MALAPs are shaping activity for looked after children in the regions

Capacity planning and benchmarking for the service capacity to support looked after health is a key step to ensure adequate arrangements are in place locally. There are currently no regional or Strategic Health Authority standards or processes for ensuring that the level of primary care trust support to looked after health is adequate or 'fit for purpose'. In Trent's

Strategic Health Authority, a set of looked after health standards has been produced, derived from the LAC Health Guidance, to inform the SHAs performance management of the PCTs in the SHA area.

In the North East a regional benchmarking questionnaire *Health Inequalities for Looked After Children, 2004* (DfES, 2004) was completed by the regional MALAPs and it identified significant variations in capacity to support looked after children's health. It identified, for example, that in some localities looked after children who needed a CAMHS service would get one immediately, and in other localities they may have to wait many months for an outpatient appointment. This regional benchmarking exercise is allowing each MALAP to consider the level and adequacy of its looked after health capacity in comparison with other localities in the region. It is thereby helping to raise the capacity in localities where it is insufficient. This 'fit for purpose' capacity audit is identifying the components of an ideal looked after health team. Table 3.3 describes, for an approximate size of looked after population of 400 children, the minimum service levels that are required. Not all councils will require the exact composition as described, but the overall capacity requirement as described is well recognised.

Apart from ensuring that the level of service capacity is adequate to deliver coordinated multi-agency support to the looked after children, the MALAPs are also coordinating other activity. They are ensuring that the MALAP Action Plans also include joined up funding links between other programmes such as between CAMHs support, Choice Protects, Education Protects, and the Healthy Care Programme. The MALAPs have also identified a key role for Looked After Training Officer roles. There is a need to link across all the professionals identified above and to deliver a coordinated programme of training and consultancy to foster carers, residential staff and social workers.

The benchmarking exercise described above is also identifying that in most of the councils the leisure support to looked after children is inadequate. The support of the council's leisure services and establishing a looked after leisure budget is essential.

Consider for a moment the level of sports and leisure equipment that is offered to children in most reasonably well-off households. There will be a regular supply of training

Table 3.3   Minimum service levels per 400 LAC

Professional	Part time/full time (%)	Hours required (hrs)
Paediatrician	80	30
LAC psychologist	200	74
LAC therapists	200	74
LAC nurse	100	37
Admin/IT/Data Set	100	37
Priority links to psychiatry	20	8
LAC leisure service	200	74
Drugs worker	100	37
Health promotion worker	50	19
Sex and relationships worker	80	30
LAC training officer	50	19

Table 3.4 Leisure budget

No. of LAC	No. of leisure officers required?	Equipment budget @ £6 pw	Equipment budget £10 pw
200	1 FTE	£120,000 pa	£200,000 pa
300	1.5 FTE	£180,000 pa	£300,000 pa
400	2 FTE	£240,000 pa	£400,000 pa
500	2.5 FTE	£300,000 pa	£500,000 pa
600	3 FTE	£360,000 pa	£600,000 pa

shoes, clothing and other sports equipment – tennis racquets, skateboards, bicycles, footballs, netballs, basketballs, hockey sticks, crash helmets, etc. Children will pick up and drop off their activity in these sports or leisure interests in seasonal or other periods as their interest develops or wanes. Most looked after children do not experience the same level of equipment support as this. It is commonly recognised that when children leave their placements they are not generally moved from one placement to another in a large van due to the vast amount of space required for all their sports and leisure equipment and clothing. An individual leisure allowance of between £300 and £500 is not unreasonable to expect councils to provide.

Table 3.4 describes the levels of funding and leisure staff required to support a population of looked after children.

Tables 3.3 and 3.4 above give some indication of the financial resources required to support looked after children adequately. It also illustrates why it is difficult to prioritise adequate services for looked after children when they are competing with other funding priorities within the council's social care, children in need and child protection services. Historically, providing adequate services for looked after children has always been a council struggle, and one where the children who are looked after are frequently losing out.

In four Government Office regions there is a regional support group based in the Government Office which is for MALAP Chairs and is supported by a number of regional key players such as:

- DfES Regional Development Worker for Looked After Children.
- Young People's Drugs Adviser.
- Regional Teenage Pregnancy Coordinator.
- Special Educational Needs Partnership Regional Facilitator.
- CAMHs Regional Development Worker.
- Sure Start Regional Coordinator.
- Connexions Regional Coordinator.
- Regional Arts Council children's inclusion lead.

An example of regional support to MALAP Chairs was the highly successful North East's Looked After Arts and Culture Festival which took place at the Gateshead SAGE Music Centre in August 2005. Each council's MALAP has nominated an Arts and Culture lead for looked after children to link to the regional Looked After Arts and Culture Forum. This regional forum is planning and coordinating activity to support each annual Festival of Looked After Arts and Culture in the region. Local MALAP funding bids have been made to regional funding bodies such as North East Museum, Libraries, Archives and Culture (NEMLAC), Arts Council England North East (ACENE), and Big Lottery Fund (BLF). This funding is linked to local libraries and museum's work with looked after children who are preparing work in advance of each regional Looked After Arts and Culture Festival.

Another example of regional-local support activity is the regionally coordinated audit of high-cost children in out of region placements. This audit was assisted and funded by the DfES Looked After Task Force. Each MALAP coordinated a detailed multi-agency case study of its 12 highest-cost children who were in out of region placements. This information was collated into a regional database and the implications for re-provision of local services was fed into the NE Regional Commissioning Unit for children in out of region placements.

In two of the North East MALAPs there are specific sub-groups for Looked After Leisure. Leisure services are leading the work of the sub-groups, and the activity is designed to coordinate improvements in access for looked after leisure activities.

There is also a North East Looked After Football network where teams from local authorities play throughout the year in a friendly 'festival' atmosphere for regional trophies. The feedback from the children involved is that they are now better at accessing leisure activities alongside their looked after peers in a way that wasn't previously as accessible or welcoming within the wider range of mainstream sports activities.

Conclusion

The Healthy Care Programme has been the prompt for establishing a large number of MALAPs around the country. At this point there are over 65 of them delivering the Healthy Care Programme – almost half of all the councils in England. These new partnerships have established a new infrastructure for multi-agency coordination and delivery of the performance improvement agenda required by *Every Child Matters* and by the Healthy Care Programme. Key to the new processes has been the involvement and participation of children and carers at the centre of this activity.

Core success features of the new multi-agency partnerships are that they were:

- Established under the oversight of the Children and Young People's Strategic Partnerships or Children's Trust Boards.

- Led by a senior officer – usually the lead officer for children's services, and supported by a MALAP Coordinator.

- Linked to the Corporate Parent Scrutiny Process (and the CYPSP) with a clear reporting mandate and terms of reference.

- Supported by a Looked After Training Officer role.

- Addressing developments within the wide looked after 'whole-system'.

- Prioritising the participation of children and carers in the planning and delivery of improvements.

- Improving the health and well being of all looked after children by adopting a wide 'well being' model of health (rather than an illness model), as required by the Healthy Care Programme.
- Addressing fragmented corporate parenting.

It is to be hoped that these new partnerships or MALAPs will continue to grow and develop in order to offer a permanent and well resourced level of support for looked after children.

References

Corbin, T., Gatward, R., Goodman, R. and Ford, T. (2003) ONS/DoH. *www.statistics.gov.uk*

DfES (2003) Statistics at *//www.dh.gov.uk/PublicationsAndStatistics/Statistics/Statistical-WorkAreas/StatisticalSocialCare/fs/en*

DfES (2004) *Health Inequalities for Looked After Children in the North-east, 2004* is available from *http://www.dfes.gov.uk/choiceprotects/publications/ http://www.publications.parliament.uk/pa/cm199798/cmselect/cmhealth/319/31902.htm*

DoH (2002) *Promoting the Health of Looked After Children: Guidance.* London: HMSO.

House of Commons (2001) *Health – Second Report.* London: Health Committee Publications.

Melzer, H. *The Mental Health of Young People Looked After by Local Authorities in England.* London: The Stationery Office.

Riley, D.A. (1997) Using Local Research to Change 100 Communities for Children and Families. *American Psychologist.* 52: 4, 424–33.

Utting, W. *People Like Us: The Report of the Review of the Safeguards for Children Living Away From Home.* London: The Stationery Office.

Chapter 4

The Need for Health Policies and Protocols and the Importance of Training

Kathy Dunnett

Local authority work is typically dominated by many policies, procedures, plans, protocols and guidance. Whilst it is essential to have a framework for everyday work to ensure consistency and safety in practice, it is also essential that these are accessible and understandable by the staff who are delivering the work. In some instances, statements of policy quoted by senior management do not translate well to the coal face where people are working with staff shortages, lack of resources, lack of support, poor working conditions and lack of key skills due to want of experience and training.

A good policy needs to be one that:

- Staff can relate to.
- Is clear.
- Is easily understandable.
- Is free from jargon.
- Is explicit in its expectations and outcomes.

This in itself is quite a challenge, as working within the 'looked after' arena will be a range of professionals from health, education, social care etc. Within those professions there will be a range of qualified and unqualified staff, who bring different skills and expertise, but also different views and attitudes, depending on their background and experience. Many of the health policies that a local authority would want to consider may involve considerable multi-agency working, therefore it is important to engage as many agencies as possible in the initial consultation stages of policy making. Any policy that is jointly agreed between different child care agencies will need to be 'officially' passed as an agreed way of working, e.g. primary care trusts need to rubber stamp policies via 'the Board'.

So why have a health policy?

Not only does it give a framework for good and safe practice, it gives staff a responsibility and children and young people an entitlement. Without a policy, the essential services may be poorly delivered or overlooked. It gives staff a standard by which to be measured, which can be addressed through supervision or governance. An example might be the case of immunisations and looked after children. This is an area of much concern for Public Health Officers and Immunisation Coordinators, and yet there is very little guidance to either health professionals or social workers on how to achieve a full immunisation programme, bearing in mind that when children move around, their health records are difficult to access and young people do refuse to get the immunisations done. There is some guidance for health professionals in the form of *The Green Book* (DoH, 1996) that is largely relevant to practice nurses, health visitors and school nurses. The importance of immunisations needs to be understood by social workers, foster carers and residential care staff. The fear of 'overdosing' on immunisations needs to be dispelled. The main outcome from too many of a particular immunisation will only be a sore arm. The devastating effects of measles, polio or meningitis (whilst still rare with 'herd' immunity) are far more serious, with the potential for disability and even death.

Sexual health is another area of high concern (see chapter on Sexual Health, Sexuality and Sex Education for Children and Young People in Care) and policy guidance here would encourage social care professionals to address this highly sensitive issue, which in the past has been extremely hit and miss, relying on the experience of individuals, but without local or national guidance or support for the work. It is only in recent years that the framework from the National Children's Bureau was published to initiate this work (Patel-Kanwal and Lenderyou, 1998) and the Teenage Pregnancy Unit issued their guide on the website (*www.dfes.gov.uk/teenagepregnancy*).

Medications, also an area of concern and failing for many residential establishments, has had very little guidance, however, in 2003 a recommended format was launched on the Royal Pharmaceutical website – *www.rpsgb.org.uk*

So who should be involved in writing health care policies for looked after children?

Depending on what the policy is about, a range of professionals could be consulted to provide expertise, practical advice and achievable aims and objectives. Carers and young people should also be consulted. This should ensure that the policy is workable and will inform children and young people appropriately, giving them the skills they need to be able to achieve good health. Research informs us that young people appreciate discussion around the issues, rather than facts and figures (Allen, 1987). Professionals to be included in any consultation should be:

- Health professionals.
- Educational/school professionals.
- Social care staff.
- Policy development officers.
- Carers.
- Children and young people.
- Ethnic minority groups.
- Specialists in learning disabilities/physical disabilities.
- Religious and cultural groups.

Anyone can initiate policy work, but it is essential to have up to date information and support from appropriate experts. Consultation should be as wide as possible, in order that everyone feels that they have had an opportunity to air their views. A timescale needs to be adhered to, so that all involved understand their responsibility about gathering information for an end product. If consultation goes on for too long, the impetus can be lost to take the work forward and enthusiasm wanes. Policies can get lost in systems where there is a high demand of work, and if the development/consultation phase goes on for too long, there is a danger that other priorities will become more important.

Other policies recommended by the Department of Health in the *National Minimum Standard for Children's Homes* (DoH, 2002a) are as follows:

- Health – immunisations and screening, nutrition and diet, exercise and rest, personal hygiene.
- Health and safety (including food hygiene).
- HIV/AIDS awareness, confidentiality and infection control.
- Care practices towards children of the opposite sex/intimate care.
- Sexuality and personal relationships.
- First aid and the administration and storage of medication.
- Smoking.
- Alcohol.
- Drugs and misuse of substances.

In the absence of national guides for residential and foster care, the following organisations may be of use:

- British Association of Adoption and Fostering.
- National Foster Carers Association.
- Champions for Children and Young People in Care (CPHVA).
- National Children's Bureau, Young Minds.
- Who Cares? Trust.

There are obvious links with local schools polices, and the Healthy Schools website. The innovation of Healthy Care (NCB) is an obvious place when beginning to look at any health issues for looked after children (see chapter on Healthy Care).

Links to training

Training in health care should be a fundamental part of any training package for both foster carers and residential care staff.

Until fairly recently training in health care has been piecemeal and without structure. It may be difficult for non-health professionals to understand the need for policies on health care and training. Children and young people are naturally fit and healthy because of their age, and it is only later, after many years of poor life-styles (smoking, substance abuse, poor nutrition), that problems will begin to emerge. There is, therefore, a huge health promotion agenda for all children and young people, but especially for looked after children and care leavers.

Looked after children and care leavers are a special case for consistency in health messages and constant health promotion. Without the safety net of ordinary family life, looked after children can grow up not knowing about the fundamental issues of home-keeping, such as; decorating, washing clothes, cleaning and hygiene, food hygiene and healthy, balanced regular meals. Even, if they are lucky enough to find a permanent or semi-permanent placement, if there is no guide or training concerning some of the more difficult issues such as sexual health or substance misuse, it is likely not to be addressed. Even within natural families, many parents may flounder without help and guidance. Looked after children whose lives are in a constant state of flux, sometimes moving to many placements or excluded from school, are likely to reach adulthood without having any consistent health messages, and in the worse possible scenario, lacking in immunisations and general health care because of lost health records and inconsistency with health planning and health promotion. It is vital, therefore, to address this gap for a highly vulnerable group of children, with sound health policies, protocols and guides, backed up with a rolling programme of robust training.

Training can be delivered in a variety of ways. For residential care staff, a certain amount of initial training can be performed within the unit with competent and experienced members of staff. Many staff/trainers have a problem with assessing staff for 'competency' after a short training session. Competency is really only possible after training and a period of consolidation of learning within an appropriate learning environment.

Let us take medications training as an example. Preliminary training could be delivered on site, with basic written guidance on the procedure, perhaps a flow chart to aid understanding. There should then be a period of time when the member of staff is supervised for compliancy in the procedure. A more in-depth training session could then be part of mandatory training offered to all new staff within the first few months of employment. Updates would also be necessary as new local and national guides are issued. Also, if medications are a rare occurrence for staff, regular training is useful to remind staff of good practice. Problems with medications should be part of a policy, which may lead to some staff members being disciplined if procedures are not followed.

For foster carers, the situation may be more complicated. Foster homes may not seem like home if too much is structured and recorded. However, there should be a standard of good practice and there are some recommendations in the *National Minimum Standards for Fostering Services* (DoH, 2002b). It is advisable that carers should at least record controlled drugs, for example Ritalin. Basic understanding of medications should be delivered within a Health Induction Programme such as that recommended by the National Children's Bureau (Lewis, 1999). Problems with medications should be addressed via supervision in the same way as with residential care staff.

Training for both residential care staff and foster carers should be challenging and thought provoking, practical and instructive. Caring for anyone, whether it be nursing, hairdressing or chiropody – cannot all be learned via a book or in a classroom. The more practical tasks must be learnt 'on the job', with experienced carers or staff. Whilst policies and procedures are important, giving boundaries and guidance for the jobs that need to be done, the training should always be linked to the more practical tasks of holistically caring for the child.

It is probably useful for carers and staff to have the training programme delivered in short bursts over a period of weeks, in order that learning can be consolidated. During this time, carers and staff should be adequately supervised and supported.

Currently, training programmes for carers/care staff are becoming more formalised through the requirement to attain NVQ 3. The programme from the National Extension College Trust (NEC)/National Foster Care Association (NFCA, 1999) is a useful tool when considering any aspect of training for carers. Up until this time, training, particularly on health care was minimal across the country. Hopefully, all carers/care staff will regard information on health and health promotion as an essential part of their training, and social services training departments will involve the designated health professionals within the programme.

What's happening in Europe?

There is a wide variety of training, qualifications and experience that is required for staff working in residential child care in Europe. There has in recent years been an international increase in professionalisation of residential child care work. This is partly due to the different use of children's homes over the years, once mainly 'orphanages', now often house the most difficult and vulnerable children and young people. Many have suffered extreme and ongoing trauma, and the previous scandal of abuse in children's residential care (DoH, 1992) has emphasised for staff to be better trained and therefore regard child care work as a profession.

The main profession covering child care in Europe appears to be social pedagogy. The social pedagogue includes some social work functions, and some education functions. Basically it is better understood in Europe to concern the 'general upbringing' of the child, rather than just education which is generally how the word is understood in Britain (Madge, 1994). But the level to which staff are trained varies. The majority of countries require a basic training, but some countries, such as Germany, Belgium, Luxembourg and Netherlands have opportunities to access degree level qualifications; whereas Denmark, France, Ireland, Italy, Spain and Sweden offer qualifications similar to a diploma. Some countries, such as Greece and Portugal are not specific about training requirements for residential child care. Even for the countries that offer a degree or diploma level qualification, it is not specific to residential child care, and will often be a very general training around education or social work.

Summary

So, to summarise, we need policies and protocols in place that have been developed in conjunction with the young people that they are designed to serve. The policies and protocols need to set out specific expectations and outcomes – deliverables – that are measurable and these need to be supported by training modules that will give the carers the necessary skills to deliver the proper service.

References

Allen, I. (1987) *Education in Sex and Personal Relationships*. London: Policy Studies Institute.

DoH (1992) *Choosing with Care: The Report of the Inquiry into the Selection, Development and Management of Staff in Children's Homes*. London: HMSO.

DoH (1996) *Immunisation against Infectious Diseases: The Green Book*. London: HMSO.

DoH (2002a) *Children's Homes, National Minimum Standards, Children's Homes Regulations*. London: HMSO.

DoH (2002b) *Fostering Services, National Minimum Standards, Fostering Services Regulations*. London: HMSO.

Lewis, H. (1999) *Improving the Health of Children and Young People in Public Care*. London: NCB.

National Extension College Trust/National Foster Care Association (1999) *Caring for Children and Young People: Standards-based Training for Foster and Residential Carers*. Cambridge: NEC.

Madge, N. (1994) *Children and Residential Care in Europe*. London. NCB.

Patel-Kanwal, H. and Lenderyou, G. (1998) *Let's Talk About Sex and Relationships. A Policy and Practice Framework for Working with Children and Young People in Public Care*. London: NCB.

Royal Pharmaceutical website – *www.rpsgb.org.uk*

Teenage Pregnancy Unit – *www.dfes.gov.uk/teenagepregnancy*

Appendix I   An outline training programme

A recommended health training programme could look like this.

Induction – day I

- Clarification of policies, procedures and local rules of engagement with particular attention being paid to actions that untrained staff must not carry out. E.g. Naso-gastric tube feeding.

Basic training (within the first few weeks)

- Personal Health Plans and the Health Assessment.
- Fraser Competency (see section on Fraser Competency in chapter on Sexual Health).
- First Aid. Training and supervision in medication.
- Emotional health and promoting health, esteem.
- Healthy Care – NCB Training Package – Helen Chambers (see chapter in this book).

Within six months

- Specialist training as required – percutaneous endoscopic jejunostomy (PEJ) feeding, rectal valium, etc.
- Healthy eating and exercise.
- Health promotion.

Within the first year

- Sexual health.
- Substance misuse.
- Immunisations.

Rolling updates

- Specialist training of whole staff teams every six months, including medications.

Section Two:

Health for Looked After Children: Everyone's Business

Chapter 5

Primary Care Trusts and the Health of Looked After Children

Liam Hughes

Introduction

Growing up fit and well both physically and emotionally is important if children and young people living away from home are to benefit from the care and education provided for them. The great paradox is that those who need it most often find it hardest of all to gain access to appropriate health services. Primary care trusts (PCTs) have had an important role in recent years ensuring the timely and effective delivery of health services to looked after children. Now there are new proposals for change following the publication of *Commissioning a Patient Led NHS*, which will separate out commissioning from provision in PCTs. The creation of Children's Trusts will also have a significant impact (DoH, 2003).

This chapter has been written at a time of rapid change. It describes the role that PCTs have taken, and looks forward to the new landscape of child care. The starting point is that in the last few years there has been real progress in delivering better education and social care to those vulnerable children and young people. Health services have also improved in many areas with the establishment of advisers and specialist teams for looked after children.

Yet despite these improvements there are still gaps in cover, and children in care continue to miss out on the basic healthcare which most parents would require for their own children. Primary care trusts and their local councils have the responsibility to set this right. They are expected to work in partnership with parents, schools and communities to secure for looked after children and young people the same five outcomes set out in *Every Child Matters* (DfES, 2003) and required for all children and young people – health, safety, enjoyment and achievement, making a positive contribution and achieving economic well being. For the PCTs this needs positive attention at Board level, clear senior leadership, effective planning and commissioning and sound processes for monitoring and review. It also requires robust local partnerships with social work and education, increasingly through the new Children's Trusts and integrated departments and led by Directors of Children's Services. In 2003 the Social Exclusion Unit published *A Better Education for Children in Care*, which provided a helpful introduction to the context in which these children and young people live and go to school.

Primary Care Trusts (PCTs)

PCTs were established between 2000 and 2002, to drive NHS improvement from the ground up. They have had three main aims:

- To identify local health needs and reduce health inequalities.

- To arrange preventive and treatment services.

- To work in partnership with patients, carers, communities and other agencies to strengthen the building blocks for health.

They are currently both commissioners and providers of healthcare services and have the key NHS role for local public health and health promotion.

As commissioners they are expected to give a high priority to children and young people who are looked after. They have a duty to ensure that structures are in place to plan, manage and monitor the delivery of health care for these children and young people. Some PCTs (usually the larger ones) have handled this work directly. Very often, PCTs have made joint arrangements for these services, planned them together and provide them through hosted arrangements. This made good sense, for example, in larger cities containing several PCTs and where there are problems of scale and geography.

As both providers and commissioners of healthcare, PCTs have operated at a number of levels to help children and young people in public care. Firstly, they have ensured general services as they would for any child needing health advice, diagnosis and treatment. PCTs are responsible for local independent practitioners – GPs, dentists, pharmacists and optometrists. Under the new GP contract, they may also arrange enhanced services and GPs with special interest are practicing in a variety of fields, including child health, drugs and sexual health. PCTs also provide community nurses, especially health visitors and school nurses (see relevant sections in this book on the role of the school nurse/health visitor). All of these frontline practitioners work with looked after children and young people as part of their daily work with all children and young people.

Secondly, PCTs have organised some specialist services for children with additional needs. Community paediatricians, for example, cover local child health clinics, provide medical services for children and young people with disabilities and complex health needs and support child protection services. They may also assist adoption and fostering agencies. In many places, speech and language services are managed directly by PCTs and there may be community audiology teams. Over and beyond these primary and community services, the PCT has the responsibility to commission secondary and tertiary healthcare from local hospitals and specialist centres. Given the complex health needs of many looked after children and young people it is vital to ensure that these services are well designed to help them, and PCTs need to be intelligent and powerful commissioners for all the children in their area.

This leads naturally to what has been the PCTs third level of involvement, that of health services provided specially for looked after children and young people. Some PCTs employ healthcare staff who work directly with looked after children and young people living away from home and with their carers – foster parents, daycare and residential child care staff. They also give support and advice to social services and education colleagues. They may work as external advisers and coordinators or within teams providing direct services. They may have a background in school nursing, health visiting, health promotion or mental health. Amongst other responsibilities, they are likely to have a key role in helping the whole PCT to meet its core obligations towards looked after children and young people. Where health teams for looked after children have been created, and properly integrated with their local authority's services, there is early evidence of better quality healthcare and fewer interagency problems.

PCTs have been expected to identify a designated doctor and nurse to provide clinical and strategic leadership for child health to a defined geographical population. They have also been responsible for sound clinical governance and audit arrangements to assure the quality of both health assessments and service planning. They have had to provide a named public health professional to advise about all children in need, including those looked after. They have had a responsibility to ensure that looked after children and young people are registered with GPs and dentists where they are living and that their clinical records are transferred quickly when they move. PCTs have also been expected to promote healthcare when a child or young person moves placement or is transferred to adult health services. Finally, they have had to provide appropriate training for health professionals, working closely with social services, the workforce confederations and deaneries for medical education.

The designated doctor and nurse roles are strategic: they are to help the PCTs to fulfill their commissioning responsibilities. They should have had substantial clinical experience of the healthcare needs of looked after children and young people and undergone relevant training. The designated doctor, very often, will have had considerable experience as a medical adviser to an adoption or fostering agency. The designated doctor and nurse work together to give advice, develop policy and procedures, manage information and audit, plan and participate in local training and liaise with social services, education, other PCTs and hospitals. They are expected to evaluate the extent to which the views of looked after children and young people really do inform and shape the design and delivery of 'local health services'. They have a duty to present an annual report to the Chief Executive of the PCT and the Director of Social Services or the Director of Children's Services (see chapter on the Designated Health Professionals).

The policy context

The policy context for PCTs is moving rapidly and it is an exciting time for children's policy development in England and Wales. The cornerstone document was *Every Child Matters*, the Government's Green Paper that sought both to strengthen child protection and also to reinforce preventative arrangements. It set out a vision of the outcomes to be achieved for all children and made it clear that the NHS will have a key role in helping to achieve all of them. The Green Paper influenced the Children Act 2004, which clarified lines of accountability by introducing the role of Director of Children's Services and promoted greater integration across child care agencies through the vehicle of the Children's Trust. It also established local Safeguarding Boards to oversee child protection on a statutory basis to link together public organisations in a more determined way. Sure Start schemes for young children and their parents have already made a significant impact. By 2008 there will also be over 2,500 children's centres and a rapid expansion of extended schools offering a range of additional help to pupils and families. These improvements alone would represent a major improvement in services for children and young people.

Alongside the Children's Act, the *National Service Framework for Children, Young People and Maternity Services* has been published and this will be discussed in detail below. This dovetails closely with the health improvement White Paper *Choosing Health: Making Healthy Choices Easier* (DoH, 2004). This includes in chapter three an important plan of action for children and young people, which contains the strengthening of school nursing, the introduction of Children's Health Guides and the promise of new guidance for carers of children living away from home. Finally, a cross-government Green Paper *Youth Matters* on a new Youth Service has been published, which sets out specific new proposals to improve health and provide alternatives to risk-taking behaviours.

All of these policies have the potential to improve the well being of children and young people in general. These policies will have very significant implications for looked after children and young people and together they constitute the greatest opportunity we have been given to improve the health and well being of vulnerable children and young people since the Children Act 1989.

For its time, the Act was quite visionary. It provided the modern foundations for a comprehensive framework for the care and protection of all children and young people in need. It set out expectations in relation to those living away from home and required councils with social services responsibilities to promote the health of looked after children. The NHS was to respond by assisting them and in particular undertaking health needs assessments. Unfortunately, policy and practice soon diverged. By 1999, when a consultation document *Promoting the Health of Looked After Children: A Guide to Health Care Planning, Assessment and Monitoring* was published, it was clear that there had been very little systematic monitoring of health progress and outcomes for looked after children. This echoed wider failings in the public care system, identified in Lord Utting's report *People Like Us* (DoH, 1997). These included multiple placements, scarcity of adoptive and foster parents, poorly managed children's homes, limited training for staff and organisational cultures that allowed abuse to grow unchecked. The *Quality Protects* programme that was introduced in response, required systematic action to improve services and it identified health as an area of general concern.

Research had been limited but at the turn of the century evidence was accumulating about a number of health deficits – neglect of routine immunisation screening, limited attention to chronic ill health, poor diagnosis, significant dental neglect and limited attention to mental health problems. A small local study by Hill and Walters in 2004 found that less than half of health care plan recommendations had been implemented. The Loughborough study commissioned by the Department of Health showed that more than half of the looked after children needed outpatient consultations and treatment. Studies related to national targets for health improvement revealed that teenagers in care found it difficult to get relevant advice about their emotional problems and about safe sex and the avoidance of pregnancy.

Sometimes they spoke to school nurses or youth workers and sometimes to foster parents and unidentified staff; rarely did they talk to teachers. They reported feeling uneasy in many GP surgeries because of concerns about privacy. General advice about healthy living was patchy. Because many were not attending school consistently, school-based health education often passed them by. Pupil referral units were attempting to fill the gap but the picture was uneven.

There was another side to the coin. Local authorities had been working hard to improve outcomes for looked after children. PCTs inherited many examples of good practice, with advice available to residential care homes and to foster parents. The guidance *Promoting the Health of Looked After Children* (DoH, 2002) augmented the statutory framework by setting out explicit duties and responsibilities. It provided a strong platform for PCTs and local authorities as they worked together to plan improvements. Some of the specific themes are explored in the next sections. Subsequently, the creation of Joint Area Reviews, examining health, education and social care in an integrated framework, set up mechanisms to seek assurance about progress.

Contribution of primary care trusts

PCTs are responsible for the overall arrangements for health services for looked after children and young people in their areas. They are expected to ensure that primary care teams are available and working as health advocates, arranging timely and sensitive access to GPs and other health professionals, overseeing that clinical records are well-maintained and that health assessments have been done promptly, leading to health plans that are implemented.

Councils have a duty to put in place arrangements for health needs assessments and health plans and PCTs have an obligation to assist. Increasingly these will be built into the new Assessment Framework and constitute part of the overall plan to meet the child's developmental needs. These requirements need to be covered properly in the PCTs clinical governance framework and audited. It is important that any service level agreements are specific about timescales and mutual responsibilities and that the designated doctor and nurse are given sufficient assistance by the PCT to deliver these services effectively.

The preparation of a health assessment often involves the collation of information from a variety of sources, including community health services, GPs, community dental services and family dentists, local hospitals and accident and emergency departments. This process needs to be well organised, with clear protocols about responsibilities. The PCT needs to know that this process is being handled well and that health assessments are child focused, appropriate to their age and sensitive to the child's particular needs and fears. The plan that is produced ought to balance carefully the confidential nature of the information about individual children and young people and its integration into the overall plan. Sound arrangements for reviews are required, that are sensitive to the wishes of the child or young person about attendance and information sharing.

It is expected that PCTs will provide access to a range of services and advice for looked after children and young people and this expectation has been reinforced by the new White Paper on Public Health and the National Service Framework both of which will be discussed below.

Health promotion

The new White Paper *Choosing Health* puts great emphasis on providing sound information and advice to all parents and carers and to children and young people themselves. It promotes the ideas of personalised care and choice. These are reinforced in Standard One of the NSF, which introduces the Child Health Promotion Programme. *Youth Matters* complements both of these. Looked after children and young people are more vulnerable because of the levels of deprivation and disruption they have experienced. They are more prone to risky behaviours such as misusing alcohol, volatile substances and illegal drugs, to self-harm and suicidal behaviours, to juvenile crime and to unsafe sex and sexual exploitation. Their confidence in cooking and maintaining a healthy diet is often low and many have problems managing their weight as a result of poor diet and lack of exercise.

What they need is what all children and young people need – to develop an understanding of how to maintain their own health, make healthy choices and access support. However, looked after children and young people also need additional support in developing personal and social skills, handling risky situations and moral dilemmas and keeping safe despite often low self-esteem and peer pressure. Young people in care repeatedly say that what they value most is a trusted adult who has relevant knowledge and will treat them with respect. Carers may be able to provide this themselves but they certainly need to be able to put up signposts to other services. Very often youth workers can develop the right relationships and offer sound advice and there are now many local services staffed by multi-disciplinary teams of nurses, health promotion specialists and youth workers working together. Mentors in the Connexions Service are another important resource for health promotion and so are Youth Justice staff in relation to looked after young people who have offended.

Contraception and sexual health can be difficult areas for all young people and especially so for those looked after. Specific advice for social work and social care staff and foster carers has been provided by the DfES Teenage Pregnancy Unit (DfES, 2001). There is currently a debate about a purposed requirement to report under age sexual activity; this may be a source of tension with birth parents and other relatives. Young women who are in care are more likely to become pregnant early and deliver prematurely. Both young men and young women are more sexually vulnerable and more at risk of being drawn into prostitution. PCTs therefore need to ensure that they are giving support to their Children's Services and Youth Services colleagues and that Primary Care itself offers discrete and appropriate services to young people in general which can be accessed easily by looked after young people. Advice shops, health buses and outreach sessions at youth centres may all help. School nurses are well placed to talk in confidence with young people.

Looked after children and young people may be less likely to receive drug education and support at school because of disruption to patterns of attendance. The role of residential care workers and foster parents is consequently very important and advice is available from Drugscope (2002) and the National Children's Bureau. Research shows that looked after children and young people are more likely to come from families where drug and alcohol misuse was common and to have engaged in more drug use themselves and at an earlier age than their peers. Solvent abuse is a significant problem. Local drug services in the past often missed out the under 16s and only relatively recently have Drug Action Teams been required to produce young people's substance misuse plans (see chapter on Substance Misuse).

PCTs as partners, planners and commissioners are in a key role to support this work. They need to demonstrate that they are contributing to the delivery of effective health promotion for looked after children and young people and supporting them to make healthy choices in the spirit of the NSF and White Paper. The NHS is expected to be involved with education and social care colleagues in providing health in schools and care settings.

The National Healthy Care Standard developed alongside the National Healthy Schools Standard, provides a useful vehicle for achieving this and both need active encouragement from the PCTs.

National Services Framework for Children, Young People and Maternity Services

The *National Services Framework* published in October 2004 is a ten year programme for health improvement. It is remarkably comprehensive and for the first time sets national standards for children's health and social care and also deals with maternity services. Given the evidence about the increased vulnerability of looked after children and young people right across the health spectrum, the whole of the NSF is relevant to them. The NSF encourages increased power, information and choice for children and young people. It gives a strong emphasis to health promotion pre-birth to adulthood. It requires that all pregnant women including those looked after should receive high quality care and be involved in decisions about what is best for them and their babies. It supports particular emphasis on children and families likely to achieve poor outcomes, including children living away from home. It also recommends improved access to better co-ordinated services e.g. by the co-location of provision and by developing clinical networks.

The tone of the NSF, therefore is to encourage PCTs and other parts of the NHS to focus on the needs of the whole child and young person, picking up problems early and responding in close partnership especially with schools, social services, the youth services, leisure services and relevant voluntary organisations.

Part One of the NSF sets out five standards to help local agencies achieve high quality services. Standard One deals with co-ordinated programmes of action to ensure long-term gain, including prevention and early intervention. This introduces a new Child Health Promotion Programme, multi-agency health promotion and information and services to prevent risky behaviours and promote health lifestyles.

Standard Two covers information and support for patients and carers. It emphasises support for parents with specific needs such as mental health problems, alcohol and drug misuse, relationship conflict and the particular problems found by teenage parents or parents of disabled children. It also highlights the needs of adoptive parents and adults (including paid staff) caring for looked after children.

Standard Three promotes person-centred care, respect and dialogue. It emphasises the need for sensitive and accessible services based in appropriate locations, including Children's Centres and Extended Schools. It also requires robust multi-agency planning and commissioning arrangements and arrangements channelled through Children's Trusts. Finally, it specifies knowledge and competencies for staff across all agencies dealing with children.

Standard Four describes the need for developments and age-appropriate services as young people grow up into adulthood. It reinforces policies and practice guidelines on consent and confidentiality. It requires better health promotion for young people, in particular to reduce teenage pregnancy, smoking, substance misuse, sexually transmitted infections and suicide. It emphasises access for looked after children and young people and disabled young people and those in rural areas. Finally, it draws attention to the importance of effective transition to adult services.

Standard Five deals with safeguarding and promoting the welfare of children and young people. It requires that all agencies working with children should give priority to protecting children who are being or who are likely to be harmed. This involves joint planning, the clarification of agency roles and responsibilities, local profiling to identify vulnerable children and young people, the presence of high quality and integrated services, effective staff supervision and robust record-keeping.

Although Standard One to Five deal with all children and young people and their parents and carers, their significance for looked after children and young people is of particular importance. Three examples will underline this:

- Good parenting is important for all children and especially important when the 'parent' is the local authority. Foster carers and residential care staff need information and help to cope with both minor illnesses and more serious health problems.

- Dental health of looked after children has often been poor and needs attention urgently.

- Safeguarding children and young people in care is more difficult because according to the evidence they are more vulnerable to exploitation and their problems are more complex.

Part Two of the NSF addresses children and young people with particular needs.

Standard Six requires that ill or injured children and young people should have access to appropriate health care and related services to address their health, social, educational and emotional needs. It envisages growth in community and home based services.

Standard Seven, published early in response to the Kennedy Report, covers hospital services and discharge home. Both are important for looked after children and young people, who are more likely than others to need treatment.

Standard Eight covers those who are disabled or have complex health needs. It emphasises family-centred services which promote social inclusion. These children and young people are to have increased access to hospital and primary health care services, with earlier interventional support to parents and carers. Special attention should be given to palliative care, safeguards because of particular vulnerabilities such as communication problems and to multi-agency transitions into adulthood. This standard is of central importance given the profile of looked after children and young people.

Standard Nine, on mental health, is discussed in the following section.

Standard Ten refers to safe medication practice and good multi-agency policies in place. It refers specifically to care settings and requires local health professionals to give advice, support and training to carers.

Part Three of the NSF is about maternity services. In Standard Eleven the emphasis is on woman-centred services and easy access to information and support. All women are to be supported by a known midwife throughout their pregnancy. Clearly, local services will need to plan sensitively for young mothers who are themselves looked after and for those babies who become looked after.

The NSF represents a major step forwards for all children and young people. It should be of special relevance in ensuring that looked after children do not get left out or left behind and current PCTs clearly have the responsibility to ensure that this does not happen. It will be important for the new Commissioning PCTs to carry this forwards.

Mental health

Mental Health is clearly an area of great importance for looked after children and young people. It is covered in depth in Standard Nine of the National Service Framework for Children, Young People and Maternity Services. PCTs are expected to work closely with social services and education departments and to provide high quality, multi-disciplinary Child and Adolescent Mental Health teams. Many areas have developed local networks of professionals working across a range of agencies such as schools, health centres and children's homes. They offer support to frontline staff and direct work with children and carers where appropriate. Some children and young people need more specialist help from psychologists and psychiatrists and from higher tiers of the CAMHS.

Whilst being in care by itself need not be associated with poor mental health, the evidence about risk factors does demonstrate that looked after children and young people tend to demonstrate heightened vulnerability. Some of this relates to their previous life histories, to family influences and to environmental risk factors. Unfortunately, some also relates to their circumstances in care e.g., the stability and quality of their placements and the nature of their current links with families, friends and peers. PCTs need to ensure that there are effective mental health services in place that recognise the special risks faced by looked after children and the imperative for multi-disciplinary work.

The DoH published *Making it Happen: A Guide to Delivering Mental Health Promotion* in 2001. It identified ten elements that could promote or undermine good mental health. This was a response to growing evidence about poor mental health and poor mental health services for children and young people. For example, the Audit Commission Report *Children in Mind* (1999) described the uneven and fragmented nature of mental health services for under eighteens and drew attention to the high rates of diagnosable psychiatric disorder amongst looked after young people. This was amplified in the SEUs Policy Action Team 12's report (2000) on *Young People* and by the Young Minds report *Whose Crisis?* in the same year (see chapter on Mental Health).

Looking backwards, looking forwards

Primary care trusts were created to promote fair access to the NHS and to reduce health inequalities. Children and young people in public care have been overlooked by health organisations in the past, with detrimental consequences all round. The new policy mandate provided by the Children's Act, National Services Framework, *Youth Matters* and the White Paper *Choosing Health* requires every PCT to take an active role in improving the health of looked after children and young people. This responsibility clearly rests with the Board supported by the Management Team and Professional Executive Committee and should feature in their work programmes and arrangements for governance and risk management. Given the clarity of the new policies and the overall increase in NHS resources, there should be no excuses.

This imperative is being highlighted as Children's Trusts are being brought into existence with designated Directors of Children's Services. The PCTs are expected to transfer funding to the Board of the Children's Trust to be used to commission a range of locally agreed services from health and social care agencies. Very often this will include Community Child Health Services, School Nursing, Child and Adolescent Mental Health Services, Therapy, Child Protection and Specialist Health Support for Looked after Children. In some places, service provision is also being integrated. The benefits from closer working and more integrated planning between the NHS and local authorities is likely to be very significant. The concepts of a school, and of the curriculum, are being reshaped as extended schools are being developed, sport and activity are being promoted and community links strengthened. New children's centres are being created at a rapid pace.

Whilst this is happening, the NHS itself is changing rapidly. New, bigger PCTs are being created as commissioners, and the future of provision is currently uncertain and open for debate. The new PCTs will work closely with their practice based commissioners. New forms of provider organisation will emerge, inside and outside the NHS. Great clarity will be needed about the responsibilities of each party in the new ecology of Children's Services, to ensure continuity and safety for vulnerable children. The recent and controversial White Paper provides the opportunity for closer parental and community involvement in education. Public health will be revitalised, following the Wanless Report and White Paper, and will guide more intelligent commissioning, as well as influencing the building blocks for health more powerfully.

Whatever transformations are provided, the new commissioning PCTs will need to pay careful attention to looked after children, who are children and young people with additional needs who are equally entitled to high quality NHS care.

References

Audit Commission (1999) *Children in Mind: Child and Adolescent Mental Health Services*. Wetherby: Audit Commission.

Chambers, H. (2004) *Healthy Care*. London: NCB.

DfES (2003) *Every Child Matters*. London: DfES.

DfES – *http://www.dfes.gov.uk*

DfES (2001) *Guidance for Youth Workers on Providing Information and Refering Young People to Contraceptive and Sexual Health Services*. DfES/ConneXions.

DfES (2004) *The Children Act* (2004) London: HMSO.

DoH – *http://www.dh.gov.uk/*

DoH (1998) *The Quality Protects Programme: Transforming Children's Services*. London: HMSO.

DoH (2001) *Getting the Right Start: NSF Emerging Findings*. London: DoH.

DoH (2001) *Making it Happen: A Guide to Delivering Mental Health Promotion*. London: HMSO.

DoH (2002) *Promoting the Health of Looked After Children*. London: DoH.

DoH (2003) *Getting the Right Start: National Service Framework for Children*. DoH.

DoH/Welsh Office (1997) *People Like Us. The Report of the Review of the Safeguards for Children Living Away from Home* (Lord Utting) London: HMSO.

DoH (2005) *National Healthy Schools Status: A Guide for Schools*. London: DoH.

DoH (2005) *Commissioning a Patient Led NHS*. London: DoH.

DoH (2004) *Choosing Health: Making Healthy Choices Easier*. London: HMSO.

DoH (2004) *National Services Framework for Children, Young People and Maternity Services*. London: DoH.

National Children's Bureau (General Publications) (2002) *Drugs Scope*. NCB.

Social Exclusion Unit (2000) *Position Action Team 12 – Young People*. London: ODPM.

Social Exclusion Unit (2003) *A Better Education for Children in Care*. London: ODPM.

Teenage Pregnancy Unit (2001) Loughborough Study. Teenage Pregnancy Unit – *www.dfes.gov.uk/teenagepregnancy*

YoungMinds (2000) *Whose Crisis?* London: YoungMinds.

Chapter 6

The Designated Health Professionals and Others

The role of the designated doctor for looked after children

Barbara Mary

There is some debate nationally as to whether there is a need for a designated doctor for looked after children, or whether it would be more cost effective to employ more nurses. I believe that there is an important role for a designated doctor, who should be of consultant level and that community paediatricians are particularly well placed to do this work. The role of medical advisor to adoption and the designated doctor role, gives valuable experience and insight into the needs of the looked after population, and benefits from long-term working relationships with the relevant colleagues in other agencies. It has always been a very specialised field of paediatrics and needs continuity to work effectively. There are doctors who have worked for years in the field all over this country, and who have very valuable experience and expertise to bring to the job. Their work needs to be recognised and given the consultant status it deserves. The role has too often been added to an already overloaded job description for a consultant paediatrician post, and has not been able to be prioritised over child protection and disability work.

The Department of Health Document, *Promoting the Health of Looked After Children* (DoH, 2002) recommended the appointment of a designated doctor and a designated nurse, to promote the health of these children and young people. Experience of working with a team for the health of looked after children, has shown that both positions are valuable and work well together. The recommendation was that the designated doctor role should be a non clinical one, and that the sessions allocated should be used to produce protocols and liaise with colleagues particularly in social services and education, and raise the profile of the looked after children in their area.

In practice the designated doctor has benefited greatly in also having the opportunity in other areas of the job, to work clinically with the young people by doing some of the more difficult health needs assessments, as well as sharing medical histories with them. The combination of medical advisor to adoption with the designated doctor role is appropriate, as there is much overlap in the work and also the working relationships with foster carers and social workers in the field is invaluable.

The work of community paediatricians is ideally suited to the role as they have expertise in developmental and educational medicine, as well as in child protection, and social and behavioural paediatrics. They have working relationships with many other professionals working in the community as well as with acute services, primary care and Child and Adolescent Mental Health Services. They have always worked closely with nursing colleagues in health visiting and particularly school nursing, whose work compliments each other's. Medical advisors who have been working alone for years have long been asking for a designated nurse to be appointed, and where this has happened exciting and innovative work has been produced benefiting the looked after population of that area. It is particularly essential for areas that have a high population of looked after children where health visitors and school nurses have agreed to undertake health needs assessments, and where training and research is needed.

There is no doubt that a paediatrician with the medical advisor to adoption and fostering role, has much to offer in promoting the health of looked after children. However in areas where a team for looked after children has limited funding and includes a designated doctor, then double the sessions could be provided by a designated nurse for the same money. Perhaps the best scenario is one where the role of medical advisor is part of the contract of a paediatrician and funded separately from a specialised team for looked after children.

Dreams, which were impossible to realise alone have been realised in part, and an agreed structure is in place for delivering the statutory requirements for health needs assessments for looked after children and young people. More importantly there is the opportunity to work innovatively with and on behalf of these young people in ways which do not show up on the statistics but which do make a difference to their well being both now and in the future.

The role of the designated nurse for looked after children and young people

Imelda Callowhill

Introduction

This section is an overview on the role of the designated nurse for looked after children and young people. Key to the many challenges ahead it is written with the framework of the guidance, *Promoting the Health of Looked After Children* (DoH, 2002). The optimum being guidance for delivering services from health and social services. This is where the designated nurses' role is recommended. Many PCTs across the country do not have such a role, however some nurse consultant posts have been created to excellent effect (Hill et al., 2002).

Background

In 1998 the government responded to many of their key difficulties by launching its initiative *Quality Protects*, driving forward the idea that 'vulnerable' children and young people should be securely attached to carers capable of providing safe and effective care from a holistic remit. Legislation, targets and guidance have promoted permanence through adoption, the turnover in foster care and better support for those leaving care. Yet, there is evidence to suggest that the number of children and young people in care is growing. The number of placements a child experiences is on the increase. Anecdotal information from colleagues in various parts of the country suggests that the growing numbers of children are not matched with increased posts per capita. The role and responsibilities are wide and varied and will be examined in more detail later in this chapter. The *Agenda for Change* has also had an influential place in determining whether they stay in post or revert to their former role, involving issues around trust and continuity.

The designated nurse

According to the Guidance (DoH, 2002) of *Promoting the Health of Looked After Children* the designated nurse will:

- Be a senior nurse or health visitor.
- Have substantial clinical experience of the health needs of looked after children.

It is further suggested that the designated nurse should maintain regular contact with local health staff undertaking health assessments and will liaise with social services departments and other PCTs over health assessments and health plans for out of authority placements. There is also an unwritten requirement for the nurse to assist medical colleagues in the production of an annual report, evaluating the delivery of health services for children in the care system. The production of training packages is also required to ensure that all relevant staff are appropriately trained.

Responsibility

Britain was, of course, one of the last European countries to appoint a Children's Commissioner. Professor Al Aynsley Green was recently appointed to this post and he sees this delay as symptomatic of a society in which children's services are fragmented, lack real responsibility for children, lack planning, fail to listen to patients and carers and lack effective leadership.

These are, he admits, 'pretty scathing comments', but he argues that in spite of the lack of a commissioner, no one should have any doubt about responsibility. Nurses can not shoulder this alone and must be included in the wider discussions in service development. In many places this theory has not materialised and now with the fast changing NHS 'sands' as PCTs merge, borough council departments become streamlined into Children and Learning Departments, reporting lines will change and goal posts moved. Who will be the designated nurse? Is there such a person? Who knows? Positive relationships and a caring community is a must. In order to meet the health care, educational, and welfare needs of children, staff must be supported to embrace attitudes, skills, experience and practices which create a caring environment in which each member of staff understands their role and feels confident to fulfil it.

The role of the nurse and duties to children

Nurses require a range of skills and qualities that should be a focus in the training and support of new nurses and the continuing professional development of the whole multi-agency arena.

Nurses should target health promotion and include other key life success indicators:

- Build positive relationships with individual children and young people and understand the importance of this in their lives.

- Encourage and support children and young people to take responsibility for their own learning and progress and plan their own next steps in learning about health care and related issues.

- Be an open and accessible source of information and support, provide confidentially, and ensure children and young people know they are willing to listen.

- Be able to identify needs and concerns regarding children's and young people's welfare and personal development, as well as their personal and social education progress.

- Understand the role of specialist staff in schools and other agencies and have the ability to support children and young people to seek or accept their help.

- Be ready to involve specialist staff in schools in supporting children and young people, support children and young people to approach specialist staff and refer to them appropriately.

- Be able to communicate effectively with parents, carers and other professionals, with and on behalf of the child or young person, sharing information on progress as well as problem solving.

- Be accountable for the identification of children's and young people's needs, and subsequent responses and actions, in partnership with others in the school community and other services as required.

The actual role and strategic thinking

Feedback from the young people confirms that they find the current system of dealing with the nurse as much more helpful and satisfactory. The former system of a health care service based on the 'annual medical' was seen as stigmatising and impersonal and more importantly to the child or young person without any recognisable outcomes for them. Nationally a more hands on and personal approach has emerged since the development of the nurse role in 1997. Much has happened to drive and shape future services against strong competition around star rated services e.g. coronary heart disease and stroke. Executive Committee Nurses at PCT Board level are well placed to influence the commissioning debate around the local delivery plan for health care needs. Additionally the public health paper, *Choosing Health* (DoH, 2004) is another conduit in achieving outcomes for looked after children and young people. With the strategic restructuring processes further underway again, nurses will face the challenge of understanding the complexity of the changing tides against the need to keep focused on clinical delivery or the clinical/management interface.

Conclusion

Looked after children and young people have multiple and complex mental health, social and educational needs because of their exposure to a range of vulnerable factors including loss and trauma, as well as the secondary effects of care placements and further experiences of adversity. In my experience as a former nurse post holder, in asking any child or young person in the care system what is really important to them and in the main their response will be 'I want be loved, I want to belong'. On reflection when I consider my knowledge base when I was first appointed in December 2000, did I have the skills to respond? Mental health issues were a real challenge and luckily I could refer to my colleague in CAMHS (see chapter on Mental Health). Further training in mental health for many nurses would narrow that gap and would narrow the field even more if a multi-disciplinary approach was followed. Much has been achieved but so much more needs to be delivered.

A foster carer's view of health for looked after children

AC has been a foster carer for 10 years and has had approximately 15 placements. Below is a summary of an interview with her on her experiences of some of the problems she had with her placements and her access to health care for them. The names have been changed as appropriate.

> *The hardest thing about fostering is picking away at what it's all about.*

This sentence sums up the difficulties that foster carers are faced with when they are encouraged to accept a new placement. Looked after children often come with a variety of baggage, but the reality is that foster carers rarely have much health information for the children that they have in their care. Quite often the behaviour the child or young person presents with is the biggest problem and foster carers are unsure as to what the behaviour really means. Is there emotional damage? Are there mental health issues? Do they have a particular condition that makes them behave like this? Do they have an attachment disorder? It appears that many professionals are reluctant to label children, but the reality is that help, support and sometimes benefits are attached to a label (Attention Deficit Hyperactive Disorder). Foster carers also feel more secure with a label, and feel that they know the boundaries within which to work, and the limitations of the young people.

When new carers are faced with complex young people, it must be even more difficult for them as they lack the benefit of experience. Mental health support seems the hardest of all the services to access. Child and Adolescent Mental Health Services (CAMHS) has become easier in some areas it seems, due to many local initiatives of having a fast-track service for looked after children. However, once a young person reaches 17, the services are sporadic and confusing, as neither CAMHS nor the adult services seem to want to accept responsibility.

> *We had a girl placed with us. We knew some members of her family had mental health problems and that she'd recently been diagnosed with Bi-polar disorder. Her behaviour was quite challenging, but often similar to that of a lot of teenagers who have experienced disruptive lives. It was hard to get a picture of how she used to behave before her diagnosis. Her view was that she'd always behaved that way and although we were getting a different view from her school, who said her behaviour was out of*

character, her psychiatrist supported her view of the situation and took no action. The worst thing was that she had no allocated social worker, and so nothing was coordinated. By the time she was allocated a social worker, her behaviour had progressed to such an alarming level that she had to be sectioned. She was writing in blood on her bedroom walls. The whole experience was very detrimental to the whole family, and almost destroyed our relationship with her.

When it comes to physical health issues, the problems are just as difficult. If foster carers do not have the right knowledge about the child's health history, then when they attend for hospital appointments, etc., with the child, carers will not know what questions to ask. Foster carers say they need a health professional to advocate for each child, to be able to do a search for a basic health history such as immunisations, accidents etc. There appears to be a discrepancy in what foster carers say they need in the way of health history, as to what they are told by social workers. It may be that social workers are concerned with issues of confidentiality, but there should be no problem in sharing the majority of information with a carer, otherwise it becomes increasingly difficult for carers to actually do their job and care for the child. It is vitally important for foster carers to know if a young person in their care is HIV positive, as the chances are they will be involved in some treatment. It is not possible to take a young person for treatment and not know what it is for.

It appears that often foster carers have to take things into their own hands, and try and access a health history from the parents or other family. Foster carers become an advocate for the child, pushing all the professionals to make appropriate referrals, pushing professionals to undertake tests to ascertain what condition the child has. Even the child's general practitioner does not necessarily have the information that is needed, as if the parents have been neglectful, the health problems have not necessarily been addressed.

Training on health issues for foster carers is very disparate across the country. For staff in residential establishments, there is a move to encourage all residential care workers to train for a Level 3 NVQ (see chapter on Training, Policies and Procedures). This is not always the case for foster carers. It appears to be mainly optional as to what is accessed and what is not. However, until a health course is accessed, carers do not know what they don't know. An example of this is with blood borne viruses. Carers should know to treat everyone in the same way, with 'Universal Precautions' (see Appendix 2 in the Sexual Health chapter in this book). This means to treat everyone the same, that is, as a possible source of infection. In this way, even if we are unsure of a young person's HIV or hepatitis status, the risks are minimised, because of safe practice with body fluids. Some areas do have a training strategy, with various recommendations, but the reality is that this is not implemented, perhaps due to lack of foster carers, lack of supervision, lack of compulsion. NHS Direct is perceived as being very helpful, but unfortunately there are many other highly unreliable websites that carers and non health professionals can access and obtain very inaccurate information. Carers should be warned about using other websites. The TCI training appears to be helpful, and has helped to change practice in a positive way. This training should be given very early to new foster carers, as sometimes it comes too late in a difficult placement and the child still has to be moved, because relationships have broken down.

We had a very angry and violent young boy with us. When things got difficult for him he would run away. The policy on what to do when this happened was unclear and interpreted differently by the police and emergency duty team. This was very frustrating and added to the trauma we were feeling. He wrecked our home and inflicted injuries on me before we seemed to get any real help . . .

On the yearly health assessments, it often seems a tick box exercise. Often it is only remembered at a review that one needs to be done, and is therefore done in isolation of the rest of the work, and then loses its impact and importance. The use of nurses instead of doctors appears to be an improvement, as in many cases it is the school nurses that undertake this work, so it is a familiar person, in a familiar place, and the child does not need to be taken out of school for a whole morning or afternoon. Sometimes, carers feel that these health assessments seem rather superficial, but helpful if they do focus on health promotion issues, such as sexual health and substance misuse.

It is felt that health needs a similar arrangement to education. In every school there is a designated teacher and looked after children also have an advisory teacher that can help them and the carer. Within health it is very different across the country as to what help is available, if any, as some areas still do not have any designated health professionals, whereas some areas have teams. Things do appear to be improving in education, but only after a lot of investment and work. The same needs to happen in health.

References

DoH (1989) *The Children Act*. London: HMSO.

DoH (1998) *The Quality Protects Programme: Transforming Children's Services*. London: HMSO.

DoH (2002) *Promoting the Health of Looked after Children*. London: HMSO.

DoH (2004) *Choosing Health: Making Healthy Choices Easier*. London: DoH.

DoH/Welsh Office (1997) *People Like Us. The Report of the Review of the Safeguards for Children Living Away from Home*. London: HMSO.

Hill, C. et al., (2002) The Emerging Role of the Specialist Nurse: Promoting the Health of Looked After Children. *Adoption and Fostering*. 26: 4.

Chapter 7

The Primary Care Team
The role of the GP in the care of looked after children

Jeremy Cox

Looked after children will have all of the health needs of any child. Almost all child health is provided by the primary care team (which in this particular context means the primary care team based around GPs). This team includes GPs, health visitors, practice nurses and practice ancillary staff.

The basic aspects of child health in terms of surveillance and preventative care will be provided in primary care. This will include routine immunisation and child surveillance services; practices may provide regular clinics for weighing and general health enquiries. GPs can undertake special training in Child Health Surveillance and most if not all practices will have one or more GPs with those qualifications. An important part of the primary care team's role in this regard is to facilitate the looked after child's access to these services to ensure as much continuity as possible. Part of this will be the timely passing on of records and information from one practice to another and the involvement of other agencies as required. The team may well also flag up these children and follow them more carefully than usual with home visits or by offering particular appointment slots.

The primary care team may also be asked to perform medicals on these children and these should be carried out in a timely and full manner. Some of the items may be beyond the knowledge or experience of the GP in which case further guidance may have to be sought from other services. They may also be asked to do reports that may contribute towards other agencies assessments. The main difficulty with these is to provide accurate and objective information especially when some of the information regarding the child may be somewhat 'soft'. The problems in this, for the GP, are very similar to those in child protection where they have to contribute to the jigsaw of information but have to balance the rights of their other patients and their responsibilities to the child. Again, changes in legislation and working practices may make these processes easier to follow and more to the advantage of the child.

Contribution of primary care teams

The primary care team have an important role to play, particularly in many instances in providing continuity before, during and after the child is looked after. They should:

- Act as advocates for the health of each looked after child or young person.

- Ensure timely, sensitive access to an appropriate member of the team.

- Ensure referrals to specialist services are timely to address the inequalities of looked after children.

- Provide timely summaries of health information.

- Maintain a record of the health assessment, and contribute to any action in the health plan as necessary.

- Ensure clinical records identify the 'looked after' status of the child or young person, so that their particular needs can be acknowledged.

- Regularly review the clinical records and contribute information to each review of the health plan.

(*Promoting the Health of Looked After Children*, DoH, 2002)

This leads on to the importance of tagging the child's record so that their status can be recognised and the whole team can be made aware that they may have particular needs and difficulties. Part of this process is also to have mechanisms in place so that request for information or transfer of notes can be dealt with speedily. In the future these potential problems may be reduced as the medical record for children becomes electronic and the records may well be held centrally as part of the National Program for IT in the NHS.

All members of the practice team must also be aware that these children may have particular health needs of many sorts and that timely intervention may be of great importance. This may be as an advocate with other services or assisting in the guidance of the child and its carers through the referral process into secondary care. In the future these processes may be improved as links between different agencies dealing with these children improve and Children's Trusts and common assessment frameworks are introduced.

In summary the primary care team should and can have a pivotal role in the care and support of looked after children. The importance of this work and the placing of it at the forefront of the team's thoughts is the challenge that needs to be met.

The role of the health visitor with looked after children

Christine Jackson-Hayward

The NHS is constantly evolving and in recent years more health services have been developed, especially with particular reference to meeting children's mental and emotional needs (Child and Adolescent Mental Health Service). The realisation of the impact of early childhood trauma and parenting on a child's mental health are now better understood. However, specialised mental health provision for the under fives is still poor (YoungMinds, 2004), though prevention or early detection and intervention can often improve the child's emotional and mental health prior to the need for a more specialised intervention. The health visitor is already at the forefront of early detection and intervention. Health visitors already provide, often without acknowledgement and support, a Tier 2 and, at times, a Tier 3 service to some of their families. With the fostering family, there would be no difference in the roles and services health visitors are already providing, but early recognition of who the foster carers are on their caseload would be beneficial to the local health visiting team (see chapter on Mental Health).

Developmental factors

Neglect and abuse have a huge impact on the developing child's brain and can often lead to emotional or mental health problems. We are well aware that maltreatment or trauma early in life physically alters the wiring and chemistry of the brain (Balbernie, 2001; Blows, 2003). Repeated experiences of terror, fear, neglect and emotional deprivation early in life causes severe problems within brain growth, which can affect a child's future life. The restricted brain growth not only causes physical problems such as speech, language and visual disturbances (Balbernie, 2001), it also affects emotional, behavioural and mental development, which can impact on the quality of the child's later life. Children can be very resilient, the trauma of early life events can cause some children in care very little problems but, for others, every day is a battle to be heard and understood. The role of the health visitor is paramount in these early years for supporting these children and their foster families and also in identifying early health and emotional problems. It has already been highlighted that health services are not geared up for the mental health needs of the under fives (YoungMinds, 2004). However, the health visitor is in a unique position to observe the dynamics within families. Combine this with support, continuing education and regular supervision from the Child and Adolescent Mental Health team, and the health visitor's skills would be further enriched in providing their service. The support and education from the Child and Adolescent Mental Health Service would allow earlier referral to more appropriate services and also give the education and support that foster families need to meet the emotional health needs of the child under five.

Foster carers

The percentage of foster carers on any one caseload is very different. This is due to the local authority recruitment and retention of the carers. Some areas also have private fostering agencies that often recruit on a regional basis rather than local. The same laws and minimum standards regulations that govern local authority teams also govern private agencies, and the Commission for Social Care Inspectorate ensure that they are meeting these standards, by inspecting all agencies.

The health visitor needs to be aware of the foster carers on their caseload to ensure they have knowledge of the transfer in of placements and the transfer out. This allows for easy transfer of case notes and an awareness of when health needs have not been met in a particular placement. Building a relationship and communication system not only with the child protection team but also the family placements team within the local authority will allow the health visitor an insight into who is a foster carer and possible placements. It will also be in keeping with the guidance laid down by *Every Child Matters* (DfES, 2003) and *Promoting the Health of Looked after Children* (DoH, 2002). This relationship will be of mutual benefit for both the health visitor and the local authority with the implementation of the guidelines on private fostering (Children's Bill, 2005).

To enable many foster families with under fives to build and sustain a good relationship with the health services, health visitors and general practitioners need to build and maintain an effective communication system and an awareness of the importance of each other's roles. A communication system between these professionals will ensure the child and family are not compromised or disadvantaged within an often disjointed community health care system (Butler, 1997) (see section on The Role of the GP).

The role of the school nurse with looked after children

Jane Walton and Kathy Dunnett

The role of the school nurse has changed and developed rapidly during the last 5 to 10 years. At one time the school nurse was seen as an assistant to the health visitor, who concentrated on physical inspections, such as lice and verrucas: they are now viewed as public health team leaders. They are ideally placed to straddle health, education and, increasingly, social care, and have a frontline opportunity to support communication around health issues and to give common sense answers to the practical management of health problems in school and other educational establishments.

The importance of the role of the school nurse with vulnerable children was emphasised more recently by the Chief Nursing Officer in her report (DoH, 2004a). The recent government White Paper *Choosing Health* (DoH, 2004b) stressed the need to aim for a workforce which included 'one school nurse for every secondary school, and their cluster of primary schools'. In reality, this is difficult to deliver. Whilst central government recognised the urgent need for health input in education, the recently allocated funds were not ring-fenced and did not reach the school nurse team in most areas.

Historically, the value of the role of school nurse has been questioned: it is difficult to prove the benefit of preventative work. However, when one health authority did remove the service, it was soon apparent that there were problems. School nurses had been working quietly for many years, providing opportunities for young people to discuss issues that concerned them, such as contraception and substance misuse. They also talked to parents and educationalists about the importance of health, enabling children to fullfil their full potential by addressing health issues and it was only when this service disappeared that the value of it became apparent. Unfortunately, it will probably take many years to claw back the lost opportunities of the period when there was disinvestment in such services.

The recent government publication *Common Core of Skills and Knowledge for the Children's Workforce* (DfES, 2005a) stresses the essential skills that all children's service professionals need to have in order to be able to work competently with children, young people and their families. These are:

- Effective communication and engagement.
- Child and young person development.
- Safeguarding and promoting the welfare of the child.

- Supporting transitions.
- Multi-agency working.
- Sharing information.

School nurses have been communicating effectively with children and young people for many years. Sometimes their communication may be mis-interpreted within the school by educationalists. It is important to remember that children and young people will have different relationships with adults, depending upon their professional role. It is not sufficient to simply 'tell' a child what do, but it is important to understand that '. . . some children and young people do not communicate verbally and that you may need to adapt your style of communication to their needs and abilities' (DfES, 2005a). Some children and young people have very inadequate communication skills as a result of lack of nurturing and good parenting. They do not have the language skills to be able express themselves adequately, or the knowledge to understand their feelings. Quite often, then, they will resort to abusive language and challenging behaviour. This reaction in young people needs careful handling in order to not escalate the situation, and to show them a better way of managing difficult situations (Dunnett in Wheal, 2005).

School nurses are trained in child development and child protection issues. Within the school environment they can often bring an alternative perception to that of the teachers and social workers. A balanced and informative view is essential in situations which require sharing information and multi-agency working.

> *A young girl in school began to lose interest in her school work. From being a high achiever, she lost homework, didn't pay attention in class and would stare rudely at the teacher when spoken to. Her parents had noticed a change, but considered she was just 'being a teenager'. However, in an information sharing meeting, the school nurse identified the behaviour as a possible form of epilepsy. The school nurse contacted the parent, and the diagnosis was confirmed by the hospital. Subsequent medication probably prevented a difficult situation from exacerbating.*

At times of transition, multi-agency or partnership working becomes even more essential, particularly for children and young people moving back home and care leavers (see section on Leaving Care and After Care). School nurses have long been working in partnerships and are adept at doing so.

> *No one agency alone can meet the needs of all children. Working in an integrated way enables professionals to develop a way of working where the sum of their efforts transcends their individual contribution.*
>
> (A Children Partnership Toolkit, LGA and ADSS, April 2004)

Current government thinking places multi-agency working as a priority, in order to prevent a repeat of the Victoria Climbié tragedy (DoH, 2003). Presently there are excellent examples of partnership working, which unfortunately, is often reliant on individual champions (CPHVA, 2005). The move to Children's Trust arrangements encourages all children's services to join together formally, to enable the child or young person and their family to have their health needs, along with other needs, met in a holistic and more efficient way (DfES, 2003).

School nurses are ideally placed to be able to undertake the annual looked after child health assessment. The annual medical for looked after children by doctors continued for many years before its usefulness began to be questioned (Bamford and Wolkind, 1988; Mather et al., 1997). In some areas, this led to exploration of a different model, with exciting results (Dunnett and Payne, 2000). The school nurse, is far better placed to have an ongoing knowledge of the child, and 'familiarity' with children and young people who have difficulties with relationships is crucial. They will have a record of the child's health, probably a rapport with both child and carer, and be able to address pertinent public health issues such as sexual health, smoking and diet. This work needs to be undertaken under the jurisdiction of the designated nurse or doctor for looked after children so that some of the more difficult issues which occasionally looked after children experience, can be dealt with effectively. Whilst the general health levels of the majority of children are now improving, some of the more vulnerable children are particularly susceptible to risks of teenage pregnancy and child sexual abuse (DoH, 1998).

School nurses are now often known as 'school health team leaders' and many head teams of nurses including qualified staff nurses, nursery nurses and sometimes nursing assistants. Having a range of staff and skills within a team enables the school nurse to delegate the more routine work to junior staff. This wide range of skills and knowledge enables the school health team to deal efficiently with the wide range of problems that working in a non-health environment can bring.

References

Balbernie, R. (2001) Circuits and Circumstances: The Early Neurobiological Consequences of Early Relationship Experiences and how they Shape Later Behaviour. *Journal of Child Psychotherapy*. 27: 3, 237–55.

Bamford, F. and Wolkind, S. (1988) *The Physical and Mental Health of Children in Care: Research Needs*. Unpublished. London: Economic and Social Research Council.

Blows, W.T. (2003) *Child Brain Development*. www.nursingtimes.net 28–31.

Butler, J.R. (1997) Child Health Surveillance in England and Wales: The Bad News. *Child Care Health and Development*. 23: 4, 339–54.

CPHVA (2005) *Partnership Working*. Bromley: Community Practitioners and Health Visitors Association.

DfES (2003) *Every Child Matters*. London: DfES.

DfES (2005a) *Common Core of Skills and Knowledge for the Children's Workforce*. London: DfES.

DfES (2005b) *Private Fostering Arrangements: Guidance Notes*. London: The Stationery Office.

DoH (1998) *Modernising Social Services*. Cm 4169. London: The Stationery Office.

DoH (2002) *Promoting the Health of Looked after Children*. London: DoH.

DoH (2004a) *The Chief Nursing Officer's Review of Nursing, Midwifery, Health Visiting Contribution to Vulnerable Children and Young People*. London: DoH.

DoH (2004b) *Choosing Health: Making Healthy Choices Easier*. London: DoH.

DoH/DfES/HO (2003) *Keeping Children Safe: The Government's Response to the Victoria Climbié Inquiry Report and Joint Chief Inspectors Report Safeguarding Children*. Cm5861. Norwich: HMSO.

Dunnett, K. (2005) The Health of Children who are Fostered. In Wheal, A. *The RHP Companion to Foster Care*. Lyme Regis: Russell House Publishing.

Dunnett, K. and Payne, H. (2000) How Can we Make Health Assessments More Acceptable to Looked After Young People of Secondary School Age? *Adoption and Fostering*. 24: 3.

Hall, D.M. and Elliman, D. (2003) *Health for All Children*. 4th edn, Oxford University Press.

Hewitt, O., Roose, G. and John, A. (2004) *View Finder*. YoungMinds 71, July/August.

Local Government Association and Association of Directors of Social Services (2004) *A Children Partnership Toolkit. www.creativeexchanges.com*

Mather, M., Humphrey, J. and Robson, J. (1997) The Statutory Medical and Health Needs of Looked After Children: Time for a Radical Review? *Adoption and Fostering*. 21: 2, 36–40.

Section Three:
Health Issues

Chapter 8

The Mental Health Needs of Looked After Children

Sharon White

Young Minds, the UK's leading authority on the mental health of our youth, define children's mental health as 'the strength and capacity of children's minds to grow and develop with confidence and enjoyment. It consists of the capacity to learn from experience and to overcome difficulty and diversity. It's about physical and emotional well being, the ability to live a full and creative life and the flexibility to give and take friendships and relationships'.

Research shows that more looked after children suffer from mental health problems than other young people including severe and long-term mental illness. However, their mental health needs frequently remain unmet (Mental Health Foundation, 2002).

This chapter aims to explore why children in public care are over-represented and the pre-disposing factors that make them more vulnerable and at risk. It will also define, by looking at research-based practice, what works, what doesn't and how we can positively move the agenda forward to change this unacceptable picture.

Introduction

There are three terms commonly used in relation to mental health issues:

- Mental health problems.
- Mental disorders.
- Mental illness.

These refer to differing levels of distress, confusion and inability to cope with every day events that children and young people may experience.

Mental health problems

It is estimated that 25 per cent of all children experience a mental health problem. These affect their ability to learn, to have and sustain friendships and to deal with difficulties and challenges that they are faced with.

These are borne out in the way they feel and behave. Some become over-anxious and afraid, find it difficult to trust and become angry. They may lose interest in hobbies, friendships and find it difficult to concentrate. For some this manifests in deteriorating behaviours such as aggression and criminal activities.

The Social Services Inspectorate report (1997) found that 38 per cent of young prisoners had been in care and, concluded Gunn et al., (1991) one-third of young men within the criminal justice system had a primary mental health disorder.

Mental disorders

Children and young people whose difficulties are more severe, complex and long-lasting are referred to by psychologists as having a 'disorder', this is approximately 10 per cent. Their daily lives are seriously affected and they require treatment and specialist services. Emotional problems such as depression, anxiety, social phobia and conduct disorders such as aggression, bullying and destruction are the most common types. For many of our children in care this is frequently exhibited in 'deliberate self-harm, the most common form being self-poisoning (NHS, 1998).

Mental illness

This affects a much smaller number of children and young people. Their illness is so severe that it causes them, and the people who care for them, great distress and confusion. Many have a significant biological cause for their difficulties. Examples of this may include clinical depression, psychosis and advanced cases of anorexia nervosa. Parental mental illness is often a reason for children being placed into care and they have a higher risk of developing mental illness (Rutter and Quinton, 1984). There is a risk of inheriting this through parental genes but the higher risk, suggest Joachim and Richardson, is from the effects of the parent's moods or behaviour, frequently coupled with the child assuming a carer's role for their parent.

Overall, it is estimated that 64 per cent of children in care will have a mental health problem (DoH, 2003).

What makes a child in care more vulnerable to mental health issues?

There are a number of risk factors that put any child at risk of developing a mental health problem, some exist within the child and may include temperament, learning difficulties, neurological or chronic illness, and developmental delay.

Some of the factors come from within the family e.g. parental conflict or family breakdown, poor parenting, abuse; physical, sexual, emotional, neglect, substance abuse and parental mental health problems. Other influencing factors come from within the community such as living in poverty; poor housing, unemployment, lack of economic or social support.

For looked after children it is frequently a combination of these factors that puts them at more risk to developing mental health issues.

The following diagram illustrates how these risk factors work together to increase the likelihood of a mental health problem arising. Having risk factors in two areas seriously erodes children's resilience (Vellacott, 2004).

Children and young people who enter into the care of the local authority have already suffered trauma and challenges over and above those experienced by the majority of their peers. They will frequently have been abused or neglected, suffered bereavement, disability or serious illness of one or both of their parents. Many are from poor socio-economic backgrounds and are affected by the impact of poverty and associated social exclusion.

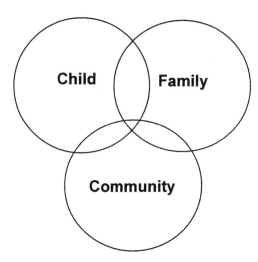

Figure 8.1   Risk factors

Bowlby (1969) and Howe (1995) identified that these children are unlikely to develop secure early attachments and will go on to have difficulties forming secure relationships. Many will develop attachment disorders.

Moving into care itself is a major emotional and physical upheaval for any child/young person to endure. Despite their abusive and neglectful home situations they often find it very difficult to accept, to settle and also blame themselves, leaving them with feelings of guilt and shame (Who Cares? Trust, 2004).

Social care staff face difficulties in providing appropriate placements that meet the basic emotional, physical and cultural needs. Lack of and unsuitability of placements often necessitates frequent move of foster, residential or secure home. Often there is also change of the professionals i.e. social worker, nurse or school. This leaves the child further unsettled, unhappy and disempowered so that they feel they cannot ask for the help they may need and lack the motivation to access any services that may, in fact, be offered to them. The stigma and shame associated with the care system that they endure is a further inhibiting factor (Mental Health Foundation, 2002).

The high levels of mental health needs in the looked after population are related to their early adverse family experiences as well as the secondary effects of their experiences within the care system, particularly frequent moves and placement breakdowns (Minty, 1999; Rutter and Quinton, 1984). These are interrelated with social, educational and relationship difficulties. Vice versa, children with mental health problems are difficult to achieve placement stability for, thus often entering a sequence that is difficult to break (Barber, Delfrabbo, and Cooper, 2001).

For many the resulting low self-esteem leads them into risk-taking behaviours including unsafe sex, self-harming, substance and alcohol misuse (DoH, 2003) (see section on Risk Management/Harm Minimisation).

Case study 1

Sarah was the eldest of three, with two brothers, and, at age 12, she went to live with her maternal aunt and uncle whilst her birth mother went into 'rehab' for 'doing long-term hard drugs'. She suffered both sexual and emotional abuse in their care and was moved into a foster home. She 'didn't fit in', they all talked with 'posh voices' and the school work was 'too hard', she didn't have 'any mates' and her foster sister 'ignored her'. Sarah missed her mum and brothers but each time they met up they 'blamed her' for splitting up the family and for 'telling lies'. Her social worker was 'kind' and her foster parents tried hard to understand but no-one could get 'inside her head'. When 'bunking off' school she met a 'great crowd', she 'showed *them*' how to do 'real drugs', and it was 'a breeze' doing the 'robbing to get the cash . . . they all had loads of money in that area'. Sarah served a two year sentence in a youth secure unit. She is now 16 and moving into her own flat.

Care leavers go through the normal problems experienced by most young people as they journey through to adulthood, however, there are also key differences. Generally they have to leave home and live independently at a much earlier age, and of these 20 per cent experience homelessness or have regular moves. They have poorer educational attainment, fewer go on to further education, experience higher unemployment rates, have unstable career patterns and, as a result, many are dependant on welfare benefits.

Leaving care, coping with the challenges and responsibilities of setting up home, leaving school, searching for employment and, for many, becoming parents at a younger age than other young people are, suggests Stein (1997) major contributory factors to the high levels of mental health problems suffered by these young people. There are also significant continuities with mental health disorders after leaving the care system (Buchanan, 1996; Cheung and Buchanan, 1997) (see section on Leaving Care and After Care).

The evidence base

Whilst it is important to remember that just because a child is looked after we should not assume they have a mental health problem, as this can lead to further stigmatising, we can conclude from research that looked after children have greater mental health needs than their peers (Brand and Brinich, 1999; Richardson and Joughlin, 2000; Roy, Rutter and Pickles, 2000). A significant number of these have more than one condition or a serious psychiatric disorder (McCann et al., 1996).

In 2002 a survey commissioned by the Department of Health was conducted by the Social Survey Division of the Office of National Statistics (ONS). Their findings showed that among young people, aged 5–17 years, looked after by local authorities, 45 per cent were assessed as having a mental disorder; 37 per cent had clinically significant conduct disorders; 12 per cent were assessed as having emotional disorders such as anxiety and depression, and 7 per cent were rated as hyperactive. The less common disorders such as 'tics' and 'eating disorders' were attributed to a further 4 per cent of the sampled population. The overall rate of 45 per cent included some children who had more than one type of disorder.

Analysis of this data to illustrate how the prevalence of mental health disorders differed between the survey of the children looked after by the local authorities and the 1999 ONS survey of those living in private households showed huge discrepancies:

5–10 year olds
Emotional disorders: 11 per cent compared with 3 per cent
Conduct disorders: 36 per cent compared with 5 per cent
Hyperkinetic disorders: 11 per cent compared with 2 per cent

11–15 year olds
Emotional disorders: 12 per cent compared with 6 per cent
Conduct disorders: 40 per cent compared with 6 per cent
Hyperkinetic disorders: 7 per cent compared with 1 per cent

Therefore, they concluded, conduct disorders seem to contribute to the largest difference in childhood psychopathology between local authority and private household populations. (The 16–17-year-olds comparison could not be made as they were not covered in the 1999 survey.)

(The term 'mental disorders', as used in the report by the ONS was as defined by the ICD-10 Classification of Mental and Behavioural Disorders, to imply a clinically recognisable set of symptoms or behaviour associated in most cases which has a considerable impact on the child's day-to-day life.)

Prevalence of mental health disorder was also analysed in relation to placement in foster, residential, with natural parents, or living independently. The distributions were found to be significantly different according to placement with:

Children living with natural parents or in residential care being twice as likely as those in foster care to have emotional disorders (20 per cent and 18 per cent compared with 9 per cent).

Children in residential care were far more likely than those in foster, natural family or independent care to have a conduct disorder (56 per cent compared with 33 per cent and 28 per cent).

They further concluded that the prevalence of mental health disorder reduced significantly the longer the child remained in the same placement provision.

Children placed in 'specialised residential care' in order to address particular types of problems such as; abused children, autism, behavioural problems, learning difficulties, physical and mental disabilities, were more likely to have mental health problems; 74 per cent compared to 60 per cent. However the major difference was in those suffering from hyperkinetic disorders: 12 per cent compared with 1 per cent of those children placed in generalist care.

It is anticipated that these worrying statistical findings from 2002 will, in actual fact, have increased. In a study conducted by Blower et al. (2004) that used both a qualitative and quantitative approach to assessing the need for mental health services for looked after children, they discovered that 56 per cent of their sample (48 children and young people) were suffering from significant 'psychological morbidity'. 44 per cent had a definite, probable or self-resolving diagnosis of at least one psychiatric disorder with impaired psychosocial function. They concluded that the 'majority' of the children and young people were suffering from 'chronic and disabling' mental health problems.

The response/What works?

Traditional services have had limited success for looked after children. It is now acknowledged that services need to be sensitive, flexible and available if service users and their carers are going to benefit from them. To this end there is a clear move to improve on the services offered, including reducing waiting lists experienced by many. This also includes a more pro-active approach that, it is anticipated, will assist in the prevention of mental health problems (DoH, 2003). Coupled with this the past decade has seen an increase in the recognition and of the importance of the mental health of all children and young people including those 'looked after'.

In response to this the government has introduced numerous strategies and policies that seek to improve on the previous inefficiencies within the care system. This began in earnest with the launch in 1998 of the *Quality Protects* programme, The Children (Leaving Care) Act 2000 and most recently the *National Service Framework for Children* (DoH, 2004) to name but a few.

Within the guidance document; *Promoting the Health of Looked After Children* (DoH, 2002), improving their health is recognised as a multi-agency responsibility and it provides a clear framework for practice across health (including mental health services) care and education services.

With this in mind training in the early identification of mental health problems is required by all health, social services and education professionals working in this field. Resources to provide this can be found within the *Choice Protects* programme (DfES, 2002) which aims to improve the quality and, in turn, reduce the number of placement moves.

Carers will also require this and additional training that assists them in promoting the child's emotional well being and when to seek expert advice.

For interventions to be effective we are strongly advised (*Quality Protects* programme) to consider the views of the children and young people themselves who can offer us a wealth of experience and guidance. An engagement with services, as previously discussed, is frequently the barrier to access, so active participation in the development of such services will encourage more participation and benefits.

Equitable and accessible CAMHS services should be offered to all looked after children and their carers, including 'fast tracking' on a needs basis. Services need to be considerate of the specific needs of disabled, black and ethnic minorities, asylum-seekers and refugee children. For those leaving care there should be a seamless provision and transfer from CAMHS to appropriate adult mental health services, though this remains a problematic area (Williams and Kerfoot, 2005).

In more recent years, CAMHS in the UK have grown and developed models of direct provision in primary care settings as well as to vulnerable client groups, including looked after children (Callaghan et al., 2004). However, as these are often supported by short-term funding initiatives, they are frequently not sustained. The LAC CAMHS grants (2004/5) have been significantly increased this year and it is hoped, therefore, that some of these may become financed longer-term.

Joint approaches to commissioning and planning involving health, education and social services are recommended for children with high levels of mental health need. This enables specialist provision for some of our most complex young people (DoH, 2003).

There are pockets of good practice emerging, particularly in areas that have seen the emergence of dedicated health/mental teams. One example of this is borne out in the findings of the *Evaluation of a New Mental Health Service for Looked After Children*. The team combines primary mental health workers (PMHW), psychology and psychiatric skills. It offers telephone and face-to-face consultation to local authority staff, assessment, treatment and training. Of the 45 children and their carers included in the research at referral and five month follow-up, they found a significant improvement in the children and carers perceived the interventions as appropriate (Callaghan et al., 2004).

Specialist therapeutic services are having a positive impact for children and carers alike. One such service in the North of England is delivered by a therapeutic social work team. Although still in its infancy, interim results suggest positive results including, significantly, a reduction in the number of placement moves for the children and young people. The model includes:

- Direct therapeutic intervention to individual children.
- Regular psychologist consultation to residential home staff.
- A 'fostering surgery' to support task, fee-paid, remand and assessment foster carers.
- Specialist training for carers.

There are also a number of successful community based services that highlight the need to work both with the child and with their support network. This may include their youth worker, education staff etc, a multi-agency approach has been found to best serve this (Sheffield Support Service for Looked After Children, as cited in *Promoting the Health of Looked After Children*, DoH, 2002).

Dedicated health teams are emerging across the UK, some including mental health workers. Key to their work is the introduction of an holistic health needs assessment (HNA), statutorily required for all looked after children, that gives an opportunity for the children and their carers to identify and discuss their mental/health needs. Some HNAs incorporate a mental health needs assessment, such as Goodman's Strengths and Difficulties Questionnaire (SDQ) (DoH, 1999).These act as a screening tool to identify mental health needs and support referrals to mental health services. Tools such as the SDQ also identify positive aspects and improvements, therefore, in themselves can promote the child's resilience. A recent small-scale audit on the use of the SDQ has shown that it identified previously undetected high mental health needs, failure to refer and discrepancies in child and carers perceptions (Butterfield, Share and White, 2005).

There are many other successful initiatives, and further examples can be found on the NHS Beacons' website via *www.dh.gov.uk*

Case study 2

Robert was four when he first came into care. His mum was 'depressed' all the time, and his dad had died when he was two. They said he had ADHD and they put him on 'tablets to stop him buzzing about'. His foster carers were 'cool' but when Tom, foster dad, had a heart attack, Robert had to move to another placement, he was 12. They still saw each other every other weekend, he saw his mum on the others, and he was 'spoilt rotten'. His social worker talked to everyone, including school people, new carers, the nurse and the GP about him, and they all got together with him and made a plan. Robert struggled to make friends at home though he had loads at school, because his new placement was on a farm. His care nurse got him into a youth club and basketball club, the 'social' even 'coughed up for his fees and transport'. Robert is 16 soon and looking forward to staying with his current carers, he is going on to college, 'I shocked myself with five GCSEs', he is studying towards becoming a social worker.

Building resilience

There is much that can be done to protect children from experiencing mental health problems, suggest Young Minds (2004) and to build up their resilience, even in difficult circumstances. They go on to say that a number of protective factors can work to offset the risk factors, previously discussed in relation to looked after children.

For most of the children within the care system this will often mean rebuilding resilience that has either never been achieved or has been eroded as they experience their loss of self-esteem and, sadly, feelings of hopelessness.

All agencies; local authority, education and health must take a clear role within this.

The importance of a child enjoying at least one good 'parent/child' relationship is paramount (Rutter et al., 1998; Young Minds, 2005). For those in the care system this may be their main carer, social worker, independent visitor, nurse, etc. Children who feel emotionally secure are better equipped to grow up with confidence. They also respond positively to parents who are clear and direct in what they expect of them and who are able to set realistic limits on what is and is not acceptable in terms of behaviours. For our carers then, this demands the delivery of expert, uniform care supported by training and education.

Healthy Care

This programme, funded by the DfES, aims to promote the well being of looked after children and young people. It provides guidance and support to local Healthy Care partnerships to develop a programme of work which works towards a national Healthy Care standard. It can be used as a key mechanism for the delivery of promoting the health of looked after children and contribute to the government's required *National Minimum Standards for Residential Care* (DoH, 2002) and *National Outcomes for Children* (DfES, 2003).

Education

Schools with positive policies on behaviour, achievement and anti-bullying play a crucial role in promoting children's mental health (Young Minds, 2004). Encouraging this culture is a key aim of the Department for Education and Skills (DfES, 2002) and supported in its publication *Promoting Children's Mental Health within Early Years and School Settings.*

Education Protects (DfES, 2002) aims to help local authorities raise the educational attainment of children and young people in care and has further supported the development of dedicated teams who monitor, improve and advocate for the educational provision for looked after children. Due to frequent placement moves and behavioural problems, looked after children are often excluded from the education system or, if they remain within it, fall behind and fail to meet their potential with only one per cent of school leavers who are in the care system achieving one GCSE (DfES, 2004).

Due to their experiences, many looked after children do not fit well within mainstream education. In some areas there are specific services that such looked after children can access; Behaviour Education Support Teams (BEST) Pupil Referral Units (PRU). For some of our most disaffected young people early access (pre-16) to more preferred and suitable alternatives such as mechanics courses, beauty therapy and craft trades are being offered by some higher education institutes.

Leisure

Leisure is an important factor in the promotion of one's sense of well being, self-esteem and promotion of resilience. For looked after children and young people leisure services have a corporate responsibility to provide for these children as, often, they have had little or no experience of them.

Some areas give free of charge provision as it is recognised that the financial implications on foster, family and residential budgets can often act as a barrier to access. The MAX card is one example that provides free access for looked after children, their carers and their families to museums and art opportunities (*www.nemic.co.uk/resources/maxcardleaflet.pdf*). Transporting and chaperoning also place demands on carers, however, partner agencies need to identify creative ways, such as working with youth services, independent visitors etc. with which to overcome these in order to give these children the equal opportunity to experience what the majority of their peers do.

One could argue that, due to the predisposing factors affecting their mental health, that they should be given priority provision. For this to be recognised, partner agencies need to have in place a 'preventative strategy' and should be considered within Primary Care Trusts' (PCT) responsibilities.

Leisure assessments

Some areas working in close partnership with their leisure services are able to offer health needs assessments utilising leisure centres including gym equipment. This not only introduces the children to the services on offer that they frequently miss out on due to absent parenting or lack of resources within their placement, but also to the concept of exercise as part of a healthy life-style. This empowers and informs them so that they can make healthy choices that, in turn, promotes mental resilience.

Youth services

Every Child Matters; Change for Children (DfES, 2004) sets out a national framework for local programmes of change to be led by local authorities and their partners. 'Working with voluntary and community organisations to deliver change for children and young people', and the Green Paper on Youth (2004) places clear responsibilities on youth services to target support for the young people who are deemed to be most 'at risk'. This will include a significant number of looked after children.

Working in close partnership with their youth services via their multi-agency health forum, one residential home has successfully disengaged a number of their young people from criminal activity and diverted them into other recreations such as basketball, tall ship sailing, photography, drama and music. This is a proactive model whereby the youth services highlight their local and other relevant forthcoming activities to the children and young people within the home. Recognising that they are amongst their most vulnerable target audience they then direct them towards the most suitable activity. The improvement in their behaviours, social skills, school attendance and lessoned criminal activity is tangible.

Culture/religion

The Mental Health Foundation (1999) reminds us of the importance of considering mental health within a cultural setting as each culture has its own ideas and beliefs about well being and what promotes this. Differing cultures have different views on the roles and responsibilities of children within it. A lack of sensitivity to such cultural differences can lead to a sense of dislocation for children and a sense of distrust of professionals on behalf of the parents. It is generally accepted that religious faith, a sense of humour and an ability to reflect can act as resilience factors within a child.

Conclusion

Despite the overwhelming evidence base, the extensive mental health needs of looked after children and young people remains largely unmet (Harman et al., 2000; Payne, 2000; Richardson and Joughlin, 2000).

There is substantial variation in the provision of Child and Adolescent Mental Health Services (CAMHS) for looked after children, the interventions offered and the disciplines and agencies involved (Minnis and Del Priore, 2001).

Problems in accessing CAMHS include narrow referral, reluctance by referrers' to pathologise children's behaviour, mobility and engagement (Hatfield, Harrington and Mohamad, 1996; Mather, Humphrey and Robinson, 1997; Nicol et al., 2000).

However, clear research can now be used to guide continued investment into developing responsive services to begin to respond to this challenge and 'positively move the agenda forward to change this unacceptable picture'.

References

Barber, J.G., Delfrabbo, P.H. and Cooper, L.L. (2001) The Predictors of Unsuccessful Transition to Foster Care. *Journal of Child Psychology and Psychiatry* 42: 6, 785–90.

Blower, A. et al. (2004) Mental Health of Looked After Children: A Needs Assessment. *Clinical Child Psychology and Psychiatry*, 9: 1, 117–29.

Bowlby, J. (1969) *Attachment and Loss, Volume 1, Attachment.* New York: Basil Books.

Brand, A. and Brinich, P. (1999) Behaviour Problems and Mental Health Contact in Adopted, Foster and Non-adoptive Children. *Journal of Child Psychology and Psychiatry* 40: 8, 1221–9.

Buchanan, A. (1996) *Intergenerational Child Maltreatment: Facts, Fallacies and Interventions.* Winchester: Wiley.

Callaghan et al. (2004) Evaluation of a New Mental Health Service for Looked After Children. *Clinical Child Psychology and Psychiatry*, 9: 1,130–48.

Cheung, S.Y. and Buchanan, A. (1997) High Malaise Scores in Adulthood of Children and Young People who have been in Care. *Journal of Child Psychology and Psychiatry*, 38, 575–80.

DfES (1998) *Quality Protects.* London: HMSO.

DfES (2002) *Education Protects.* London: HMSO.

DfES (2002) *Promoting Children's Mental Health within Early Years and School Settings.* London: HMSO.

DfES (2003) *National Outcomes for Children.* London: HMSO.

DfES (2004) *Every Child Matters: Change for Children.* London: DfES.

DoH (1999) *Strengths and Weaknesses Questionnaire.* London: HMSO.

DoH (2002) *National Minimum Standards for Residential Care.* London: HMSO.

DoH (2002) *Promoting the Health of Looked After Children.* London: HMSO.

DoH (2000) *The Children (Leaving Care) Act.* London: HMSO.

DoH (2003) *Guidance on Accommodating Children in Need and their Families.* London: DoH.

DoH (2004) *National Service Framework for Children, Young People and Maternity Services.* London: HMSO.

Gunn, J., Maden, A. and Swinton, M. (1991) Treatment Needs of Prisoners with Psychiatric Disorders. *British Medical Journal*, 303: 338–41.

Harman, J., Childs, G., Kelleher, K. and Kelly, J. (2000) Mental Health Care Utilisation and Expenditures by Children in Foster Care. *Archives of Paediatrics and Adolescent Medicine*, 154: 11.

Hatfield, B., Harrington, R. and Mohamad, H. (1996) Staff Looking after Children in Local Authority Residential Units: The Interface with Children's Mental Health Professionals. *The Journal of Adolescence*, 19: 2, 127–39.

Howe, D. (1995) *Attachment Theory for Social Work Practice.* Basingstoke: Macmillan.

Mather, M., Humphrey, J. and Robson, J. (1997) The Statutory Medical and Health Needs of Looked-after Children: Time for a Radical Review? *Adoption and Fostering*, 21: 2, 36–40.

McCann, J.B., James, A., Wilson, S. and Dunn, G. (1996) Prevelance of Psychiatric Disorders in Young People in the Care System. *British Medical Journal* 13, 1529–30.

Mental Health Foundation (1999) *Bright Futures: Promoting Children's and Young People's Mental Health.* London: MHF.

Mental Health Foundation (2002) The Mental Health of Looked-after Children. London: MHF.

Mental Health Foundation (2002) *Children and Young People with Mental Health Problems.* London: MHF.

Minnis, H. and Del Priore, C. (2001) Mental Health Services for Looked-after Children: Implications from Two Studies. *Adoption and Fostering*, 25: 4, 27–38.

Minty, B. (1999) Annotation: Outcomes in Long-term Foster Family Care. *Journal of Child Psychology and Psychiatry*, 40: 7, 991–9.

NHS (1998) *Managing Deliberate Self-harm in Young People.* Report CR64. London: Royal College of Psychiatrists.

NHS Beacons website via *www.dh.gov.uk*

Nicol et al. (2000) Mental Health Needs and Services for Severely Troubled and Troubling Young People including Young Offenders in an NHS Region. *Journal of Adolescence*, 23, 243–61.

Payne, M. (2000) *Teamwork in Multi-Professional Care.* London: Palgrave Macmillan.

Richardson, J. and Joughlin, C. (Eds.) (2000) *The Mental Health Needs of Looked-after Children.* London: Gaskell.

Roy, P., Rutter, M. and Pickles, A. (2000) Institutional Care: Risk from Family Background or Pattern of Rearing. *Journal of Child Psychology and Psychiatry*, 41: 2, 139–149.

Rutter, M., Giller, H. and Haggell, A. (1998) *Anti-social Behaviour by Young People.* Cambridge: Cambridge University Press.

Rutter, M. and Quinton, D. (1984) Parental Psychiatric Disorder: Effects on Children. *Psychological Medicine*, 14, 853–40.

Social Services Inspectorate Report (1997) *Better Management, Better Care.* 8th Annual Report. London: DoH.

Stein, M. (1997) *What Works in Leaving Care?* Barkingside: Barnardo's.

Who Cares? Trust (2004) *Carezone.* London: The Who Cares? Trust.

Vellacott, J. (2004) Something Inside Us. *YoungMinds*, 77.

Williams, R. and Kerfoot, M. (2005) *Child and Adolescent Mental Health Services: Strategy, Planning, Delivery and Evaluation.* Oxford: Oxford University Press.

Young Minds (2005) Child and Adolescent Mental Health Problems: Key Facts about Childrens Mental Health. *www.youngminds.org.uk*

Chapter 9

Substance Use/Misuse and Drug Education for Children and Young People in Care

Andy Betts

Terminology

In the field of drug education, semantics and euphemisms are frequently used with flippant regard, and can conjure various images and meanings depending on the audience and the setting. It is important that certain words and phrases, for the purpose of this chapter are briefly defined as a pre-commencement.

Drug – Drugs are defined as substances both legal and illegal, including alcohol and tobacco as well as solvents and narcotics.

Substance misuse – 'Substance taking which harms health or social functioning is described as "substance misuse". Substance misuse may be dependency (physical or psychological) or substance taking that is part of a wider spectrum of problematic or harmful behaviour' (Britton and Castleton, 2002: 7).

Substance use – 'Substance use is the taking of a substance, which requires a lower level intervention than treatment. Harm may still occur through substance use, whether through intoxication, illegality or health problems, even though it may not be immediately apparent. Substance use will require the appropriate provision of interventions such as education, advice and information, and prevention work to reduce the potential for harm' (Britton and Castleton, 2002: 7).

Background

All children and young people are entitled to and deserve drug education. This is emphasised by the government, which is committed to providing drug education and information to young people in a range of settings (Home Office Fact Sheet, 2003). Education forms an integral part of the government's national drug strategy for England *Tackling Drugs to Build a Better Britain* (1998) updated (2002).

A strategy which: 'has a vision to create a healthy and confident society, increasingly free from the harm caused by the misuse of drugs. One of the key elements is to help young people resist drug use in order to achieve their full potential in society' (Britton and Noor, 2003: 4).

Although drug education has become a focus for many schools, via the Personal, Social and Health Education framework, it is a fact that many looked after children have their schooling disrupted, thus may receive limited or zero drug education via schools. Other agencies, such as the youth service may pick this up – but again this depends on attendance. Thus; it is important that workers in the care environment have an understanding of drug related issues, feel confident and are able to talk openly to young people. This issue increases with significance, as research conducted by the Health Advisory Service (HAS, 1996) has demonstrated that looked after children have the potential to greater vulnerability to problematic substance use. Protective factors, such as a supportive family environment and enhanced positive individual and social factors may enable young people to be more resilient to problematic substance use. The influences of these factors are possibly limited for looked after children. For example, young people may be introduced to and drink alcohol at home. However, for looked after children in a children's home this is not an option, they may first be introduced to alcohol via peers often in the parks or the streets with obvious additional health and legal risks (Britton and Castleton, 2002: 26). Thus preparing young people with accurate drug education is vital, as knowledge can empower young people to undertake their own 'self-risk analysis', helping them to make an informed choice which can aid in resistance to substance misuse. Indeed, research has indicated that where support is provided for young people in care, especially in the transition phase to independent living, that any drug taking may become a passing phase which is greatly reduced with the onset of stability (*Findings No. 190*, Home Office, 2003).

A further consideration is when young people have been (or are in) a family environment where one or more of their parents/carers have been a problem drug user. It has been estimated that there are between 250,000 and 350,000 children in the UK in this situation (ACDM, 2003: 2). This can have a negative consequence on the young person's development; in addition there are strong links with socio-economic deprivation (ibid.). In this situation it is vital that agencies work together to support both the parents and young people. At present guidance and support is limited as legislation and support agencies either focus on the parents or the child. Nevertheless, agencies such as schools and social services are an important support mechanism and drug agencies are increasing their scope to create a 'family friendly' environment, while agencies such as the Youth Service and Connexions can provide excellent support for the young person. A recommendation of the report has been for agencies such as social services to be more flexible with the range of care offered, such as day fostering, as a way to support both the parent and young person, with the inclusion of drug education when required (ibid., 9).

Legal issues and guidance on drug education and 'treatment'

Existing guidance for statutory agencies demonstrates the support and indeed the encouragement for workers to provide drug education to young people in their care. This is emphasised in the *Quality Protects Programme* (objective 4) (DoH, 1999a) and the *Working Together to Safeguard Children* (DoH, 1999b). This is further portrayed in the *National Minimum Standards for Children's Homes* (DoH, 2002) which has a subsequent emphasis not just to provide drug education, but that young people should be 'actively discouraged from smoking, alcohol and illegal substances' (Britton and Castleton, 2002: 14). To aid in the implementation of national to local strategies, Drug Action Teams were created and it is the responsibility of the DAT to produce a Young Peoples Substance

Misuse Plan, a plan that has to target vulnerable groups of young people, with clear and specific outcomes.

However, despite the national guidance and local strategic plans, adults are often nervous and/or cagey discussing drug related issues. It is important to be aware (aptly summarised by FRANK, see website) that, 'Drugs are illegal. Talking about them isn't'. In addition, parental/carer consent is not required for the provision of advice and information with regard to substances (ibid.: 21). National and local guidelines, however, should still be adhered to. It is vital that the young person can converse in a free and open environment and be assured that discussions are confidential. Nevertheless this should be set firmly within the context and guidelines of the Children Act (1989). Agencies frequently have policies and guidelines, which dictate that the worker should sever confidentiality if they feel the young person is in danger of harming themselves or others. If such a protocol exists, it is essential that the young person is aware of this prior to any drug education/discussions. This will help to avoid any connotations of mistrust if confidentiality does have to be breached.

However, if the young person were to be referred on to treatment, such as counselling, then parental or carer consent would be required, unless the young person is deemed competent. Without these safeguards, a legal challenge could arise. Briefly, adults (over 18) are regarded as competent; and are able to seek treatment, as they desire. Generally, young people (16–18) are seen as competent in law under the Family Law Reform Act, 1987 to seek or withhold treatment. Young people under 16 are not deemed as competent under law to receive self-consenting medical treatment. However, it is possible for a professional to provide and refer for medical treatment under the Fraser Guidelines (see appendix in Sexual Health Chapter) where the provider has assessed that the young person is competent to give their consent. This can only be conducted on an individual basis and not through group sessions.

It is clear that work in the field of substance use/misuse can be extremely varied. Ranging, for example, from a comparatively simple intervention of explaining the effects and harms of tobacco, to complex dependent poly-drug use, where the user has many underlying issues. To aid workers in their comprehension of the range of interventions, HAS developed a four-tier model. It was envisaged that workers in the care environment would be able to conduct substance use/misuse work at Tier 2, if required, and have in place a procedure to refer the young person to a Tier 3 service if necessary (see Appendix 1). In order for these to occur workers should be versed in providing an initial assessment or screening of the young person in relation to substance use/misuse. This will ascertain any relevant gaps in knowledge around substances and any direct or indirect needs of the young person. Many local authorities have developed their own screening tool, to help workers through this initial assessment.

Legal issues – drugs and the law

Legislation and guidelines continue to change and grey areas in law may have to linger for a test case to achieve clarity. However, it is important to be aware of the fundamental laws concerning drugs, which should be kept up to date, and this can easily be achieved by referencing a recent leaflet or website. From personal experience, a frequent reason why workers are dubious about discussing drugs is that they are concerned that incorrect information may be provided. Whilst it is very important to avoid mis-information, basic facts on drug laws are readily available and if during a discussion you are unsure, why not look the answer up together? This can only help to create an atmosphere for further discussion.

For the reason cited above, it would be unwise to dictate the drug laws in great depth here. However, as a brief reference one should be aware of the following:

The main legislation, which governs illicit drugs, is the Misuse of Drugs Act (1971). Offences include (among others) those from unlawful possession of a substance, to unlawful supply and intent to supply. Penalties are more severe for supply than possession, and they also differ depending on the class of the drug. The law classifies illicit drugs into three categories:

- Class A – maximum seven years and/or unlimited fine for possession, life and/or unlimited fine for production or trafficking.

- Class B – maximum five years and/or unlimited fine for possession, fourteen years and/or unlimited fine for production or trafficking.

- Class C – maximum two years and/or unlimited fine for possession, fourteen years and/or unlimited fine for production or trafficking.

A further consideration for care homes and foster carers is Section 8 of the Misuse of Drugs Act. This places an obligation on the occupiers and those concerned in management to discourage drug use on premises for which they are responsible. A person may be at risk of prosecution if they 'knowingly permit or suffer' the taking, supply, preparation or production of a controlled drug. Although it is clear a worker cannot be responsible for every activity that takes place, if a charge were made they would have to prove reasonable steps were taken against the activities. For all care homes a clear and up to date drug policy is essential.

Legislation also covers other substances such as alcohol and tobacco, but these substances are not deemed illicit. In addition, regulations on medical grounds can allow a person to possess and use certain controlled drugs (i.e. with a prescription); these drugs are clearly defined through current legislation.

The effect of drugs

As this chapter is primarily concerned with drug education it would not be prudent to provide information in intricate detail on the effects of drugs and this information is also readily available via leaflets and websites. As a brief reference however, the effects of drugs are divided into three categories depending on how the substance alters the nervous system:

- Depressant drug – Here the drug depresses the nervous system. Effects include reduced heart rate, tiredness, relaxation, and loss of body co-ordination, slurred speech, and relief from tension and anxiety. High doses can result in unconsciousness and even fatality.
    Examples: Alcohol, heroin, and solvents.

- Stimulant drug – Here the drug stimulates the nervous system. Effects include increased heart rate, increase alertness, reduced appetite. High doses can increase nervousness and anxiety.
  Examples: Amphetamines, cocaine, and caffeine.

- Hallucinogen – Here the drug alters the perception of the user. Effects include distorted perception and heightened sensory awareness. Can result in anxiety, paranoia and panic attacks, especially if the user is experiencing a 'bad trip'.
  Examples: Cannabis, magic mushrooms and LSD.

With all drugs other variables can affect the users 'experience', for example, the environment, the persons mood and the quality of the drug. Ironically, it is often the adulterated drugs that can result in detrimental experiences, for example Ketamine masquerading as Ecstasy, as the user would experience the effects of a drug that is utilised as an anaesthetic in veterinary surgery, rather than the expected Ecstasy sensation! In addition poly-drug consumption can be an unpredictable variable, which could result in both a physical and psychological shock for the user.

When delivering drug education or being part of a drug related discussion, the issues relating to the effects of drugs, and the legislation with regard to drugs, will invariably surface. It is important to have, or to have access to, accurate and up to date information, as this is an essential component to the quality of the drug education (*Protecting Young People*, DfEE, 1998, cited in Drugscope, 2005). Thus the above extracts on the law and the effects of drugs serves as a baseline reference for any drug education planning.

Why do young people take drugs?

Facts and figures alone, however, are insignificant unless one has a basic understanding on why young people take or desire to take drugs. This could be seen as the 'million dollar' question, but the reality is of course there is not one answer, and it is often a complex conundrum of reasons and underlying issues (Drug Policy HSCC, 2004). For example, a young person who is using solvents could be doing so as a way of coping with physical or sexual abuse within the family. In addition, one should not underestimate the scope of peer influence/pressure. Other reasons often cited include the 'rite of passage' the desire to experiment, escapism, boredom and availability. As stated, it will frequently be a combination of reasons, suffice to say that a person undertaking drug education sessions should be aware of possible underlying issues, as until these are addressed a young person would be more prone to experience the consequences of possible substance misuse.

Let's get down to business – drug education

Like the word drug, drug education can conjure different images and even opposing viewpoints. However, before one embarks on the types of drug education available and an ensuing quest to solve the world's drug problems via education, it is important to first undertake a 'reality check'.

Research indicates that drug education is unlikely to prevent a young person from experimenting with drugs. However, good quality drug education can delay the onset of experimentation and prevent the extension to problematic drug use. In addition, education

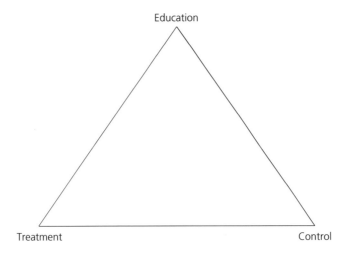

Figure 9.1

can have an impact upon drug use patterns, resulting in decreased harm and increased awareness of safety (Drugscope, 2005). Working together with agencies providing treatment and those involved in control, it is clear that drug education is a vital component in tackling the problems associated with drugs. For example, it is a losing battle if dealers are arrested only to be replaced in the future by today's young people – education linked in with the other agencies can help tackle this potential cycle and vice versa (certificate in drug awareness studies, accredited by NCfE, 2000).

Whatever style or type of drug education that is conducted one could argue that an educational rather than a propagandist approach should always be adhered to. An educational approach endeavours to provide 'accurate and balanced information' (Drugscope, 2005). It encourages debate and free discussion, recognising that people have different opinions concerning drug use. As a consequence this helps young people develop social skills, such as confidence, enabling them to articulate opinions whilst participating in discourse – the wider virtues of social education. In contrast, a propagandist stance would distort figures and exaggerate the dangers of drug use, talking 'at' young people, rather than 'to' them. This approach does not encourage debate and discussion and stifles the development of social skills, not allowing the development of opinion, and devaluing any stance that contravenes the already arranged agenda. In this situation, it could be argued that young people 'switch off' as they are being patronised and not being instructed with sincerity (Drugscope, 2005). Indeed, from my own personal experience in delivering drug education in youth projects, initially I frequently encounter resistance from the young people – such as, 'oh we're not going to talk about drugs are we', 'we did that at school. It was boring'. However, after the session the young people were pleased and said they learnt and felt their opinions were valued; thus helping the young people to make their own informed decisions. Although polemic, this is of course a random example, I do not wish to universally criticise drug education in schools, as I know that some excellent education has been developed in those establishments.

As a final notion connected with the propagandist approach, one should also be cautious with an over emphasis toward shock tactics and the 'just say no' answer. Again, this stance can distort the truth and stifle development of opinion, reducing the potential of young people making their own informed choices. It is the opinion of the author, that if young people are excluded, for example in making their own informed decisions, they will naturally rebel. Thus, this approach can actually be counterproductive.

The reality is of course that nobody (and I mean nobody) can be totally objective, as we will all deliver a drug education session with our own prejudices and values. However, it is important to strive for objectivity and to create an environment where people's opinions are valued, even though you may disagree with them.

Drug education may be summarised as 'the acquisition of knowledge, understanding and exploration of attitudes and values which facilitate young people to be able to make informed decisions about their own, and other people's use of drugs' (Drugscope, 2005).

Types and styles of drug education

Young people are not all at the same level of awareness in relation to substance use/misuse; furthermore this is not as simple as an age barrier. For example, a young person at the age of thirteen may be a regular tobacco and cannabis user, but another young person at fifteen may have never tried tobacco and never been offered cannabis. Therefore it is imperative to gauge the awareness level of the young person/people – this can aid in the appropriateness and relevance of the education and the information and resources provided. For example, a young twelve-year-old may enquire what heroin is? This can be simply explained and supported with a suitable leaflet. It would not be appropriate to explain how to inject heroin safely, then provide a harm reduction leaflet aimed and written for adult intravenous drug users.

It is my firm belief that assessment should be completed by involving and consulting with the young people, for if the educational session is aimed at them, surely they are the best people to explain their level of awareness. This can be done simply through a questionnaire or even a quiz (don't forget the prizes! This can prove to be really popular). Example questions could be:

- What class drug is cannabis?

- What are the effects of cannabis?

- Is alcohol a depressant, stimulant or hallucinogenic drug?

- What are the possible social consequences of alcohol abuse?

These are just examples, which can easily be added to or replaced by another drug. But they do cover key elements; legal awareness, and the effects of drugs and possible wider social repercussions, for the individual and the wider community. If the work is conducted on an individual basis, the utilisation of an appropriate screening tool may also be of assistance in assessing the level of awareness.

So . . . The assessment has been completed and there is a firm understanding of the young people's level of drug awareness. Will the ensuing educational session be preventative or focused on harm reduction? Probably a combination of both, but it is important to be coherent on both approaches.

Preventative drug education

Fundamentally this has the aim of preventing young people from using drugs. An example of this would be conducting a 'No Smoking' session to a group of young people who do not smoke. The aim – To re-enforce and to praise their existing stance on smoking, providing examples of the negatives of smoking, but also emphasising the positive virtues of not smoking such as enhanced physical fitness, especially if they are interested in sport. The session may also include aspects of social education, for example, supporting the young person's confidence to resist the intrigue or temptation of smoking. This could be conducted through role plays, or drama work. It is hoped the drug education would help prevent the young people from smoking, or at least delay the onset.

Harm reduction

In contrast, harm reduction recognises the fact that many young people will take drugs, both legal and illegal. As such, this approach is aimed at the 'prevention of harm rather than . . . use' (Cohen, 2001: 8). It is an admission that the ethos and delivery of preventative work, although important, will not eliminate drug taking among young people. The session will be about the drugs, rather than against them, supplying accurate and open information on the substances under discussion. Recognising the fact that the young people are using, or contemplating using certain substances – from the educational session, the young people will be able to make their own informed decision to take or continue to take drugs, based on accurate information. In a sense, the young people will conduct a 'self risk assessment' – Will the benefit of taking this drug outweigh the risks? This approach could become more conflicting and controversial for the worker, especially if it involves illegal substances.

A personal example of this work can be supplied. After a drug education session at a youth club, a young person approached me and said 'I'm going clubbing at the weekend and I'm planning to take Ecstasy with a group of friends. Could I explain the health risks?' I myself had to undertake a 'self risk analysis'; should I supply this information? I would be informing this young person how to take Ecstasy; is this condoning the use of a Class A substance? I had visions of the young person rushing home, informing their parents that they have just had an explanation on how to take Ecstasy, by a youth worker at their local youth club. After briefly analysing their awareness age and the integrity of their intent, I decided to proceed.

I commenced by explaining that the best way to reduce the risks involved is not to take the drug at all. 'However, if you intend to do so' – I then proceeded to explain the risks of over-heating, the importance of water consumption, but not too much, and to allow the body time to recover and recuperate after the effects have expired. I firmly believed I formulated the correct decision on the basis of harm reduction, allowing the young people to make their own informed choice. The fact remains, however, I informed the young person how to take Ecstasy, but at least I did not read in the papers of a young person dying from an Ecstasy induced heat stroke.

In reality, a drug education session, whether for an individual or a group will probably involve both types of approaches. Hypothetically, I may attend a drug education session where many of the young people regularly smoke cannabis. Here I will do harm reduction work, explaining the health and legal risks, but recognising the fact they are taking cannabis. It is too late for preventative work, the aim is to reduce the harm cannabis can cause on the individual. However, in the same session and recognising the fact that some young people are being offered other illegal substances, I may adopt a more preventative approach. For example, the young people may query cocaine and its usage and although I will explain what it is, the effects and legal status, I would not elaborate on how to 'cut it up' and snort it safely. On this occasion that level of response would be inappropriate. The explanations and discussion should always be balanced toward the awareness of the young people.

As workers, it is important to be mindful of your agency drug policies, as some institutions shy away from the harm reduction ethos. This is largely due to the fear of a media or political backlash, especially as young people are involved. In addition it is useful to be aware of the resources that you are employing, as certain leaflets for example, are aimed at and written for older young people with a focused harm reduction message. Whilst other leaflets are aimed at a younger age group and lean to a preventative model. On occasion agencies may become extremely offended that certain leaflets are being used on their premises. This once again re-iterates the importance of pre-planning. If visiting another centre, be aware of their drug policies as they may be vehemently against any harm reduction messages. If you are unsure on the material you are utilising, refer to the local Primary Care Trust, or Health Promotion, they can be an excellent source of information and advice.

What you aim to achieve

Whether preventative or harm reduction sessions, certain areas of substance misuse should be targeted, as this will help the young person to make their own informed decisions in the **key areas** as outlined below. This can largely be achieved with a homemade set of cards. These methods have been personally tried and tested in a wide set of environments, including youth clubs, schools, colleges and voluntary organisations. It can be a great tool in the learning process, especially if vital ingredients are included, such as the education is conducted in an environment where the young people feel their opinions are valued and respected, debate and discussion to each answer is encouraged, but perhaps most importantly of all, it should be fun!

Key area – what is a drug?

First and foremost a drug education discussion should commence by clarifying what a drug is. This may sound simple at first, but invariably people, including academic institutions and dictionaries have varied definitions on what a drug is.

For the purpose of the session this can easily be resolved. Ask each member of the group or individual for words and phrases that describe drugs. Common responses are:

> . . . *something that gets you stoned*
> . . . *it makes you drunk*
> . . . *something that's illegal*

All these are examples, and I predict, also the ones presented to you, will have an element of truth. Simply write down the key words on a piece of paper, such as 'stoned' and 'illegal' and once completed attempt to construct a sentence from the key words. This sentence can then be compared with definitions from a dictionary. This serves the purpose of allowing young people to contemplate and discuss what a drug is, whilst demonstrating how definitions will vary, an illustration that the term 'drug' will create a varied response from different people – depending on their own life experiences. For example, if someone has recently been arrested for possession of cannabis, the term 'drug' will mean 'illegal', yet if another person has just received life-saving antibiotics the interpretation may contain a medicinal perspective. As a guide the range of the sentence should include key words, such as legal/illegal, natural/synthetic and effect mind/body. The words do not have to be exact, an indication will suffice, and again this can be achieved through discussion during the exercise.

Key area – legality

It is vital that young people have a basic understanding of the law. For example, if a young person believed cannabis was legal, they may take the decision to smoke a joint openly on the street, which could result in arrest. They were thus unable to undertake a 'self-risk assessment' based on correct information. The young person may have reversed this decision if they had had accurate information, based on legal risk, this could be a life changing moment, whilst the arrest resulted in a criminal record.

To demonstrate the law I play a card game. Cards are written out with the following:

Class A, Class B, Class C and legal (I use a sheet of A4 paper for each).

I then write down names of substances on other cards, this can be as many as you like, but at least focus on the drugs that are relevant to the group (again on a sheet of A4, but a different colour this time). I commence by briefly explaining the Misuse of Drugs Act. The Class A, B, C and legal cards are then placed on the floor or table. The game is then easily played. One at a time read out the names of the 'substance' cards. Once the correct answer has been deduced, the 'substance' card is then duly placed on either A, B, C, or legal card, thus illustrating the legal status.

Key area – effects

Akin with fundamental legislation it is paramount that young people have an understanding of the effect of drugs. Again, a young person should have an awareness of the consequences of drugs, both good and bad, in order to allow a 'self-risk analysis' based on correct information. A young person may not decide to consume a depressant style drug, as later in the day they will be operating machinery. In this setting they now realise the dangers, such as drowsiness, slowed reaction and body co-ordination. But without this information they may have succumbed to a peer influence situation, not been aware of the dangers, unable to make an accurate 'self-risk analysis'.

To demonstrate the effects I continue with the card format. Write out the words depressant, stimulant, and hallucinogen on three separate pieces of paper. The cards with the substances written on can be utilised again.

Initially I instigate a group discussion on what happens to the mind and body under the influence of drugs. For example with depressant – phrases such as 'slows the body down' and 'makes you tired' should be aimed for. Once this is completed the card game imitates the same format as the 'legal card game' – with the correct card being placed on the appropriate effect card, once the answer has been deduced via group discussion.

Key area – risk to the individual and the wider community

The next stage is to attempt to broaden the perspective, rather than concentrating on just the individual. To focus on the consequences of drugs to other people, such as how drugs can damage and stigmatise estates. Do not solely concentrate on illegal drugs, as passive smoking can damage other people's health, and abusive and anti-social behaviour is often connected with alcohol abuse. In addition, expand on the individual, apart from consequences of the effect of the drug and the legal risks, what are the social implications? Possible expulsion from school/college, or stigmatised by the family?

A simple card game can once again be applied. On this occasion only the 'substance' cards are required. Ask the group to create a 'risk ladder' on what they perceive to be the most dangerous drugs. Thus, the cards eventually form a continuum from the least harmful at the base, to the worst substance at the apex. This is a fantastic opportunity for discussion and debate, now the group will not just have to consider the consequences for the individual, but also the wider community. After completing the 'risk ladder', invite the group to justify their decisions. Why has substance X been placed at the top? Why is substance Y situated at the bottom?

A further aid to develop discussion and to encourage the young people to articulate their opinions is what I label the 'debate game'. Again this is very simple and no resources are required. Request that everyone stands in the centre of the room, and explain that you are going to read a statement. If you agree, go to the right of the room, if you disagree, re-locate to the left of the room, those unsure remain in the centre.

Example statements can be:

> *All drugs should be legalised.*
> *Cannabis should be legalised.*
> *Those who smoke do not deserve NHS treatment.*
> *People should not be permitted to smoke in public.*

Once the group has re-located, again, invite them to justify their decisions. This can create an excellent atmosphere for discourse amongst the group. The advantage of this exercise is that the statements can be concurrent to the present social and political agenda.

Extra resources

The above exercises are simple to conduct and require minimal resources. This is deliberately so; it is to encourage the fact that every worker can undertake drug education. It is not necessary to have gizmos, gadgets and an extremely large in-depth knowledge of the subject. What you are not acquainted with, or cannot remember, can easily be checked against a current leaflet or website. Indeed, it is futile to have masses of information and facts and figures if these cannot be delivered to young people, via an educational environment that is conducive to the young people's learning skills. If you already have a good established working relationship with the young person, you may be the ideal person to deliver the drug education, as the young person already relates and listens to you.

That is not to say, however, that extra resources should not be employed, it is merely postulating that a far greater asset are the personnel skills that young people can relate to. If, however, you decide to utilise extra resources, from my personal experience, I find that resources that are interactive and/or visual can act as an aid and/or icebreaker to the session.

These include a 'drug case', a 'smokerlyzer' (measures the Carbon Monoxide levels in the body due to smoking) 'Tar Jar' (a visual illustration of the tar the body consumes through smoking), and 'drunk glasses' (a personal demonstration of, when worn, the disorientation that the body experiences with the effects of a depressant drug, such as alcohol). However, these items are inanimate on their own and should only be used as part of the educational session. For example, the glasses are fun to wear, but it should be explained about how the body loses co-ordination with a depressant drug, to illustrate how vulnerable that young person appears whilst staggering (due to the glasses). Although it is fun, when the glasses are removed the effects are eliminated, that is not the case if someone is intoxicated with alcohol. To access these resources, refer to your local Health Promotion, which should stock and supply a range of materials to help in the delivery of drug education.

How do you know you have achieved anything?

A major question that you may ask yourself following the session is did the young people learn anything? Did the education have an impact? The first question is easier to measure as it is a quantitative indicator. One could conduct a quiz or questionnaire prior to the session and re-conduct the same questions after the session to analyse any improvement in knowledge.

Measuring qualitative material, such as intrinsic awareness on substance related issues and how this will affect behavioural patterns could be far more difficult. In addition, any possible changes may be in the 'long-term'. Indeed, do not expect miracles, since a young person will rarely initially demonstrate a behavioural change due to an input of drug education. For example, at one of my first sessions, I attended a youth project and focused on the issues around smoking. Although I explained the dangers of smoking and methods of 'giving-up', none of the young people said they were intending to quit and were content with smoking. I departed quite despondent. What was the purpose of the session? What did I do wrong? Approximately six months later I re-visited the club, and during the session I was approached by one young person who had attended the previous meeting. He said he had reduced the amount he smoked, and was intending to quit altogether. After the first session he had returned home with images of the effects smoking could cause. This illustrates a long-term consequence of drug education, and in fact it was only measured as the young person decided to inform me of his actions, otherwise it may have never been recorded. To conclude, you may have a positive impact, although you may never know!

In an attempt to combine both qualitative and quantitative material I designed a Recorded Outcome sheet (see Appendix 2). This is a measurement of learning, the 'distance travelled' in knowledge and awareness from the commencement to the culmination of the drug education, with a focus upon the key areas previously listed. When utilising this tool, always invite the young people to complete it. I have found that to achieve a greater degree of accuracy, ask the young people to complete the entire sheet following the session, even the 'knowledge prior to the session' sections. It is, in my experience, that people often over-state their knowledge/awareness levels when it concerns drugs. It is only after the session that people innocently realise that their awareness was not as complete as they may have perceived.

The frequently asked question

A brief reference should be dedicated to the frequently asked question – '*Have you ever done drugs?*' (The question always refers to illegal drugs). The following extract is my personal belief, and should not be seen as advice, but as a point of reference. I am not concerned if the reader has consumed drugs, or has never even seen an illegal drug; the response is the same.

If asked I always reply, 'what I have, or have not done is irrelevant, as this session is about you and about you at this moment'. 'I will leave you to draw your own conclusions'. Why this response? Firstly, if you deny (truthfully or not) that you have taken drugs, the young people, especially those who do take drugs will find it difficult to relate to you. They may argue, 'how can you conduct an educational session about the dangers of substance abuse, if you've never experienced the drugs'? Or (the continued thought pattern) even suffered life's hardships that may lead to substance use/misuse? If young people do not relate, the drug education session will become far more challenging. Secondly, if you admit to drug taking in your youth (truthfully or not) then this too, I believe, could be detrimental. Similarly, young people may withdraw their respect, especially those who abstain from drugs, both legal and illegal. Those who have been resisting the temptation toward substance experimentation may question their stance; even their support worker took drugs! In addition, the young people may view the fact that you once took drugs, but you are fine now, you even have a professional post that allows working with young people. It contains a message that 'it is ok to do drugs at present, even if I have a difficult time, I'll get by and get a decent job just like my support worker'!

Finally – A word on slang

The drug culture (especially the illegal drugs) has created in a sense a whole new language. But why? The answer is simple, to alienate those people who are not part of it. Words and phrases can be utilised to disguise people's intent from those who are not part of the group or culture. As with 'Cockney Rhyming' slang, people could converse amongst themselves without 'outsiders' understanding the conversation or being able to 'fit in'.

Certain slang words for drugs are national and will mean the same where ever you are in the country, such as *Hash* (meaning cannabis resin). However, others are very local and can be peculiar to a particular town, estate, or even unique to a group of friends. In addition slang words are constantly changing and updating, and what may have been vogue when you were 'young' and 'hip', can seem extremely out of date if used today. Slang is intrinsic to young people's culture and will always remain so, whether it is about drugs or not, or whether the young people are using drugs or not. Slang is a fact, do not be fearful of it, do not take it personally! In addition, websites such as Frank have a section on slang, and latest used words, so if you desire a greater awareness of the latest slang terminology, this can easily be referenced.

Conclusion

- The field of drug education is very wide and varied, which can contain opposing viewpoints. Be aware of the different philosophies, as your approach and the agencies may be different.

- The level at which the drug education is delivered should match the awareness of the young people.

- It is not illegal to talk about drugs; in fact government documents support such an approach. 'Treatment' however, does contain legal restraints.

- It is important to undertake basic drug education training, but you do not have to be a 'drug expert' to deliver drug education. If required, there is someone you can always ask for advice.

- Drug education is not a 'magic wand' and behavioural changes with regard to substance use/misuse may not be seen at all in the 'short-term'.

Training

Many agencies offer drug awareness training sessions, which can be offered to focus on a particular area of work, for example issues around a residential centre or a youth club. The local Drug and Alcohol Action Team should provide this information.

As a recommendation the NCFE Level One in Drug Awareness Studies is an excellent course, which also provides accreditation. For more specialist workers the NCFE Level Two in Drug Awareness Studies is ideal (some further education colleges offer these courses) (see chapter on Policies, Protocols and Training).

References

Advisory Council on the Misuse of Drugs (2003) *Hidden Harm: Responding to the Needs of Children of Problem Drug Users*. Executive Summary. London: Home Office.

Betts, A. (2004) *Drug Issues and the Youth Work Curriculum. Hertfordshire Youth Service Drug Policy*. Unpublished.

Britton, J. and Castleton, J. (2002) *Taking Care with Drugs: Responding to Substance Use Among Looked After Children*. London: Drugscope.

Britton, J. and Noor, S. (2003) *First Steps in Identifying Young People's Substance Related Needs*. London: Drugscope.

Cohen, J. (2001) *Drug Education: How to be Effective*. Liverpool: Healthwise.

DfES (1989) *The Children Act 1989*. London: DfES.

DfES (2004) *Drugs: Guidance for Schools*. London: DfES.

DoH (1999a) *Quality Protects*. London: DoH.

DoH (1999b) *Working Together to Safeguard Children*. London: DoH.

DoH (2002) *National Minimum Standards for Children's Homes*. London: DoH.

Drugscope (2004) *Druglink: Guide to Drugs*. Drugscope.

Drugscope (2005) via website *www.drugscope.org.uk*

Frank website: *www.talktofrank*

Health Advisory Service (1996) *Children and Young People: Substance Misuse Services: The Substance of Young Need*. London: HMSO.

Health Services Consultative Committee (2004) *Drugs Policy*. Isle of Man: HSCC.

HMSO (1987) *Family Law Reform Act*. London: The Stationery Office.

HMSO (1971) *The Misuse of Drugs Act*. London: The Stationery Office.

Home Office (1998) *Tackling Drugs to Build a Better Britain*. London: HMSO.

Home Office (2003) *Fact Sheets 1–40*. London: Home Office.

Home Office (2003) *One Problem among Many: Drug Use among Care Leavers in Transition to Independent Living*. Findings No 190 London: HMSO.

Appendix I   Hertfordshire's HAS Four Tiered Model

Tier 4
In-patient or residential assessment, treatment and care for those with significant, complex and often multiple problems.

These services may be provided by very specialist youth oriented, or other highly specialised agencies such as secure provision or substance treatment clinics.

Tier 3
Multi-disciplinary response involving components of specialised youth or substance treatment services for young substance users with complex needs. Specialist assessment and referral.

These services might involve young people's substance misuse treatment services, child and adolescent mental health teams, youth offending teams, youth counselling teams and outreach workers.

Tier 2b
Multi-disciplinary response involving individual and group-work interventions from dedicated youth or substance misuse services for vulnerable young people whose substance misuse is high risk and a significant factor in their level of need. Specialist assessment and referral.

These services might involve young people's substance misuse prevention and intervention teams, child and adolescent mental health teams, youth offending teams, youth counselling services, social care providers and young homeless organisations

Tier 2a
Substance misuse education targeted at drug users or those most at risk, harm minimisation advice and simple interventions such as one to one conversations, diary keeping and planned education. Substance misuse screening (could be part of a general assessment) and referral.

Provided by youth oriented services with some knowledge of drugs and alcohol, and skills in working with young people's problems. Key professionals include youth workers, connexions advisers, school nurses, counsellors, educational welfare, health visitors, social workers and psychologists.

Tier 1
Universal Drug Education, assessment and referral.

Provided by generic services such as education, youth services, general practitioners, social workers, sports coaches, volunteers, in fact anyone working with young people.

Appendix 2   Recorded outcome in drug education

Name _____   Age _____

Youth Club/Project _____   Date _____

Key: 1 = poor, 2 = average, 3 = good, 4 = very good

'I feel my level of drug awareness was/is?'

Before the session   *After the session*

1   2   3   4   1   2   3   4

'I feel confident that I know/knew about the dangers of drugs'

Before the session   *After the session*

1   2   3   4   1   2   3   4

'I feel confident that I know/knew about drugs and the law'

Before the session   *After the session*

1   2   3   4   1   2   3   4

'I feel confident that I know/knew the effects drugs have on the body'

Before the session   *After the session*

1   2   3   4   1   2   3   4

When thinking about your knowledge/skills before and after the session do you have any other comments?

Chapter 10

Sexual Health, Sexuality and Sex Education for Children and Young People in Care

Kathy Dunnett

This chapter should contain enough information for a range of professionals to gain information on sex and sexual health issues, to enable them to consider working with children and young people in care, e.g. designated health professionals, school nurses, health visitors, social workers and foster carers. This chapter will also identify all the groups who have additional needs in the field of sex education. The designated health professionals should also be an appropriate source of advice around training and policy development.

Background

Children and young people need sex education from their parents or carers, teachers, peers, health professionals and the media. Legislation such as the Education Act 1996 and the Children Act 1989 supports the sex education of children and young people, and places a duty on workers to talk about sex and relationships. The Guidance and Regulations to the Act, Volume 4, states that:

> The experience of being cared for should also include the sexual education of the young person. This may, of course, be provided by the young person's school, but if it is not, the social services department, or other caring agency responsible for the young person should provide sexual education for him.

However, looked after children often have their schooling disrupted, and the sex education programme in schools is still patchy (Patel-Kanwal and Lenderyou, 1998). 'Workers', or the 'department' should be interpreted as any person representing the work of the department. This interpretation puts a responsibility on care staff in children's homes, social workers, family placement teams and foster carers.

Research states that most young people would prefer to receive sex education from their peers than from school, parents or the media (Wellings et al., 2001). Peers are not necessarily a good source of advice, they may be misinformed and inaccurate. Many of the children and young people who we have in our care are disaffected with schooling, estranged from their families or parents, and the media often gives mixed messages. Thus, it falls to carers to have the responsibility for this very important part of health education. It is not enough to delegate this responsibility to the school, nurse or social worker. Responsible sexual health messages need to be consistent and constantly re-enforced. Many children and young people in the care system have not had consistent and positive parenting, and it is therefore even more crucial that this work is done. Looked after children and young people may have experienced traumatic events, some sexual, which may distort their understanding of sex, sexuality and relationships. This may lead them to behave inappropriately when forming relationships and display inappropriate sexual behaviours. These children and young people are in even more need of guidance, discussion and actual coaching around appropriate approaches with personal, caring and romantic relationships.

'Adolescent girls who have a history of sexual abuse are more likely to have sex early (before age 15) not use birth control, and have more than one sexual partner' (Stock et al., 1997). Girls with histories of sexual abuse have been found to have a greater desire to conceive than girls without abuse histories (Elders and Albert, 1998) and research also suggests that boys who become fathers in their early teenage years are likely to have lived with neither, or only one of their natural parents, and in families where discussion of sex was difficult or did not take place (*Supporting Families*, 1998). Whilst none of this research directly refers to looked after children, undoubtedly there will be many young people in the system to which this research does apply.

The lack of robust policies within social care settings to support this work is actively detrimental to the development of children and young people, who, if they do not receive truthful messages on sexuality and sexual health, will almost inevitably develop confused thoughts and behaviours, possibly contributing to the escalating need that we currently have to provide specialist placements for children and young people with sexually harmful behaviours. A sex and personal relationship policy is an essential means of supporting good practice, giving a clear framework for talking about sexual matters. It should give staff and foster carers a responsibility (with appropriate support) to know what they should do and how to do it. It will also give children and young people an entitlement, a right, to this information (Patel-Kanwal and Lenderyou, 1998) (see chapter on Training, Policies and Protocols).

Legal issues

Guidance for professionals and carers has been lacking, despite the recommendation in the Children Act (1989) and the Utting Report, *People like Us* (1997). The *Quality Protects* (1998) programme published several useful guides in conjunction with the Teenage Pregnancy Unit. The most up to date version is available on the Teenage Pregnancy Website, published by the DfES in 2004, 'Enabling young people to access contraceptive and sexual health information and advice: legal and policy framework for social workers, residential social workers, foster carers and other social care practitioners'.

For many years the Local Government Act 1988, 'Section 28', was understood to disallow work on homosexuality within schools. Within social care settings, this Act scared professionals and carers into avoiding the topic if possible. Lack of training and local policies, fear of misinterpretation of intention with subsequent disciplinary action, and sheer embarrassment, ceased development of health promotion in this subject for many years. This Act was repealed in 2003.

House rules for children in care

Young people need to understand that sexual relationships in the same household cannot be condoned. This rule may need to be made very clear and could possibly result in one of the young people changing their placement. The possibility of coercion and abusive sexual relationships is extremely high in multi-placement establishments.

Young people, sexual health, statistics and being in care

The United Kingdom has the highest teenage birth rate in Western Europe (Social Exclusion Unit, 1999) and although some young parents manage extremely well, teenage births have increased health risks for the young women and their babies. Teenage parents are also more likely than older parents to live in poverty and to be unemployed (DfES, 2004). Sexually transmitted diseases are on the increase amongst 16–19 year old women, particularly chlamydia. At least 10 per cent of sexually active young people are estimated to have an STI (DfES, 2004).

Accurate data on young women pregnant in care or as a care leaver is difficult to obtain, since local authorities do not routinely record this. There is probably a need, however, for the new designated health teams to consider collecting this information, in order to provide an appropriate service. Many looked after children have mental health needs that will need to be worked with in order to deal with any aspect of their care. Research does indicate, however, that children who have been looked after are around 2.5 times more likely to become teenage parents than those brought up with both natural parents (Social Exclusion Unit, 1999).

Young people who are looked after worry less about the possibility of pregnancy than those who are not looked after, feeling rather fatalistic about life in general (Corlyon and McGuire, 1999). This is probably due to a variety of reasons – education may have been disrupted, resulting in few qualifications and poor prospects of employment; young people in care often having less opportunity to make decisions and small mistakes that young people not in care have the opportunity to learn from; young people who have no sense of belonging will constantly search for this, forging inappropriate and sometimes exploitative relationships in order to find what they think is love, and just to be part of something (Scambler and Scambler, 1997). Both looked after girls and boys aspire to have a child so they can have 'something to love' (Corlyon and McGuire, 1999) but sometimes to 'prove' to 'people' that they can achieve parenthood:

> . . . *It'll be good to have a baby, 'cos I can love it, and it can love me back . . . an' I'll be better than me mum ever was wiv me . . .*
>
> (Female, 16, in care 10 years, no support networks)

Policy development

Policy development for sex education etc. is essential to support good practice, ensure conformity and consistency, keep professionals and carers safe from litigation and give children and young people a right to this very important health promotion work. An effective policy should support, encourage and expect professionals and carers to undertake this work, and should be accompanied with training and appropriate supervision (see chapter on Policies, Protocols and Training).

Training

Training on sexual health, sex education and talking to children and young people about sex is offered on a regular basis to foster carers and residential care workers (see chapter on Training, Policies and Protocols).

Sex education at school

All educational establishments, whether they are educational support centres, pupil referral units, youth programmes etc., should have some form of sex education for the young people that are their client group. Many of the young people being educated in these circumstances will have had disrupted education and may have missed vital information. There are many equally vulnerable young people being educated in colleges during their Year 10/11, but unfortunately they do not always have access to sex education lessons. Some of the alternative residential/educational establishments do not have the facility of the school nursing service, to assist and support sex education through Personal Health and Social Education (PHSE), such as secure units or learning support centres or pupil referral units. All schools are now being encouraged to have a policy that clearly states which topics will be covered. It may be important for carers to telephone the school and ask what topics are being covered in order that they can know how to give further input. Sex education often begins around Year 5–6 and quite often the school will invite parents and carers into school to discuss what will be taught.

Sexualised language

Many adults worry about the language of young people, and yet the use of language is continually changing and refining. What was regarded as an insult many years ago often becomes subsumed into almost normal language, e.g. fiddlesticks, an acceptable expletive in the 1960s, is a Victorian term, 'to masturbate'.

When young people tell you to f*** off what does it mean?

Ordinarily, particularly in schools, adults react angrily with heavy discipline. Yet young people do not have the language skills of an adult, nor the social skills, nor the control. Those children who have been subjected to some form of abuse are more likely to be more emotional and immature in their responses in social situations. It is worth giving the young person some time to reflect on an alternative response, to reflect on their feelings, and not to get angry. When a relationship has been formed, the use of swearing can be challenged – 'swearing only insults people and makes them angry, it does not tell them what you are feeling, or what they have done to upset you . . '.

Sexuality

The word 'sexuality' often means different things to different people. Many will determine it as whether an individual is homosexual (gay/lesbian) heterosexual (straight) or bisexual. Other studies will refer to sexual orientation, sexual behaviour or activity and sexual identity as being part of an overall sexuality.

Sexual orientation is defined as a pattern of arousal that includes sexual feelings, affectionate attraction, and emotional or romantic feelings (Remafedi, 1985, in Owens, 1998). Sexual orientation is not a choice (although for some, sociological factors may have some influence) and is evident at a very early age. There may be a genetic link (Burr, 1996). Whilst some children or young people may develop same sex crushes at different times in their lives, sexual orientation is more persistent and permanent.

Sexual behaviour or activity is the expression of sexual feelings by the individual. Sexual behaviour of an individual will depend on a variety of issues, such as family, culture, religion, situation, etc. Individuals will engage in sexual behaviour for a number of reasons – such as love, affection, loneliness, societal expectations, experimentation, power, etc. When a young person's sexual behaviours appear diverse, professionals may often believe that that person is 'confused' about their sexuality. The reality is that whilst the young person may have more feelings of homosexuality or bisexuality, they will try to behave in a heterosexual way.

Sexual identity is a consistent sense of sexual orientation, sometimes at odds with sexual behaviour depending on the situation. For example, within same sex prison settings, same sex activities will occur, yet not many of the inmates will define themselves as homosexual or lesbian. Sexual activity is a powerful physical need, which can drive some individuals to behave in ways that would be less acceptable to them if there was more choice.

Many Western societies would like to put sexual orientation into defined boxes of homosexuality, heterosexuality or bisexuality, but the reality is that sexual orientation is a continuum, with individuals having a variety of preferences around sexual activity. What is acceptable and preferable to one individual, is totally unacceptable to another individual.

There is no doubt that many children/young people may come into care through problems, disagreements and concerns about their sexual behaviour or sexuality. It is vitally important that these young people are given the help and support that they need to be able to develop and grow into happy and healthy adults. The alternative may be family alienation, homelessness, homophobic bullying within education and subsequently reduced employment opportunities.

Teenagers and pregnancy

Who is notified when it is discovered that a looked after girl is pregnant will depend very much on the circumstances of the pregnancy (are there child protection concerns?) and the girl's wishes. It is recommended that news of the pregnancy is not made common knowledge, at least until the girl has decided that she intends to continue with the pregnancy when, of course, others, such as her school, will need to be informed. Is it possible that she may also have acquired a sexually transmitted infection? If this is likely, she will need to be encouraged to attend the local genito-urinary clinic (GUM) look in the Yellow Pages, or speak to the designated nurse or school nurse.

Young women that are in care are more likely to fall pregnant as a teenager, than girls not in care. There may be a number of reasons for this, but for many girls it is a need to feel loved and wanted. There is some evidence that young men feel like this also. Girls will often use the idea of pregnancy to gain themselves attention and excitement; it is often difficult to know how to deal with these issues, as the roots are deep within a girl's personality, relating to poor self-esteem and self-worth.

Girls that persistently request pregnancy tests should be encouraged to attend the local family planning clinic. In this way, if they are pregnant, they can immediately have access to a range of information that they will need (abortion, health issues when pregnant) and if they are not pregnant, they can receive good advice on contraception (condoms, pill, injection, implants).

If a pregnancy is confirmed by the clinic, then the girl will need to sort out her feelings about whether or not to continue with the pregnancy. It is useful at this stage *not* to talk about 'the baby', but rather 'it', and 'the pregnancy'. Realistically in the early stages of pregnancy, it is just a collection of cells and girls may find it harder to decide to terminate a 'baby', than a 'pregnancy'. Foster carers can play an important role in discussing alternatives with her.

A useful exercise that can be done with girls considering options is given at the end of this chapter in Appendix 1.

Do remember that if a boy in your care becomes a father, he too may have difficult feelings towards the pregnancy and feel left out and rejected. It will be important for carers to support boys as much as they can, or arranging counselling if requested.

Abortion and adoption

If the girl decides that she wants an abortion, this can be arranged through her GP. She will also have to consider future contraception, and emergency contraception should be explained to her.

Abortion is another difficult issue that carers and professionals may need to face. One of the biggest problems is who to tell? Looked after children often have highly personal health issues shared very publicly, which embarrasses them and encourages them not to share concerns appropriately.

The earlier that the girl can be encouraged to consider the pregnancy the better, and easier options for terminating a pregnancy are available. For some girls, this is a challenge. Many girls almost seem to deny the act of sex and possible pregnancy. They seem unable to make a decision, so don't do anything, thus the pregnancy continues until the option for abortion is no longer there.

> . . . *I don't remember having sex* . . . *he must have done it to me when I was asleep* . . .
>
> (13 year old girl in residential care)

A fifteen year old girl, when asked why she had not asked for emergency contraception:

> . . . *I just didn't think about it really, I just didn't think that it was going to happen to me* . . .

Young people in care seem to have more difficulty in making decisions (see Appendix 3, Fraser guidelines). Perhaps, because of past abuse, these young people can so effectively block off difficult things that have happened to them, issues that need a decision, unfortunately also become blocked off.

> . . . *A young girl of 16 texted her designated nurse on a Sunday to inform her that she had unprotected sex, the nurse immediately texted back to make an arrangement to*

> *meet the girl and her boyfriend on the Monday, to attend the clinic . . . The good point of this scenario, is that this particular girl had already had two abortions, but had finally found the courage and maturity to acknowledge the consequence of her behaviour.*

As soon as a girl acknowledges her pregnancy, she should be encouraged to attend either the family planning clinic or her general practitioner. If she is undecided whether or not to continue with the pregnancy, the family planning clinic may be able to give a young girl more time than a busy GP. As mentioned, the earlier that the pregnancy is acknowledged, the more choice the girl has. The abortion pill (early medical abortion) must be taken within nine weeks of conception, but is not available in all areas, and some young girls will have to travel to another area to access this option. There are still variations across the country with regard to quick and easy terminations, and some girls may have to wait many weeks before it can take place. She will need considerable support during this time, and may change her mind several times. She should certainly have the support of an adult to accompany her to appointments – the initial consultation and the termination. This may need to be a special arrangement within health, if the young girl does not want to inform her carers of the termination, and wishes to keep everything confidential. All services offering abortions should undertake their own counselling, to ascertain whether or not the young girl has really made up her mind. Sometimes girls will also need to access further counselling after the event. Carers and local authority departments, before referring to a non NHS facility, should reassure themselves that very young girls are being supported and treated appropriately whilst on site. Some private clinics do not allow adults on the ward whilst the girls await their procedure. This situation should be questioned and challenged, as it is not in keeping with the current recommendations of children as inpatients in the *National Service Framework for Children: Standard for Hospital Services* (DoH, 2003).

For girls who feel unable to have a termination, the option of adoption must also be discussed. Unfortunately, for some young girls who later find they are unable to cope, this becomes a decision that is sometimes made for them, initially the baby being taken into foster care, then subsequently placed for adoption.

It is interesting that whilst many young people are inclined to adopt an anti-abortion attitude, this is much more evident with looked after children. Because of the rejection that they themselves had suffered, the girls often do not consider adoption as a possibility (Corlyon and McGuire, 1999). For some young girls, carrying on with the pregnancy is the easiest option, and this may be due to the fact they feel they have little control in their lives, and are unfamiliar with long-term planning (Corlyon and McGuire, 1999).

Confidentiality

Some highly personal health issues should not be shared with a whole staff team unless they have a specific reason for needing to know. It is *never* appropriate to share personal health issues during a statutory review, although some problems will need to be discussed in a more private setting, either before or after the review. Some personal health problems should not be passed from carer to carer as foster children move, which may be difficult for family placement teams feeling that carers are unable to care for a child adequately unless they are fully informed. However, children and young people should also have a voice in what gets passed on, and what does not, and there must be a way of alerting carers to issues *without* necessarily knowing intimate details. Looked after children and young people should be able to have access to a confidential health service in the same way as any other young person does.

Special needs

Learning difficulties

Young people with learning difficulties have the same sexual preferences and behaviours as non-disabled people (Brown, 1994) and should have the same rights to sexual expression as anyone else. However, society more often views them as needing to be protected from sexual information and relationships. Young people with severe learning difficulties are not usually encouraged to consider long-term sexually active relationships and the possibility of marriage and parenthood (Douglas-Scott in Burtney and Duffy, 2004).

For children and young people who have learning difficulties, the constant re-enforcement of simplified sexual health messages is even more important due to perhaps their limited abilities to retain information and skills. Much of the inappropriate behaviour (for example, masturbating in public, touching and exposure) is due to lack of information rather than sexual abuse (although this should not be overlooked) or being over-sexualised. The difficulty of finding appropriate resources for children and young people with learning difficulties can be a challenge, as there is such a wide variety of abilities, and some children and young people may have other disabilities, such as communication, sensory and physical problems. Sex education must be explicit and clear, not relying on innuendo or inference. It should be delivered in small steps, beginning with the basics of names for body parts, safety and privacy issues, nice touches and nasty touches. If this work is not done, it can lead to those with learning difficulties being more at risk from sexual abuse, because they will not fully understand what is happening to them, and may not have the language to explain it. It may also not prepare them for the possibility of intimate examinations or relationships in the future, should this ever be necessary, and they may be fearful of taking off their clothes.

There are some legal issues relating to people with learning difficulties:

- If a man were married to a woman with learning difficulties, then sex is legitimate.
- For unmarried women it depends on an assessment of the level of the woman's impairment of intelligence and social functioning.

(Mental Health Act 1983 in England and Wales; Mental Health (Scotland) Act 1984)

If a woman, therefore, was assessed as 'having arrested or incomplete development of mind, including significant impairment of intelligence and social functioning', then it would be illegal for a man to have sex with her. If she were deemed 'capable' then it would not be an offence (Douglas-Scott, op. cit.). With same sex relationships, the Criminal Justice Act 1980, section 80 makes 'homosexual acts' with a man with learning difficulties an offence if he cannot consent. An assessment of capacity would be required.

It would seem sensible to try and delay sexual relationships with young people who have severe learning difficulties until we are sure they have reached a level of understanding and emotional maturity that will enable them to cope. This will only be achieved through good sex education delivered and supported, consistently and repeatedly via all the adults associated with these young people – carers, teachers, health staff, family, etc. However, if these needs are ignored, then this may lead to confusion, frustration and challenging behaviour (Moore, 1991). Young people with learning difficulties must also be given the opportunity to cope with other small acts of independence and decision-making, just in the same way as any other child or young person who does not have learning difficulties.

Mild learning difficulties/specific learning difficulties

There are many young people that present very normally within society, and will attend a mainstream school, apparently operating at an average, or slightly below average level within school. There may be some behavioural problems, and there may be apparently minor problems with poor handwriting, concentration or laziness, and forgetfulness.

It may be that these young people have an as yet undiagnosed specific learning difficulty. As young people get older, these types of learning difficulties will be harder to diagnose, as young people develop compensatory skills to overcome their difficulties. These difficulties may be very specific, affecting short-term auditory and visual memory, but will have an effect on the way that young person absorbs and understands information. These young people represent a particular challenge when giving information on sexual health, as whilst they may appear to take in the information, the reality may be that they can only remember very little. It is even more necessary to engage these young people in conversations about sex and sexual health, in order that you can be sure that they have all the information they need to make sensible choices for themselves.

Physical disability

Children and young people with a physical disability also have the right to sex education, physical relationships, marriage and parenthood. However, there are obvious difficulties of the mechanics of a sexual relationship when young people have limbs missing, or restrictions of movement make quite simple movements very difficult (such as putting on a condom). Privacy may also be difficult when young people need lots of help with basic functioning. From the very beginning, parents and carers need to acknowledge the difficulties of children and young people and not ignore them. Disabled young people should be encouraged to engage with their own age group (disabled and non-disabled) and to form ordinary relationships. Family planning clinics may be able to explore with physically disabled young people how sexual satisfaction can be achieved, perhaps not necessarily by sexual intercourse if this is too difficult for a disabled couple. The Family Planning Association now sells a range of sexual aids which can enable disabled young people to experience their sexuality in a way that may not be possible through an ordinary relationship. Specialist counsellors may also be able to advise. It is imperative, however, that the sexual needs of disabled young people are not ignored.

Sensory disabilities

Depending on the degree of sensory disability or disabilities, sex education may have to be given with a range of methods. For example, young people with hearing needs will need access to sub-titled videos, Braille books and carers (ideally) that can sign. Young people that are blind should have the opportunity of access to models, in order that they can have more accurate explanations of what to expect. A range of specialist resources may be available via the designated health team, the health promotion department, or the appropriate specialist agency (blind society) may be able to give appropriate advice. Specialist advisory teachers may also know of appropriate resources on sexual health.

Complex needs case study

. . . A young man of 15 was showing extremely difficult and challenging behaviour in his residential home . . . he masturbated in public and tried to touch and mount female staff. It transpired that he had never been given any sex education, either via his parents, the school or the staff in the home . . . the other difficulty was that not only did he have severe learning difficulties, but he was also registered blind, and only had limited hearing . . . Because information had not been given earlier, it proved very difficult to undertake this work, and appropriate resources seemed impossible to find . . . After months of very difficult behaviour, giving the staff a lot of stress, he was finally moved to an adult establishment early, where the staff ratio was greater, and they were able to manage him better . . .

Religion, race, castes and culture

When discussing issues of sex, sexuality, and contraception, it is important to remember that some races, cultures and religions may find discussing it embarrassing, even offensive. However, this does not mean that children and young people should be denied the opportunity of having the information. At least if they are aware of what is available, they can then make an informed choice as to how to use the information. It is important to remember that in all religions and cultures there are a range of views and values held, from those that uphold strictly all the rules of their particular belief, and those that are more flexible. Clarification will need to be sought from parents and young people, and even if the parents are reluctant for information to be passed on, it may be decided that this needs to be done in the 'best interests' of the young person.

Social services departments may come into contact with families that forbid contraception and abortion, expect virginity until married, support circumcision of both boys and girls (female circumcision is now an offence in this country (Prohibition of Female Circumcision Act 1985 s 1(1), see Fortin, 1998), refuse to acknowledge homosexuality, and refuse teaching on sex until marriage is imminent. Professionals need to be open minded and unbiased when encountering extremes of beliefs. Many cultures would require a female doctor to examine a female, and young females would need to be given this facility to save severe embarrassment.

It is essential for carers to be informed concerning the values and beliefs of the family, then to consider the nature and detail of the information that should be given, depending on the wishes of the family, and the needs of the child or young person. Advisory teachers would be able to give more specific guidance on the traditions of races, religions and cultures with regard to sex education.

If young people are requesting information/services that are against their parents' wishes, staff should assess the young person's competence, bearing in mind that if young people are asking for information, it is unlikely that this is the first occasion that they have needed it! And therefore, probably fairly essential that the information is given! It is equally essential that once the decision has been made, that this is documented and the young person is supported properly and confidentiality is maintained.

If English is not the first language of the young person, it may be necessary to work through an interpreter, and find culturally and linguistically appropriate materials.

Traveller culture

There are a variety of beliefs and understanding of sex, sexuality and sexual health within the travelling communities, and it is essential to keep an open mind and possibly broach the subject with parents or relatives to try and glean cooperation at an early stage if their children are taken into care. Some of their ideas seem very old fashioned such as '. . . the menfolk do not discuss such issues (menstruation) with the women . . . it is dirty talk and people do not like to hear it . . .'. Some cultures will go much further, even to the point of arranged marriages and insisting that the girl is a virgin on her wedding day.

If this rather sensitive topic is not discussed with them, it can often become an issue that the family will argue about and become a further barrier to prevent other work being done with them.

Contraception

Teenagers in care may need advice and support on this issue. It is important that this subject is not shied away from. Research states that young people often begin a sexual relationship before they seek contraceptive advice (Wellings et al., 2001). We must try to ensure that this does not happen, and look for opportunities to give older children advice before they need it. This does not encourage young people to have sex, but it will encourage them to seek appropriate advice. Young people should be encouraged to visit family planning clinics for information. Some professionals are concerned that by allowing them to visit the clinic, we have made a decision concerning their level of competence. This is not the case. The staff at the family planning clinics are trained to access competence, and will deal with that issue. Visiting the clinic is merely accessing information, in the same way that you would attend a library. The DfES *Framework for Social Workers, Residential Social Workers, Foster Carers and other Social Care Practitioners* supports this work and so should local policies (DfES, 2004). Just because you are not an expert on sexual health, does not mean you cannot advise on this subject – your advice is simple, '. . . always use a condom, and for extra protection you should attend the GP or family planning clinic for a choice of contraceptives – the pill, the contraceptive injection or implants, are the most reliable and easy to use . . .'. There are some excellent leaflets for young people now, not forgetting information about the emergency contraceptive pill, which can be taken 72 hours after unprotected sex, and considerably reduces the chances of pregnancy if taken properly. This is available from the GP, family planning clinic and most accident and emergency departments.

Sexually transmitted infections

If young people continually risk their sexual health by having unprotected sex with multiple partners, then the chance of them acquiring a sexually transmitted infection obviously becomes much greater. Many young people also have concurrent partners, which increases the risk even further (Wellings et al., 2001).

Sexually transmitted infections (STIs) are an increasing cause of morbidity among young people 16–25 and rates are rising among younger teenagers also (PHLS, 2002).

Since 1996, the rates of chlamydia increased for young people, and in 2002 it was estimated that 1.2 per cent of 16–19 year old girls were infected with chlamydia. Males aged 20–24 are more affected than the younger males, perhaps merely reflecting that in relationships the girls are more likely to date males slightly older than themselves. Whilst some of these statistics are obviously reflecting better testing facilities, it is important to remember that the real numbers are hidden, due to chlamydia being virtually symptomless.

Most STIs are easily cured provided that it is diagnosed early on in the disease and treatment is effective. Some sexually transmitted infections are resistant or difficult to treat, such as genital warts and herpes (unfortunately these can also sometimes be caught despite wearing a condom – due to the possibility of sores and warts being located in areas of the genitalia not in contact with a condom – outer labia, base of the shaft of the penis) also HIV and hepatitis, whilst technically being a blood borne virus, can be passed on sexually and can have life-changing effects.

Carers often have concerns about the possibility of acquiring the blood borne viruses during their caring duties. The reality of this happening is rare, provided that carers follow 'Universal Guidelines' (see Appendix 2). These are sensible straightforward rules, which should prevent infection from child to carer, or even carer to child (a carer positive for hepatitis or HIV should not necessarily rule them out from a caring role, provided all understand the risks and take the necessary precautions). However, all carers should be encouraged to be immunised against hepatitis B, which will need to be checked every few years (carers should receive individual advice).

Young people that persistently refuse to protect themselves by using a condom should be encouraged to attend regularly at the genitourinary clinic for screening. Your designated health professionals/school nurse will be able to locate the nearest clinic, or the website *www.playingsafely.com* is a useful resource.

Alcohol, substances

It is important to discuss important issues such as alcohol and substances, and how they relate to sexual health. People who are under the influence often do not make good decisions for themselves, and safety and accidents can be particularly problematic. The relationship between risky sex and alcohol and substances affects adults as well as young people. Both alcohol and some substances can appear to enhance sex and sexuality, but more often it can be associated with sex that is regretted, exploitative, abusive or violent (Alcohol Concern, 2002). Young people report having more risky sex when they are under the influence of alcohol (Traeen and Kvalem, 1996; Hibell et al., 2001) and also that alcohol is the main reason for having early sex or sex with someone they had not known that long (Ingham, 2001).

Some of the reasons for this link between alcohol and risky sex are that:

- Alcohol lowers inhibitions (Plant, Bagnall and Forster, 1990).

- Alcohol reduces the sense of self-control (Rhodes and Quirk, 1995).

- Alcohol affects judgement (Alcohol Concern, 2002).

- Alcohol can affect dexterity – trying to put on a condom.

- Being drunk provides a legitimate excuse for behaviour that might otherwise be seen as unacceptable (Rhodes and Quirk, 1995).

It is imperative that young people are given this information in order that they consider their own risks around sexual health and being under the influence of alcohol.

> . . . A boy of 15 had unprotected sex with a girl of 15 after a group of them from the Children's Home had absconded and managed to buy a large quantity of alcohol. The next day, the girl alleged that the boy had 'raped' her. He fervently and consistently denied the accusation, but was moved from the Children's Home (where he had lived for two years), to a specialist unit many miles away . . .

For more information on Substance Misuse, see relevant chapter.

Difficult/dangerous/upsetting situations

(See section on Risk Management/Harm Minimisation in Chapter 13.)

Children that engage in sexually harmful behaviours

Occasionally, you may suspect, either because of inappropriate behaviour or questions, that the child/young person in your care may have been sexually abused. Do make a note of your concerns. Try to be as objective as you can in the description of the behaviour. Children and young people do behave inappropriately and do make mistakes with sex, but it is important not to jump to the wrong conclusions. If inappropriate sexual behaviour is continually repeated, after you have spoken to the child/young person and asked them to stop the behaviour, then it is important to pass this information on, so that it can be investigated to ascertain whether or not further help, advice or treatment is necessary. It is essential that children and young people with inappropriate sexual behaviours are given the correct information on all issues relating to sexual health, according not only to their age, but also their experiences. Often this work can be difficult, as to discuss sexual issues may remind children of abusive experiences, and they may try and involve carers/ professionals in a flirtatious way (Vizard, 1997, in Estela et al.). It is important that carers and non-specialist professionals react objectively, and are not drawn into detailed discussion of grooming or abuse, but gently and firmly bring the discussion back to the topic being taught. All disclosures need to be reported, and carers and non-specialist professionals (school nurses, social workers, etc.) should be supported by specialist professionals, either from CAMHS, or specialist agencies, such as NSPCC, Barnardo's or other children's charities. Children and young people who have problems in this area, are often put in placements which remove temptation (single placement), but often these problems may not be resolved unless the young person is given support and guidance. Sometimes, when the young person leaves the supervision of care, they revert to old habits, and may eventually become imprisoned.

> *A boy of 14 in a residential establishment was urgently removed to a specialist placement due to a 'serious sexual assault' on a member of staff. When the staff team were challenged on this terminology, a range of interpretations were given – from touching to attempted rape. It transpired that the boy had touched a female member of staff's breasts, but it was during a restraint, and it was unclear as to the nature of the touch.*

(Dunnett, in Wheal, 2005)

Children abused and abused through prostitution

Looked after children can be more vulnerable to grooming and abusive relationships due to their searching feelings of wanting to be loved and belong.

> *. . . At the beginning I remember being in care and I can remember a girl who used to work. I used to go out with her . . . I wanted to belong, it had got nothing to do with money.*

(Scambler and Scambler, 1997)

Since the 1980s there has been a growing concern and awareness that some young people in the care of residential homes are particularly targeted (Jesson, 1991). Barnardo's were amongst the first to reject the term 'child prostitution', and instead reframe the whole issue as 'sexual exploitation of children', and later 'children abused through prostitution' (Barnardo's, 1998). Sir William Utting, in his report *People Like Us*, recommended that abuse through prostitution should be dealt with as a child protection issue.

Professionals and carers need to be alert to all forms of abusive situations, whether sexual or otherwise. Recent research from Barnardo's highlights the growing problem of sexual abuse of children and young people through the internet and mobile telephone technology (Palmer and Stacey, 2004).

Children who have been sexually abused will need extra support around sex education and relationship issues. They may have distorted views about what sex means, and may need specialist counselling and support. Children who have been sexually abused, may become distressed during sex education lessons in school, and behaviour may deteriorate. Professionals need to be patient and understanding, and may have to repeat information several times before it can be taken on board by a child that has upsetting and violent memories of sex. Again, non-expert professionals and carers may need to seek specialist support/training before feeling confident to undertake this work.

Children that have been sexually abused, or that are abusive to others are entitled to appropriate services to help them address their problems. It is better to make a referral for a child that subsequently does not need help, than not to make a referral for a child whose problems eventually get much worse. Local ACPC (now Local Safeguarding Boards), should have local policies that highlight the specialist needs of these young people, and should recommend a way forward.

Parental issues, consent and confidentiality

Parents should be informed that issues of sex and contraception will be discussed with their child when appropriate, and they should also be informed that they may not necessarily be consulted if their child wishes to keep certain information confidential, and they are assessed as being Fraser competent. For those parents that are interested in being involved in a constructive way, it would be ideal if they could attend the same training courses as is offered to foster carers or residential care workers. The Children Act 1989 emphasises the importance of working in partnership with parents on all matters concerning their children's upbringing. If a parent does not consent to their child having information about sex and personal relationships, staff will need to assess what is in the best interests of the child (see Appendix 3, Fraser Competence, previously known as Gillick Competence).

Beginning to do it!

For some, training will be essential; others may feel more able, particularly if they have managed to speak to their own children/young people on these issues. It is vitally important to feel confident, and it may be that you would need to access materials from local health establishments (Health Promotion Department) before you could begin.

Building a relationship with the child/young person is obviously an important part of the role of the carer, building a rapport is not always so easy, particularly on difficult issues such as sex. Talking about sex should be an 'okay' thing to do within the home. Topical issues in newspapers, magazines and even in soap operas, can be used to raise the topic to discuss in an informal and light-hearted manner. In this way, children and young people will have the information, hopefully, before they need it.

Do not confuse listening and giving advice. Advice and guidance can be helpful, particularly with younger children. The best decisions a person can make are those that they have arrived at themselves. The professional or carer's role is to help the young person consider all the necessary information, to sift it and represent it so that they can understand it. In this way they will feel able to make an informed decision. This is empowering for any young person, will build their confidence and self-esteem, and will give them the skills to enable them to take their life forward into adulthood.

Younger children

With younger children, it may be necessary to liaise with parents as to which words to use for intimate body parts. It is essential that we do have names, in order that children can be encouraged to keep clean, but it is also protective, because if children believe they are being touched inappropriately, they must be able to state exactly where, not just 'down below'.

If children ask questions, it is important to answer them as honestly as possible, without getting too embarrassed or even disgusted. Young children will repeat things they have heard in very inappropriate settings and will not realise that it is rude. It is also important to understand the context of the question, and not launch into too much description. A suitable answer to the question, 'Where do babies come from?' may only need a reply such as, 'A mummy grows them in her tummy'. Young children will often be satisfied with a short answer, and will ask further questions if they need more information.

Older children and young people

It is important to establish a rapport on these subjects at an early stage, and if body hygiene is an issue, this may be a less threatening way to tackle the issue. Whilst teenagers will have a variety of names for their private parts, it is useful to encourage the proper terminology, explaining that health professionals are more comfortable with these words!

Naming of body parts and talking about a range of sexual health issues can be a difficult thing to do without becoming embarrassed, and this may be worse when dealing with older children, as they often become embarrassed too. Practice makes perfect, and if you have sons and daughters, nephews and nieces of your own, you may feel more able to practice on them first. If not, practice with your partner or a friend, just get used to saying the words out loud.

A useful stalling answer to a difficult question, could be, 'That's a good question, I need to think about how to explain it to you properly. I'll speak to you tomorrow.' This will give you time to choose your words and even telephone someone for guidance. Please ensure though, that you do try and answer the question.

Conclusion

Sex, sexual relationships and relevant issues are one of those 'difficult' subjects that people (this includes many relevant professionals) do not like to think about or talk about. Views amongst different professionals can vary greatly, especially on some of the problematic issues, such as 'sexually abusive behaviours'. Depending on one's training, a social worker, a health professional and educationalist may hold very diverse views on what kinds of behaviour are acceptable or not, and may clash on decisions that need to be made concerning suitability of placements and school. It is vitally important that all relevant services try and come to an understanding of exactly what is happening for the child or young person, the risks that their behaviour presents and what, in the child's best interests, should be done (if anything). The move to children's trust arrangements should hopefully support this way of working, encouraging children's services to work together in multi-disciplinary teams (DfES, 2003).

As this work can be difficult, it is important that local champions (usually the designated health team) pull on all the relevant professionals to help them in this work –

policy writing, training, support and advice. The teenage pregnancy adviser should be someone that can advocate for this work to be given a high priority in local plans for the area.

References

Alcohol Concern (2002) *Alcohol and Teenage Pregnancy*. London: Alcohol Concern.

Barnardo's (1998) *Whose Daughter Next?* London: Barnardo's.

Brown, H. (1994) An Ordinary Sexual Life? A Review of the Normalisations Principle as it Applies to the Sexual Options of People with Learning Disabilities. *Disabilities and Society*, 19: 2, 123–44.

Burr, C. (1996) *A Separate Creation: How Biology makes us Gay*. London: Bantam.

Burtney, E. and Duffy, M. (Eds.) (2004) *Young People and Sexual Health: Individual, Social and Policy Contexts*. Basingstoke: Palgrave Macmillan.

Corlyon, J. and McGuire, C. (1997) *Young Parents in Public Care: Pregnancy and Parenthood among Young People looked after by Local Authorities*. London: NCB.

Corlyon, J. and McGuire, C. (1999) *Pregnancy and Parenthood: The Views and Experiences of Young People in Public Care*. London: NCB.

DfES (1989) *The Children Act 1989*. London: HMSO.

DfES (1998) *Quality Protects*. London: HMSO.

DfES (2004) *Healthy Living Blueprint for Schools*. London: HMSO.

DoH (2003) *National Service Framework for Children, Young People and Maternity Services: Core Standards*. London: HMSO.

Elders, M. and Albert, A. (1998) Adolescent Pregnancy and Sexual Abuse. *Journal of the American Medical Association*, 208, 648–9.

Fortin, J. (1998) *Children's Rights and the Developing Law*. Cambridge: Cambridge University Press.

Hibell, B. et al. (2001) *The 1999 ESPAD Report; Alcohol and other Drug Use amongst Students in 30 European Countries*. Stockholm: Swedish Council for Information on Alcohol and Drugs.

Home Office (1998) *Supporting Families*. London: The Stationery Office.

Ingham, R. (2001) Survey commissioned by Channel Four for the series 'Generation Sex'. 16th October, 2001.

Jesson, J. (1991) Young Women in Care: The Social Services Care System and Juvenile Prostitution. In *Whose Daughter Next?* (1998) London: Barnardo's.

Moore, K. (1991) Confronting Taboo: Helping People with Learning Disabilities to Understand their own Sexuality. *Nursing Times*, 46–7.

Owens, R.E. (1998) *Queer Kids: The Challenges and Promise for Lesbian, Gay and Bisexual Youth*. London/New York: Haworth.

Palmer, T. and Stacy, L. (2004) *Just One Click: Sexual Abuse of Children and Young People through the Internet and Mobile Telephone Technology*. London: Barnardo's.

Patel-Kanwal, H. and Lenderyou, G. (1998) *Let's Talk About Sex and Relationships. A Policy and Practice Framework for Working with Children and Young People in Public Care*. London: NCB.

Plant, M., Bagnall, G. and Forster, J. (1990) Teenage Heavy Drinkers: Alcohol-related Knowledge, Beliefs, Experiences, Motivation and the Social Context of Drinking. *Alcohol and Alcoholism* 25: 691–8.

Public Health Laboratory Service (2002) *Sexually Transmitted Infections in the UK: Data Tables*. London: PHLS.

Rhodes, T. and Quirk, A. (1995) *Drugs as 'Reason' and 'Excuse' for Unsafe Sex*. Executive Summary 40. London: Centre for Research on Drugs and Health Behaviour.

Scambler, G. and Scambler, A. (1997) *Rethinking Prostitution: Purchasing Sex in the 1990's*. London: Routledge.

Social Exclusion Unit (1999) *Teenage Pregnancy Report*. London: SEU.

Stock, J.L. et al. (1997) Adolescent Pregnancy and Sexual Risk-taking among Sexually Abused Girls. *Family Planning Perspectives*, 29: 5, 200–7.

Teenage Pregnancy Unit (2001) *Loughborough Study* Teenage Pregnancy Unit – *www.dfes.gov.uk/teenagepregnancy*

Traeen, B. and Kvalem, I. (1996) Sex under the Influence of Alcohol among Norwegian Adolescents. *Addiction*, 91: 995–1006.

Utting, W. Sir (1997) *People Like Us: The Report of the Review of the Safeguards for Children Living away from Home*. London: The Stationery Office.

Vizard, E. (1997) Adolescents who Sexually Abuse. In Estella, V. et al. (Eds.) *A Practical Guide to Forensic Psychotherapy*. London: Jessica Kingsley.

Wellings, K. (2001) *Teenage Sexual and Reproductive Behaviour in Developed Countries: Country Report for Great Britain*. Occasional Report, No.6. New York: AGI

Wellings K. et al. (2001) Sexual Behaviour in Britain: Early Heterosexual Experience. *The Lancet*, 258, 1843–50.

Appendix I   Pregnancy Options

A useful exercise with girls considering their options is to get them to make lists

- **List the six things that I really enjoy doing in my life right now.**
    1. Seeing my mates Fridays and Saturdays and going down the club.
    2. Horse riding on Sunday.
    3. Going to college in September to do the Nursery Nurse course.
    4. Going to work on Saturdays.
    5. Going out for curries at the beginning of the month.
    6. Seeing my boyfriend.

- **How would these options be affected if you chose to continue with the pregnancy?**
    1. Eventually I would have to stop doing this because the pregnancy would show. I should give up smoking and drinking.
    2. Some sports are restricted in early pregnancy and horse riding is one of them.
    3. I could start college, but wouldn't be able finish it or take the exams until I could sort out arrangements for a baby.
    4. I would have to stop this eventually – it's only a Saturday job, so they might not want me back.
    5. Curries might well make me feel sick, your tastes are all funny when you are pregnant and have morning sickness (or sometimes all day sickness!).
    6. The pregnancy is not his, I don't suppose he will want to keep seeing me.

- **How would these options be affected if you chose to keep a baby?**
    1. I may be able to go out sometimes, but I'm not sure it would be reasonable to ask someone to baby sit every Friday and Saturday. I could pay someone, but how could I afford it? How would I know they are reliable? Would I have to move placement?
    2. The birth of a baby may make me quite sore down below for a while, especially if there are stitches and if I get infected.
    3. I'm not sure what would happen to the course. I might be able to get on another course, but there is still the problem of who would mind a baby, and how will I get the homework done in the evening if it was crying a lot. Suppose it kept me up all night – how would I cope with college then?
    4. I would probably have lost this job, I might get another – but who would want to look after a baby for all day?
    5. If I breast fed a baby, I wouldn't be able to eat curries – it would give a baby colic. I'd still have to find a baby sitter!
    6. It would probably be difficult to find another boyfriend if you already had someone else's baby.

- **How would the list look if you chose to continue with the pregnancy, but have the baby adopted or fostered?**

Appendix 2   Universal precautions

Treating everyone (including yourself) as a possible source of infection

Treating everyone the same.

- Cover cuts on hands.
- Wash hands before and after first aid procedures.
- Use disposable gloves for first aid.
- Use household rubber gloves for heavily soiled material.
- No sharing of toothbrushes, razors, etc.
- Follow more detailed procedures in any local sexual health or blood borne virus policy and guidance.

Appendix 3   Fraser Guidelines/Gillick Competancy and Confidentiality for Young People

- The House of Lords made a judgement in 1985 known as the Gillick Judgement, or more accurately, the Fraser Guidelines. It relates to contraceptive advice and treatment to a person under 16.

- It states that under 16s have a right to confidentiality, whether asking for contraceptive advice or any other medical treatment such as abortion.

- It allows young people under 16 of 'sufficient understanding and intelligence' who understand the implications of medical treatment to consent to such treatment on their own behalf.

- The Fraser Guidelines are only legally binding to doctors but are considered to represent best practice for other health professionals (i.e. nurses, school nurses, all family planning and genitourinary medicine (GUM) clinic staff).

- While the Fraser Guidelines emphasise that young women under the age of 16 seeking contraceptive advice should be encouraged to inform their parents or carers, it upholds the right of doctors to prescribe contraception without parental knowledge or consent, providing that the doctor is satisfied that the young person:
  – Will understand the advice.
  – Cannot be persuaded to tell their parents/carers, or they will not allow the doctor to tell the parent/carers, that they are seeking contraceptive advice or treatment.
  – Is likely to begin or continue having unprotected sex with or without contraceptive treatment.
  – The young person's physical or mental health is likely to suffer unless they received contraceptive advice or treatment.
  – It is in the young person's best interests to receive contraceptive advice or treatment.

- Many professionals work within their own professional guidelines which prescribe confidentiality as best practice in relation to service provision. Any sex and relationships policy and guidance should always address confidentiality, particularly when it considers young people.

- A professional cannot guarantee confidentiality regarding any discussion with a child about sex and relationships if they feel that there is a child protection or criminal matter which needs to be investigated by the appropriate authority.

Whilst the original statement at the Gillick case was concerned with general practitioners giving contraceptive advice – it can be seen that the principles of deciding as to whether a child or adolescent is competent to make a decision about any aspects of their life can be applied. There are difficulties to applying this principle, however:

(a)   On a general cognitive (ability to understand) level, the competency of young children up to 11 or 12 is different from that of younger adolescents and different again with older adolescents.

(b)   Some individuals, depending on intelligence and experiences will have more competency skills than others of similar ages, so a general rule cannot be applied.

(c)   Some decisions will require more competency skills than others, e.g. Shall I get a bus or a train? Or, shall I stay on at school or go to college?

(d)   If a person is traumatised in some way through bereavement, ill health, etc., then their competency skills may be considerably reduced. Also, if they are under the influence of substances.

(e)   The UN Convention on the Rights of the Child Article 12, states that: 'Whenever adults make a decision that will affect you in any way, you have the right to give your opinion, and the adults have to take that seriously.' This may mean that we try to find a compromise with the child, acknowledging a move to independence.

(f)   Children and young people are also more influenced by many pressures, as they grow and develop more sophisticated decision-making skills. Adolescents will naturally begin to question the belief systems with which they were brought up and may discard family values, as they respond to other influences such as peer pressure. Many children and young people only have a vague notion of real but unobvious dangers, such as sexually transmitted infections. These skills develop more through maturity, but also through opportunity – identifying risks and benefits, foreseeing consequences and gauging credibility of information.

(g)   Low self-esteem can inhibit ability to make important decisions, children and adolescents showing less competence in their decision-making than their potential suggests.

(h)   Parents and carers have a duty to encourage children to develop decision-making capacities from as early an age as possible. Parents and carers may sometimes find it difficult to involve children and young people in family decisions, mainly from a 'protective' viewpoint, and not wanting the child to be hurt or upset. It may be a difficult judgement call over some issues, but some decisions should not be given to children or young people where the consequence of that decision may impair their future development or give rise to considerable feelings of guilt for many years.

Sometimes it is our role as parents or carers to make mistakes for the child/young person and *bear the blame for that mistake*, as to pass it to the child would be too great a burden. Sometimes, however, it is helpful for children/young people to make small mistakes themselves and then parents/carers can then use these situations as learning experiences, using it to further build skills. Children and young people have the 'right' to make mistakes, but . . . good parenting involves giving minors as much rope as they can handle without an acceptable risk that they will hang themselves . . . (Lord Donaldson in Fortin, 1998: 77, *Children's Rights and the Developing Law*).

Conclusion

When considering whether or not to allow a child or young person in our care to make a certain decision, we must ask ourselves some practical questions:

1. Is the child sufficiently mature to make a particular decision and understand the consequences that flow from this decision? (Bearing in mind the above guidance).
2. What will the outcome be if the decision is not one that we would want?
3. If we cannot allow the young person to make that decision then why are we offering it to them?
4. Can we stop them from making the decision, or acting on their own? e.g. We may want to stop a young person going out, but can we physically restrain them?
5. We may have to consider using 'harm minimisation' strategies. e.g. allowing them to go out (under protest), but then offering to give them a lift home early, thus minimising risk, as they are out for a shorter period.

References

Fortin, J. (1998) *Children's Rights and the Developing Law*. Cambridge: Cambridge University Press.

Chapter 11

Nutrition and Looked After Children

Mary Cooper

Introduction

Healthy Care (2003) aims to ensure that children and young people in care live in an environment that promotes health and well being and gives them opportunities to develop life skills to enable them to live independently and healthily (see chapter on Healthy Care). *Every Child Matters* (2004) also has an expectation that young people will be healthy and safe and contribute positively to society. Good nutrition, both in terms of intake and skills, are an integral part of this. Good nutrition protects against many diseases of modern life including CHD, cancers, diabetes, and asthma. Poor nutrition can contribute to ill health and be indicative in the development of obesity. It can indirectly affect education attainment due to lack of concentration and poor attendance resulting from days lost through illness. An awareness of and involvement in food and feeding issues will equip young people with the skills to help them look after themselves and their future families in a positive and health promoting way. This extends beyond nutrition knowledge and cooking skills, although both these have a place in the learning and development of young people, to the understanding of the positive and negative emotional ties and feelings we all have with food.

This chapter is not seeking to redo work that exists elsewhere. The nutritional needs of children and young people are well documented. Good nutrition is described by the health education model The Balance of Good Health and this is taken as the standard when the term healthy eating is referred to. Therapeutic advice and support is available from dietitians working with individual children and their families and carers. What the chapter will attempt to describe is:

1. What is unique about the food environment of looked after children.
2. Whether the food environment to which young people in care are exposed helps promote the best care, opportunity and learning; and if not why not.
3. Current good practice and aspirational suggestions to improve any failures identified above.

The evidence regarding the current situation, suggestions and guidance for improvements and goals have been collated from published literature, work experience in the looked after children's sector and discussions with colleagues both locally and nationally.

The nutritional requirements of children in care are the same as for the free living population. However the sequence of events that lead up to the child being designated as looked after will by definition make them more vulnerable. Health concerns may involve feeding issues and so the care and food experience offered in both foster and residential care needs to be alert to this. Living in dysfunctional, uncaring or emotionally unstable families may have affected a young person's view of food. Mealtimes may be associated with chaos, neglect, frustration and anger. Helping young people to view food and feeding as a positive, happy occasion will take time and determination from carers.

Food environments

Living in a facility that has to accommodate large numbers of young people requires different equipment, systems and organisational processes to that of the average domestic setting. Even large families will operate differently from 'institutional care'. The size of the kitchen and dining areas and the equipment and furniture contained within may not be what young people brought up in family homes will encounter. The challenge to care settings is to effectively and efficiently feed young people while at the same time exposing them to a learning environment that will enable them to learn skills, habits, attitudes and care (sometimes subconsciously) for independent living.

Domestic settings don't commonly have health and safety notices or health promotion posters on their dining room walls. Is it appropriate then that these appear in care settings? It may be better to use personal art created by residents, examples of schoolwork, photographs or bought posters, especially if the residents have some say in their choice. If educational or instructional material requires displaying it needs to be in the office or work area not the living or leisure space. Larger establishments may decide there is a need for information boards and this material could be placed here.

Establishments where the behaviour of the young people is an issue will need to resist the temptation of keeping dining room environments sterile through lack of furniture, equipment etc. Keeping crockery and cutlery locked away doesn't encourage responsible involvement by the young people in simple chores such as setting tables or putting away clean items. Locking dining rooms or kitchenette areas to make them out of bounds and keep them secure does not promote their sensible use neither does it help promote food as an ordinary everyday and potentially fun experience. It is the unacceptable behaviour that needs managing not restricting access to the facilities.

Cultural diversity

The food served and the traditions observed should reflect the cultural mix of the young people in care but this may be offered over a period of time rather than at every meal. Theme days have been used appropriately in the past to celebrate individual discrete occasions such as Chinese New Year, American Independence day and even sporting competitions. However, a different approach will be needed to ensure that young people from different cultural groups, including South Asian and Black African, have access to familiar foods. Homes may choose to look at the number of choices served over a week and ensure all groups are represented proportionally with in this. For example three choices served at the main meal means 21 dishes are served a week. If the home has a population made up of 50 per cent South Asian young people then 50 per cent of the dishes need to reflect this culture. Other homes may choose to offer all choices on one evening from the same culture to encourage all residents to experience the food. Small homes and foster care are less likely to serve a range of choices but where an individual child holds a strong belief they should be helped to follow it into practice. Cultural background may be a consideration in the choice of a foster place but this will not always be possible. If a family or small unit has to offer separate foods to a specific young person then it must be done carefully and sensitively. If the rest of the family or group are willing to eat the same e.g. meat eaters having a vegetarian meal once or twice a week then it will help an individual from feeling isolated.

However it is organised there are a few basic principles to consider:

- Ensure strict dietary laws can be followed at all times.
- Avoid tokenism.
- Encourage young people to try food from each others' backgrounds.
- Include foods from a wide variety of cultures to reflect not only the mix within the family or home but also that within society.
- Include young people in the decisions about food.

Role models, food beliefs and consistent approaches

Not every adult, youth worker or carer necessarily has an interest or ability in cooking. However, we all eat and drink so have a view about food. This is likely to colour our beliefs, habits and opinions of what is good, important and necessary. An individual may choose to eat locally grown organic food that contains little or no additives. Others may feel that the presence (or absence) of genetically modified products are more significant than aiming to eat organic items. Yet more opinions will be held about frequency of eating out, take-aways or even specific food companies. How then can a care setting hope to have a consistent approach while showing the range of values and beliefs that people hold about food? Young people need to make up their own minds when developing their personal views. One way that is becoming increasingly popular for catering providers to maintain consistency is to develop food policies (see chapter on Polices, Protocols and Training). Schools as providers and caregivers are being actively encouraged and supported to develop these (Chambers, 2003; DoH, 2005). Young people should be part of this process in order for the policies to reflect their views, be accepted and be relevant. It is as important to know why something can't be had, as it is to influence what is offered. Policies should be reviewed and adapted regularly. This may need to be more frequent where there is a high rate of change in the residents. However, care should be taken not to change direction too often or with every request, comment or complaint. Everyone has different likes, dislikes and favourites. Realistically however, in a 'multiple occupancy household' individuals have to compromise. Learning about similarities and differences, considering other people's needs while respecting their values and beliefs is part of growing up into considerate citizens.

A staff team needs to have a standard of care that reflects the overall food policy. Teams within a single establishment with different rules regarding views of acceptable behaviour at mealtimes, rewards, punishments etc is unacceptable and can only lead to inconsistency and confusion as the young people will inevitably share notes (see scenarios 1 and 2).

Individual staff who have strong personal beliefs need to be encouraged to work within the policy and standards, just as they would for any other care standard. Personal food beliefs need to be recognised and addressed before systems and processes of care appropriate for young people are developed and agreed. Their views can be expressed as part of a healthy debate, which can and should take place in the care setting. This allows adults and young people to exchange and share opinions and form/reform personal views. The difference between debate and home policy needs to be clearly identified and separate (see scenario 3). Depending on the strength of individual belief a staff member may not be willing to demonstrate practically an opposing view. It may be reasonable to expect an individual who prefers to eat organic food to use standard items during a practical cookery session with young people. However asking vegan, Jewish or Muslim staff to cook a pork casserole during such a session would be insensitive. The breadth of knowledge and experience within the staff team should be a positive contribution to home life, not a limiting factor. However food duties rotas and learning outcomes for both theoretical and practical lessons need to be aware of these strongly held beliefs and customs.

Foster care may raise issues that need to be handled differently. Within an average domestic setting it is more usual for one system of food to be in place i.e. meat eating, vegetarian, organic etc. The debates within the family will raise an awareness of opposing views. An individual carer shouldn't be expected to buy, cook and serve items that break their faith or other deeply held belief. However, as is happening more in average households, young people may start to impose their own values onto the adults; for example meat eating parents feeding vegetarian children.

Positive mealtimes and food experiences

Currently, quality standards are being set for public sector catering to achieve. School meals have compulsory standards dependant on the age of the children (DfES, 2006), hospitals are required to monitor and improve food choices offered (DfES, 2004). *Promoting the Health of Looked after Children* states 'The context in which health promotion takes place should be healthy. Talking about healthy food where the food provided is unhealthy will negate positive work' (DfES, 2004; DoH, 2004).

How can we offer child friendly meals in a way that meets all these? At home we can eat when we want, help ourselves to drinks when thirsty, see meals being prepared, help and taste during the process. Staff rotas are needed to ensure adequate levels of cover, start and finish times of shifts and mealtimes have been as much for the convenience of the workers as for the young people in care.

For example, a child wishing to attend an after school activity such as sport or hobby club should be encouraged, not penalised by missing tea. Visits to health appointments, e.g. dentist, therapist, hospital review should where possible avoid the need to miss school. What happens if this good practice then results in missing the evening meal? Not only is the nutrition 'lost' but also an important social contact with housemates and carers. Many parents will say that mealtimes are a continuous conveyor belt process with the needs of younger and older children and working parents requiring food being ready at varying times. Although the social contact is lost the meal is available. How many care establishments will be able to serve a meal of equivalent nutritional value to latecomers?

To address this problem a Leeds care home simply served its meal one hour later and included all young people in the routine mealtime.

What food is available to the young people who are hungry after an evening sports session or during the evening for a permanently hungry growing adolescent? Having catering kitchens for the production of the three main meals with access to food and ingredients locked away allows chefs to order items, keep good stock control and maintain kitchen hygiene. This is not normal in the average domestic setting. We need to provide access to drinks throughout the day and foods for occasional snacks. This needs to be more than confectionary, soft drinks, packet snacks, biscuits etc and other food that store safely and easily with a long shelf life (DfES, 2000). This may result in food storage issues to be addressed. The foods served must reflect the likes and dislikes of the young people and their nutritional needs. However offering only high fat and high sugar items contradicts current healthy eating advice. These contradictions are what have been cited to be one of the barriers to (school) children making healthy choices (*Promoting the Health of Looked after Children*, 2002).

One issue that most residential establishments need to consider is how appropriate it is to serve a cooked breakfast. A comparison with the habits of the free living equivalent group should be a guide. Information taken from surveys done by the breakfast cereal companies show that total breakfast eating is gradually declining and within this cooked items are less popular than before. Having chefs working at the start of the day may not be the best use of an expensive resource. Having catering available later in the day may provide a system more responsive to the needs of the young people.

Some units have described generous house keeping budgets that have enabled the appearance of the traditionally expensive protein items e.g. roast meats, chops several times a week. Poor and untimely communication between care staff and caterers and inflexible food service systems do result in offering unnecessarily large quantities of food for the number of diners at a meal (see Scenario 4). Such extravagance doesn't develop responsible attitudes to food or help young people to understand budgeting. Young people are often on benefits when they leave care and are therefore likely to have a restricted budget for food. If their expectation is to be able to have two or three expensive meat meals a week and not to have to worry about wasting left-over food then their ability to feed themselves adequately and healthily will be significantly reduced. There must be a balance between overly generous and elaborate meals, nutritional requirements and being too frugal.

One financial point to note is that young people in foster or residential care are not eligible for free school meals. Families and carers will need to ensure children attending school have money to pay for their meals or provide a packed lunch.

Managing mealtimes

For all users of the dining room it is very unpleasant to have serious incidents requiring invasive behaviour management techniques occurring while eating a meal. Eating as a positive, happy and fun experience can be ruined by the behaviour of another resident. Observing meal times can show a number of factors that may lead to potential flash points for poor behaviour:

- All residents are required to do an activity together.
- Timing for (hot) meals is important.
- Space may be restricted.
- Food for some can be a stressful occasion.
- Opportunities for bullying can arise when young people are in close quarters.
- Staff may be distracted with meal service duties.
- Staff *may* be at the shift change point.

Just as children can sense tension at mealtimes with their parents and manipulate the situation ('anything for a quiet life syndrome') so can young people in care. However, within national inspection documents standard 10.6 states that 'children are not routinely excluded from communal meals' (EPPI, 2003). It is therefore inappropriate to isolate individuals too frequently. Comments from a qualitative report carried out several years ago as well as personal observations from visits have produced some very practical solutions to this problem:

- Set ground rules between staff and young people at residents' meetings.
- Adults and young people eat together.
- Eat in small groups of 4–6, each responsible for timing, behaviour etc. Neither staff nor young people leave before the whole group finish.
- Staff set standards of acceptable behaviour so consistency is ensured.
- Time out to cool off after an incident then allowing young people back to eat at the same table.
- Not forcing anyone to take or eat an item they dislike but offering appropriate encouragement to try new foods.

However, some rules were seen to be too controlling by the young people and the visitors:

- Having to wait to start to eat until everyone had been served.
- Serving food from a hatch when table service would have been more appropriate.
- Asking permission to help themselves to drinks already on the tables.
- Eating in silence when noise level perceived to be too high.
- Ringing a bell to attract the eaters attention so information about activities could be explained.

Food service arrangements

If food experiences are to be normalised then queuing at a counter to be served by someone who will not be eating with the group is not 'normal' family eating. The advantages of table or family service have already been raised as a behaviour management technique. However, food once served onto tables cannot be re-served for hygiene reasons. Having food at every small table rather than at one central service point will inevitably create more waste. It is necessary to ensure that everyone has enough; seconds are shared, and unnecessary waste is avoided where there are spaces/absences on tables. The disadvantages of table service become more apparent with wider choice menus such as:

- Serving a range of main dishes to meet the needs of all cultural groups.
- Offering salad bars to attract individuals to eat more vegetables.
- Serving modified texture or therapeutic diets to young people with special dietary needs.

The age and ability of the young people, preferences of the diners and the facilities and staff available will dictate the ultimate choice of system. Continually questioning, debating and challenging the status quo with everyone involved will result in the best system being in place.

If the chef does not eat with the group then it would be good practice to ensure they are immediately available to see the reactions and hear the comments of the diners.

Food hygiene regulations and safety issues in kitchen areas

Formal settings have a duty of care to keep young people safe and free from food borne illness. Therefore young people are likely to be excluded from the main kitchen. (Although foster carers have a moral duty of care they are not bound by the legislation that applies to larger homes.) Smaller scale open access facilities need to be provided to allow residents hands on opportunities to learn and practice skills for everyday living. This option probably offers the best of all cases in that the 'professional catering kitchen' remains the exclusive domain of the trained chefs. The appropriate sized equipment for large-scale preparation, cooking and cleaning will be needed for this area. The smaller units can use more familiar sized equipment, e.g. toasters, kettles, microwaves and cookers that can be used safely and give a better training experience for family eating. Chefs are not disturbed by frequent interruptions and young people have independence in what and when they eat and drink between their meals. Those young people who desire to become chefs need to be given appropriate encouragement and support to enter catering college, not be allowed to work in the professional kitchen.

Risk assessment is not about removing danger from the lives of young people. It is about minimising unnecessary risk and finding safer ways to practice/live. Cooking involves knives, heat, electrical equipment and water to name but a few of the dangers! Showing them how to work safely, develop simple skills and confidence will help reduce the risk of accidents. The challenge is to work safely, demonstrating correct use of equipment and encouraging opportunities for them to use their knowledge and skills. The domestic sized equipment in the open access kitchens will have most relevance to them.

Preparing for leaving care

It is true that not every child leaving home is an expert chef or homemaker. One of the anxieties that many parents express as their offspring leaves home for university is that of their child's inability to cook for and feed themselves. However, there has been a relationship with a single set of carers, usually the parents, for approximately 18 years. This has resulted in an intimate knowledge of likes, dislikes, skills and the lack of them. In extended families the role of carer and/or teacher can be provided by grandparents, aunts, uncles and older siblings or cousins etc. The pool of experience and skill in the area of food and feeding is widened and the opportunities for learning are enhanced. In many families the relationships change as the family members change – new siblings, divorce, bereavement, remarriage etc. However, this happens less significantly than change of staff teams across shift patterns and with staff turnover. Written care records are not the same as personal experience and much of this knowledge is not the subject of record cards. Some practical experience will be gained from school; the quantity and content of which is currently under review. Unfortunately many young people in care are poor school attendees and miss out on health promotion experiences there. The learning gained within the care home is therefore even more important.

The 'duty of care' that requires good standards of care to be given to young people in residential accommodation must not replace the learning process. Opportunities for learning and making mistakes in the kitchen need to be offered in a safe, controlled environment. Smaller sized living sub units, friendship groups and topic teams may all offer the possibility of trying things out and getting reactions from people who are deemed to be important and whose opinions are valued by the young people. Equally antagonistic relationships between individuals in care can be very destructive if continual criticism is made. Staff need to be able to monitor and manage these interactions positively.

It is difficult to define the basic skills that are needed for independent living as individual situations, interests and finances all affect our success. What is not acceptable is giving learning opportunities in a rush and at the last minute – in the last year before leaving care. What is more acceptable is a planned, progressive set of experiences offered throughout care according to the age, abilities and interest of the young people. These experiences need to be the early building blocks that the post 16 planning teams refer to and develop when preparing young people for leaving care. Staffing levels must be arranged to enable hands on experience with food tasks such as shopping and cooking. This shouldn't be happening by chance when rotas and staff interests allow but via this consistent developmental programme offered to all young people as they spend time in a facility. Just as children in families may love or hate cooking, so will young people in care. Those young people that are passionate about food and those that with a bit of encouragement will become competent both need support.

Foster care

Most of the issues described previously are relevant to foster care. Food beliefs, customs and preferences are within every family. However differences do exist. Foster carers are not professional cooks and they don't have other colleagues within the team to help manage difficulties and solve problems. Their support networks are likely to be informal and made up of family and friends. Support for them, and their social workers, is therefore vital to ensure good evidenced based practice is shared and standards are maintained. No-one expects a parent to become instantly capable when their child is born. They are not expected to be immediately competent in dietary regimes if their children are diagnosed with problems requiring dietary adaptations or investigations. The advantage parents have over foster carers is a constant relationship. The understanding of their child's needs will develop in an incremental way. If change is needed around food and feeding issues this will be with the help and support of the clinicians. Interruptions to this will only happen with change in clinicians at a venue or if they change venues due to relocation or decision to attend another team. Their progress and understanding about the child's needs remains. Foster carers have to pick up care where parents or previous care has left off. Even if they have had previous experience of a similar condition they won't have the unique understanding of the individual now in their care. Neither do they have the opportunity of team experience and sharing. It is therefore important that foster carers are well supported and do have the opportunity to meet and learn together.

A good foster placement, known to be able to cope with feeding issues, may be given several complex needs children at one time. Their capacity to manage multiple needs within one setting as well as caring for the needs of their own family may be too great a burden and standards of care can be compromised. Situations have been observed where foster carers have not been supported and a child felt to be 'difficult' or 'demanding' has been fed less well than the families own children. Foster carers need to have a range of skills and methods of managing different combinations of difficult situations in order to maintain standards.

Conclusion

Food is a complicated area affecting our physical and emotional health. Managed well it can add value to many areas of 'healthy care' and promote positive relationships within families and homes. Training and support for staff and projects promoting healthy attitudes to food and feeding may be available from community dietitians working with agencies supporting vulnerable young people. In order to ensure food work is consistent plans and policies need to be shared with all concerned and regularly reviewed and updated.

Scenarios

1. A unit had experienced several behaviour problems during the day. This had followed a disturbed night where significant damage had been caused by a few residents. Staff on duty were tense and young people although tired were able to pick up on this. Opportunities for constructive activities before tea were not offered as other care staff were involved in the meal preparation. The behaviour observed could have been interpreted as 'rough and tumble' and on another occasion ignored. However, the young people were given the threat from the supervising member of staff 'Do you lot not want any tea?'

When discussed in a staff meeting some colleagues were happy with this approach while others were clearly unhappy.

2. Young people involved in inappropriate behaviour during one night were not allowed to join the rest of the group for breakfast. Their choice of items was removed and they were given plain toast and water to drink. This was definitely felt to be a punishment by food. However, at the time the home were trying to promote water drinking as positive and fun. This incident gave very conflicting messages to all the young people at the time.

3. A vegetarian member of care staff can be expected to encourage young people to choose a balanced meal from a carnivorous menu; or an adult who only eats locally grown organic vegetables at home may discuss their beliefs about the advantages and benefits of such food with the young people. This will not necessarily change the food served but show the residents other opinions and values. A practical experience could be offered to the young people by setting up and encouraging a gardening 'club'; they may then be able to taste their produce.

4. The chef assumes all residents will be present for lunch even though many attend school or other centres and caters accordingly. This is done in case individuals change their mind at the last minute or are sent home and need feeding. The care staff don't communicate with the kitchen to adjust the numbers. The chef always served the total quantity of food onto the tables and wasn't in the habit of refilling small bowls for self-service items e.g. salad. Everything served that was unused had to be thrown.

In discussion a system was created that ensured adequate food was available but only served onto the tables once the final numbers were known. Surplus cold items were kept chilled and used at the evening meal.

References

Chambers, H. (2003) *Healthy Care*. London: NCB.

Chartered Institute of Environmental Health (1998) *Food Safety: First Principles*. London: CIEH.

DfES (2000) *Healthy School Lunches*. London: DfES.

DfES (2004) *Every Child Matters*. London: DfES.

DfES (2004) *Healthy Living Blueprint for Schools*. London: DfES.

DfES (2006) *Nutritional Standards for School Lunches and other School Food*. London: DfES.

DoH (2001) *Essence of Care: Patient Focused Benchmarking for Health Care Professionals. Care Standards*. London: DoH.

DoH (2002) *Promoting the Health of Looked After Children*. London: DoH.

DoH (2004) *Choosing Health: Making Healthier Choices Easier*. London: DoH.

DoH (2005) *National Healthy Schools Status: A Guide for Schools*. London: DoH.

Evidence for Policy and Practice (2003) *Children and Healthy Eating: A Systematic Review of Barriers and Facilitators*. University of London: EPPI.

Inspection Standards: Children's Services 2000/01.

Save the Children (1998) *Look Ahead: Young People, Residential Care and Food*. London: Save the Children.

Sustain (2002) *Grab 5! A Model School Food Policy: A Practical Guide*. London: Sustain.

The Health Education Trust (2000) *The Chips are Down: A Guide to Food Policy in Schools*. Warwickshire: The Health Education Trust.

Section Four:
Special Considerations

Chapter 12

The Health of Unaccompanied Minors

Paula Bell

In recent years an increasing number of young people from all areas of the world have arrived alone in the United Kingdom. The manner in which they arrive is varied and their stories are sometimes harrowing.

The local social services team under various names such as the Unaccompanied Minors and Homeless Team generally support these young people. They are placed under the category of Section 20 of the Children Act (1989) as looked after children and their health needs are monitored by the local PCT as for other LAC. This group however, merit even greater assessment than the indigenous population of LAC, due to their particular circumstances.

Definitions

To avoid confusion, it is important to be clear on definitions and what different terms used really mean. Different agencies may use different definitions:

Unaccompanied children (also known as unaccompanied *minors*) are 'children under the age of eighteen who are separated from both parents and who are not being cared for by an adult who by law or custom has the responsibility to do so' (UNHCR, 1994).

Problems can arise if the authorities are not able to establish to their satisfaction the age of a young person.

Refugees, international law defines a 'refugee' as a person who has fled from and/or cannot return to their country due to a well-founded fear of persecution, including war or civil conflict.

It can be difficult for children to claim refugee status if they are not able to articulate their situation.

Asylum seekers are people who have left their country of origin, have applied for recognition as a refugee in another country, and are awaiting a decision on their application.

Illegal immigrant, this term usually refers to those who enter the country secretly and do not declare their presence. Under Article 14 of the Universal Declaration of Human Rights, everyone has the right to seek and enjoy asylum. In addition, Article 13 of the 1951 Convention relating to the status of refugees states that countries should not impose penalties on individuals coming directly from a territory where their life or freedom is threatened on account of their illegal entry.

These definitions demonstrate the complexity of the status of these children.

Variety of circumstances

For those children and families who are declared on arrival as refugees or asylum seekers there is a system and provision for planned support and care. The government has set up various centres where children and adults are accommodated and education and health provision is available. Decisions on legal status and settlement in the country are then undertaken.

While some young people are declared unaccompanied minors on arrival into the country, known as their 'port of entry,' others have a less straightforward path.

Illegal entry

Some young people are brought into the country hidden from any authorities, perhaps in a lorry. They may then be abandoned and told to go to a strategic place to ask for help. This is often a police station, a social services department or even the Home Office. They may be abandoned anywhere, unaware that the adult has no plan to return and they are left lost and terrified.

Supporting 'relative'

Some arrive in the country with an adult, who they may refer to, and even believe, is a relative. This adult may then leave the young person at a strategic place where the appropriate help could be offered. In some instances the adult may attempt to look after the young person but finds this too difficult.

Some children are abused by these adults and may be living in very harsh circumstances that leads to the child running away from the adult to ask for help from the authorities.

Vulnerability

These young people are vulnerable, often confused and frightened. They are a very easy group to exploit and in fact the authorities may not know of a child's arrival and therefore existence in the country, let alone offer any protection or safety. A child may have a poor grasp of English and the normal customs and values of the country that they find themselves in. They may be desperate to belong and do what is asked of them which could lead to others taking advantage of their situation.

Many of the young people are not aware of what is happening. They may not realise that a loving parent may have paid an 'agent' a high sum of money in order to give their child a better life, or to protect them from danger in a war-torn country where children are often conscripted into the military.

Some children flee alone or with siblings as a result of their parents going missing, being imprisoned or through their death. Concerns have been raised about the vulnerability of children and the increase in 'trafficking'. Children may never arrive at the destination that was expected and they can just disappear or become caught up in the sex trade or other abusive situations.

In an attempt to reduce the risks to this group the government announced the introduction of a National Register for Unaccompanied Asylum Seeking Children (NRUC). In future all children who enter the UK alone are to be registered, on arrival at ports or airports, on a central database, before they are passed onto social services. The scheme is due to come into operation in 2005. Peter Gilroy, the NRUC committee chair said, 'This is a modern innovative solution to the modern phenomenon of children seeking asylum on their own'. Whilst this will keep track of some of these children this will not solve and protect the unknown numbers who enter the country illegally.

Health issues

Children seeking asylum should have the same access to health care as national children.

(UNHCR, 1997)

The concept of a holistic approach to the health needs of this group is especially relevant. The broad model of health, looking at physical, emotional, social, sexual and spiritual health can be applied in order to explore fully the young person's needs.

In the child's own country basic preventative care may have been lacking and this should be rectified in a 'sensitive and effective manner in the country of asylum' (UNHCR, 1997).

Three particular issues may need to be considered at the outset:

Language: To fully engage with the young person and especially to hear what they have to say, it is best practice that a suitable interpreter should be sought if there is any doubt about the understanding and ability of the child to communicate. It may be important for cultural reasons to have an interpreter of the same gender in order to discuss sensitive matters and for reasons of confidentiality and impartiality to use someone from outside of any connection with the child (Leverson and Shama, 1999). Sometimes finding an interpreter is difficult and the use of a telephone interpreter service, whilst not ideal is better than nothing at all.

Age assessment: Many of this group arrive with no documentation and there can be some uncertainty about their age, despite what the young person declares. In the UK your date of birth is often used as a means of identification but this is not the case in other countries and a young person may genuinely not know this information. In some countries where there is no formal system for registration of date of birth 01.01. plus year of birth is often used.

Some countries, such as Ethiopia use the Julian calendar which is over seven years behind the Gregorian calendar used in the West. Therefore, in Ethiopia the year 1996 began in September 2003 in Europe.

An additional complication is that those children from Turkey, Iran and Afghanistan may declare their age one year older than the normal European standard (DoH et al., 2003).

Doctors may be asked to give an opinion on age, especially to decide if the child is under the age of 18 or not, as this is the upper age limit for support arrangements. Using growth measurements and stages of puberty as an estimate may be made but there can be a margin of error of up to five years on either side. Poor nutritional status and illness may delay puberty. Dental development may be of help, giving a smaller margin of error. The Royal College of Radiologists in 1996 advised immigration officials not to request the use of X-Rays, as it is not possible to determine chronological age from bone age (Burnett and Fassil, 2002). According to guidance for paediatricians from their Royal College, as the margin of error is wide, the best clinical judgment may be in terms of whether a child is probably, likely, possibly or unlikely to be under the age of 18 (Leverson and Sharma, 1999). According to guidance from the United Nations High Commission for Refugees (UNHCR, 1997) 'The child should be given the benefit of the doubt if the exact age is uncertain'.

Legal status: When an unaccompanied minor comes to the notice of the authorities, the Home Office assesses the child's legal status. This is a complex area and is decided on an individual basis. Under child care law this group have the same rights as UK born children in the Children Act (DOH, 1989) and should come under the category of Section 20 'Provision of accommodation' and would be 'Looked After'. This legislation places a duty on social services to promote the health of this group and work with the local health services to do so.

Physical health

As with all 'looked after children' an Initial Health Assessment (IHA) by a doctor should take place in the first four weeks after being placed in care (DoH, 2002). For this group, as Coker (2001) points out, the *gender of the doctor* may be significant for cultural reasons or if there is any history of sexual assault or abuse, and this needs sensitive consideration to avoid further emotional trauma as well as compliance with the assessment. In many respects this is a detailed and specialised assessment, which for all pre-school children should require a developmental assessment; therefore it is preferable that the doctor is trained in such assessments (BAAF, 2004). All primary care trusts are expected to have a designated doctor for looked after children, who has a role in giving expert advice and who should be contacted if necessary to support those in the assessment process (DoH, 2002). The content of the IHA will vary according to the age of the child and details are set out in the guidance (DoH, 2002). For this group however, there are special areas to highlight.

Some children may not have had access to medical services in their own country due to conflicts, natural disaster and disruption (Coker, 2001). Without documentation obtaining a clear past health history this may be difficult, and any past history given by the child is likely to be incomplete. Depending on the country of origin, there may not have been previous routine health surveillance and therefore a thorough physical examination will be necessary. *Immunisations* may not have been given or the schedule may have been interrupted. Different countries also have a variety of immunisation programmes. A website is available that holds the various immunisation programmes used in a number of countries, (*http://www.who.int/immunization-monitoring/en/globalsummary/ countryprofileselect.cfm*) and a catch up programme may need to be decided on an individual basis.

Due to recent circumstances there may have been an element of physical neglect, with poor nutrition and under nourishment. This may also be caused due to unfamiliarity of the food available. Adequate personal hygiene may have been difficult to maintain leading to dermatological problems and poor oral health with dental caries.

Throughout the world there are haemoglobinopathies, such as sickle cell disease in the Caribbean, Black Africa, some parts of Asia and some areas in the Middle East and Thalassaemia in South East Asia and Mediterranean Europe. In children from these areas or when the past history is unclear with regard to the parents' origins it is good practice to screen for these conditions to eliminate them or to counsel the child at a future date if they are a carrier (BAAF, 2004).

All children are susceptible to infectious diseases and the need to screen for these will be dependant on their age on arrival, country of origin, known family and past history and the child's health status. Tuberculosis, malaria, hepatitis B and C and HIV are common in many parts of the world and should be considered. Screening is not routine but based on the doctor's clinical judgement and always in the best interests of the child. Interagency working between health and social services to establish and collate as much past history as possible and to determine risk factors is vital to offer best care.

Advances in treatment mean that early detection can improve outcomes considerably and this should be taken into consideration in regard to blood borne diseases (BAAF, 1999). According to BAAF (2004) common infectious conditions seen within the first three months of arrival are; respiratory infections, otitis media, gastroenteritis, scabies and lice. In their own country of origin measles, mumps and rubella may be widespread and this may develop soon after arrival.

Mental and emotional health

It is difficult not to overstate the difficulties that many unaccompanied children and young people face. There may be enormous losses from separation from family, possibly by bereavement. Also the loss of the familiar, their culture, friends and they may have feelings of grief, anger, fear and disorientation. They may have witnessed serious traumatic events in war torn homelands, possibly involving family and friends. They may feel that their parents failed to protect them and some may have been abducted and forced as child soldiers to commit acts of violence (Burnett and Fassil, 2002). They themselves may have been victims of sexual assault, violence or under the threat of assault with grave risks to their life.

The manner in which they came to the UK may have been very stressful and on arrival more difficulties may have followed with the need to try to explain to authorities who they are and why they are here, without the language skills.

Basics of food and shelter may not have been available for some time. It is true to say that these children may often have suffered events outside of the experience of workers dealing with them (DoH, 2002).

It can be said that the refugee experience is made up of three parts:

- **Pre-flight experience:** that may be characterised by such events as violence, fear, oppression, torture, famine, rape or death of family and friends.

- **Flight:** this may involve escape and the fear of being discovered, possible consequences of discovery, enduring hazardous conditions, various forms of abuse, separation from family and friends.

- **Exile:** coping with the anxiety of the future, homesickness, poverty, isolation, racism, loss of family and community guilt and anxiety about those left behind (DoH and Refugee Council, 2003).

Coker (2001) points out that it is well documented that victims of such traumas are often reluctant initially to talk about events, even when they are in a safe environment and feel more secure. The effects of such experiences may manifest in a variety of ways, depending on a child's age but may include such features as:

- Being withdrawn and lacking in interest.
- Poor concentration.
- Irritability.
- Aggression.
- Breathing difficulties.
- Joint pains.
- Regression e.g. speech problems, enuresis.
- Eating problems – under or overeating.
- Poor sleeping patterns or nightmares.
- Relationship difficulties.
- Impulsive behaviour or hyperactivity.
- Fear or distrust of adults and figures of authority.
- General nervousness or anxiety.
- Repetitive thoughts about traumatic events or flashbacks.

Appropriate referrals to suitable clinical expertise are essential in order to offer the skilled help that some of these children require.

Local CAMHS services may have specific projects or teams to offer suitable help, however as Burnett and Fassil (2002) explain, a psychiatric referral is not usually required as these children are often quite resilient and learn coping strategies if general help is available. Supporting factors to help develop such resilience would be:

- Time and space to explore their own feelings about experiences.
- Having some active choices and a say in some decision-making.
- A sense of belonging, a connection to an adult, a group or the community.

These young people need sensitive care and time, and nurses in primary care may be in the best position to offer support and listening. If there is a designated nurse for looked after children, as Department of Health guidelines suggest (DoH, 2002) they can act as an advocate for the young person and liaise with other agencies and health care staff on the child's behalf. They can offer support and practical guidance for foster carers and maintain regular contact. The health visitor may need to support a foster carer with any child aged under five with any behavioural difficulties and the school nurse will need to have a raised awareness of these children in the school should issues arise.

Those over school age need to be involved in activities to use their time effectively and to attend college, language classes and recreational opportunities such as sport and youth centres.

While some young people are able to adapt and adjust to a new way of life, for some the difficulties and past experiences can prove too much and lead to more complex mental health problems (GLA, 2004). All agencies need to be alert to this possibility.

There are a number of groups in the voluntary sector who are able to offer outreach support and befriending that are also culturally appropriate but care is needed to ensure the suitability of any referral, to discuss this with the young person and to monitor the progress of such a referral. It should not be assumed that a particular cultural group will be acceptable, as in some communities there are deep divides that an outsider may not be aware of and more unintentional distress may be caused.

Uncertainty about the future is often a large factor in the emotional turmoil facing these young people and this in itself can contribute to behavioural changes. Burnett and Fassil (2002) suggest that supported listening as well as helping these young people to meet in groups to share their problems is likely to be beneficial.

Two further areas that can be significant to the mental and emotional health needs of these children are attention to their spiritual needs and their education (see chapter on Mental Health).

Spiritual health

Children have as much right to spiritual well being as to any other aspect of their life and for some their religious faith is represented by their whole lifestyle which may include; attention to a dress code, food and food preparation, time for daily prayers, the observance of particular days of worship, festivals and regular attendance at their place of worship (Crompton, 2001). The inability to follow any of these practices may cause distress and lead to further emotional problems. Encouragement and support in this area can add to the sense of belonging and of well being. Young people may develop a wider circle of friends and build other social supports and activities from within their faith communities as well as become more positive and have a greater sense of meaning in their life.

Education

For those children of school age, attending a school can provide a real safe haven offering some stability and helping them to become part of the community. There is a risk, however of these children being victims once again and suffering from bullying and racial abuse, due to their difference and possible language problems, and all schools should be alert to this and act to deal with this (Burnett and Fassil, 2002). It has been recognised that these children have a higher level of underachievement compared to their peers and therefore good practice guidelines were jointly produced by the Departments of Education and Skills and of Health in order to highlight the problems and make improvements (DfES, 2004). In response to this many schools have a designated teacher for this group of children within the school who is able to offer extra support and have a greater awareness of their issues. Local Education Authorities (LEAs) have a duty to respond to the educational needs of asylum seekers and refugees in their area through Educational Development Plans and some have teams who specialise in this work using teachers to visit schools to give extra support.

There will be many children who will need help with learning English and special teachers providing English as an Additional Language (EAL) may be available. As the Refugee Council explains, the past educational experience for this group may be very different from that in their homeland and they may take some time to settle down to new teaching methods.

A strong pastoral support may be required for this group and the school nurse has a role in offering additional advice and being available for the needs of these children in whatever area they may arise. Listening to their needs and a regular presence for the child can be invaluable as well as highlight the need for any referral or liaison with other agencies if required.

In some areas there are pressures on, and a shortage of, school places and LEAs have a duty to give the same right of access to places for this group as for any other child (DfES, 2004).

Those aged over 16, statutory school age, and who have missed out on education in their homeland or who wish to continue in education can attend college or sixth-form as appropriate and should be supported in this as any other care leaver (Refugee Council, 2003). The Connexions service should be available to give advice and support.

Sexual health

It has been well documented that many unaccompanied minors, both male and female, have been the victims of sexual assault, or sexual abuse including rape. These may be isolated incidents or even systematic over a period of time. In some cultures this results in the shunning of the victim as they are seen as defiled and are rejected by others. There is often a deep sense of shame (Burnett and Fassil, 2002).

Some children are victims of 'trafficking' having been brought to the country to be used to work in the sex trade until they have come to the notice of any authority. Evidence is growing that some children have been brought to the UK as 'unaccompanied' minors and when in the care of the local authority 'disappear' and are used for sexual exploitation. Suspicion should be aroused by any child who has unknown adults around them or who has extra money, mobile phones or unaccountable extra valuables (Somerset, 2004).

Great sensitivity is required in addressing the physical and emotional needs of such children. There is a high risk of sexual infection and a full screening at a genito-urinary medicine (GUM) clinic is advisable, and this should include a pregnancy test.

Some young girls are pregnant on arrival in the country. A termination of pregnancy may not be acceptable and no assumptions should be made. Each case will need to be carefully handled with the girl and informed decisions made about the future (Burnett and Fassil, 2002). If the pregnancy is to go ahead, as for all pregnant teenagers, ongoing continuous support throughout the antenatal period and guidance in birth preparation will aid the subsequent post-natal period and the bonding with the baby (TPU et al., 2004).

Female Genital Mutilation (FGM) is practised in many parts of Africa, in some communities in the Far East and the Middle East. There has not been any systematic research to establish in exactly which countries this would occur. FGM is best described as 'procedures which include the partial or total removal of the female genital organs for cultural or other non-therapeutic reasons' (House of Commons, 2002). FGM is a criminal offence in the UK under the Prohibition of Female Circumcision Act 1985 and this Act was repealed and strengthened by the FGM Bill in 2002, which toughened up the law and includes those assisting the process. Health visitors, school nurses and social workers should be alert to any possibility of the planning of FGM for any of these vulnerable girls. It is a complex issue as it is related to customs, traditions and fears about hygiene, health, gender and sexuality. The practice is often confused with religion but there is no unanimous view in Islam and FGM is certainly not practised by all Muslims.

There are a number of health issues that can arise from FGM such as; difficulty in passing urine and with menstruation, repeated urinary tract and pelvic infections and problems with sexual function and childbirth. Repeated infection can lead to infertility and routine cervical smears may be difficult to perform in later life (Burnett and Fassil, 2002).

Not all unaccompanied minors will have been sexually active or experienced and age appropriate sexual health promotion and advice is important (DoH, 2002). These children need to adapt to living in a new culture with different values and sexual behaviour which may be very unlike their cultural norms, where contraception may not be acceptable (see chapter on Sexual Health).

Older unaccompanied minors

The Department of Health clarified the position that social services should take for the many 16 and 17 year olds that were arriving in the UK. In June 2003 guidance was issued that stated that where children seeking asylum are alone the 'presumption should be that they fall into Section 20 of the Children Act', (DoH, 2003) and therefore are 'Looked After'.

For all those who have been 'Looked After' for more than 13 weeks after their 14th birthday and who left care after 1 October 2001, they will be cared for under the Children (Leaving Care) Act 2000 and have the same rights as other care leavers (Refugee Council, 2003). This guidance therefore removes any previous doubts about the position of unaccompanied minors and how the local agencies should respond.

Access to health

As with all 'looked after' children and young people, unaccompanied asylum children have the right to full use of the NHS, and should be registered with a local GP. GPs have the right to refuse to register any patient and in some areas of the country there are shortages of GPs and this is seen especially in certain areas of London. Coker (2001) cites the desperate problems that some refugees face in trying to find a GP practice to register with, which can lead to the unnecessary use of hospital services.

Those children living with foster carers should ideally register with the existing GP of the foster carer. The difficulty is often found with those over the age of 16 who may be in semi-independent accommodation. There is sometimes an unwillingness on the part of GPs to register such young people who may only be in the area for a short time and may be seen, not always fairly, as an extra burden on the workload.

Where a young person cannot find a GP the PCT can allocate a GP who must agree to take the patient at least on a temporary basis for three months. This is far from ideal as it is helpful for a relationship and an understanding of any health needs to be established and permanent registration should be the standard to strive for.

It should always be remembered that regardless of any registration a GP must provide services where it is 'immediately necessary'. This is treatment that cannot be reasonably left until a patient returns home, and covers some emergency situations (DoH and Refugee Council, 2003).

In areas where there are larger numbers of patients, local services have tried to find solutions. This may range from funding a salaried GP to work within an existing surgery to reduce the workload to, as in some PCTs, providing a specialist service via the use of Personal Medical Services (PMS) where a whole service is created for a particular client group. PCTs also have special funding available to offer Local Development Schemes (LDSs) which pays practices extra money when registering someone from a particular group such as asylum seekers (DoH and Refugee Council, 2003).

It is important that young people new to the UK learn and understand about the working of the NHS and how to seek help when it may be needed. They need to appreciate their responsibility in making and keeping to appointment times. Those in semi-independent living are more vulnerable as they have less adult support and they may need an advocate to help them to become registered with a GP and to understand the system in the surgery that they are with.

The appropriate use of the emergency services will also need to be clearly explained to avoid any misunderstanding. The designated nurse for LAC has a vital role in this area (see section on The Role of the Designated Nurse). There may be many gaps in the knowledge for these young people and they may need very basic explanations about how the NHS works, the use of NHS Direct and knowledge about other local services such as the dentist and the optician. Some areas for example have Minor Accident Treatment Services (MATS) that can reduce the pressure on the major hospital. With limited language skills the designated nurse can be an invaluable link between the young person and the GP practice staff in securing registration and clearing up any misunderstandings that may arise. If any hospital referrals are made, additional explanations and encouragement to attend follow up appointments can avoid incomplete treatment and wasted resources. This support by the designated nurse in linking between other health professionals, such as doctors, practice nurses, clinic and hospital staff and this sharing of information is invaluable. The nursing knowledge and access to health services is not otherwise easily available to social workers trying to achieve similar outcomes where the young person may have been disadvantaged.

Case scenarios

The young people come from a very wide range of situations:

- M is a young girl aged sixteen from Uganda. She and her parents were arrested by soldiers. Both she and her mother were raped by the soldiers and her mother was murdered. M was helped to flee the country, she was pregnant and arrived in England where her baby was born prematurely.

- L had a similar experience, arriving pregnant from Liberia, very traumatised by what had happened, and with very little English.

- T came to England from Nigeria with an 'uncle' who mistreated her, with physical and sexual abuse and she ran away to seek help.

- C is a boy of fifteen, who came to England hidden in a lorry from Romania. He had lived in an orphanage in Romania and had found life very difficult. He had slept rough for a time before coming to the attention of the authorities in the UK.

- K is a boy of sixteen from the Congo. It is not quite clear how he entered the UK. However, he had tried to survive alone on the streets, but in such despair that he twice tried to commit suicide. He is now settled in a foster placement.

These and so many more young people have uncertain futures but with support, encouragement and practical help they can be empowered to achieve and move forward from their past events.

References

BAAF (1999) *Hepatitis and HIV*. Practice Note 39. London: BAAF.

BAAF (2004) *Health Screening of Children from Abroad*. Practice Note 46. London: BAAF.

Burnett, A. and Fassil, Y. (2002) *Meeting the Health Needs of Asylum Seekers and Refugees in the UK: An Information and Resource Pack for Health Workers*. London: DoH.

Coker, N. (2001) *Asylum Seekers and Refugees' Health Experience: Kings Fund Review of Health Policy*. London: Kings Fund.

Crompton, M. (2001) *Who am I? Promoting Children's Spiritual Well being in Everyday Life: A Guide for all who Care for Children*. London: Barnardo's.

Dennis, J. (2001) *Where are the Children? A Mapping Exercise on the Number of Unaccompanied Asylum Children in the UK*. London: BAAF.

DfES (2004) *Aiming High: Guidance on Supporting the Education of Asylum Seeking and Refugee Children*. London: DfES.

DoH (1989) *The Children Act*. London: HMSO.

DoH (2002) *Promoting the Health of Looked After Children*. London: DoH.

DoH (2003) *Guidance on Accommodating Children in Need and Their Families*. London: DoH.

DoH and Refugee Council (2003) *Caring for Dispersed Asylum Seekers*. London: DoH.

Greater London Authority (2004) *Young Refugees and Asylum Seekers in Greater London: Vulnerability to Problematic Drug Use*. London: GLA.

Heath, T., Jeffries, R. and Purcell, J. (2003) *Asylum Statistics: United Kingdom Home Office Statistical Bulletin*. 2nd Edn. London: Home Office.

House of Commons (2002) *Female Genital Mutilation Bill Explanatory Notes*. London: House of Commons.

Leverson, R. and Sharma, A. (1999) *The Health of Refugee Children: Guidelines for Paediatricians*. London: Royal College of Paediatricians and Child Health.

Refugee Council (2003) *Support Arrangements for 16–17 year old Unaccompanied Asylum Seeking Children*. London: Refugee Council.

Save The Children (2000) *Separated Children Coming to Western Europe: Why They Travel and how They Arrive*. Save The Children.

Somerset, C. (2004) *Cause for Concern?* London: Social Services and Child Trafficking ECPAT.

TPU, RCM and DoH (2004) *Teenage Parents: Who Cares? A Guide to Commissioning and Delivering Maternity Services to Young Parents*. London: DoH.

UNCHR (1997) *Guidelines on Policies and Procedures in Dealing with Unaccompanied Children Seeking Asylum*. Geneva: UNCHR.

UNHCR (1994) *Refugee Children: Guidelines on Protection and Care*. Geneva: UNCHR.

Appendix I   Useful contacts

Albanian Youth Action addresses welfare issues for Albanian speaking people in the UK, and especially youth. In 1996, a specific project was launched to work against the marginalisation of young Albanian refugees. The project supports unaccompanied young refugees from former Yugoslavia – mostly ethnic Albanian minors from Kosovo, Albania, and the surrounding Balkan region.

The Strand Centre, Elm Park, London SW2 2EH Tel: 020 8674 0800 *www.albaction.org.uk*

British Youth Council (BYC) is an independent charity, which functions as a representative body for young people in the UK. It forwards their views to government, political parties, and the media. Campaigns of the BYC, such as 'End Child Poverty', 'Beat Poverty' or 'Sport Relief' address a wide range of social and political issues.

BYC, The Mezzanine 2, 2nd Floor, Downstream Building, 1 London Bridge, London SE1 9BG Tel: 0845 458 1489 Fax: 0845 458 1847 *www.byc.org.uk*

Medical Foundation for the Care of Victims of Torture aims to provide survivors of torture in the United Kingdom with medical treatment, practical assistance and psycho-therapeutic support, document evidence of torture, provide training for health professionals working with torture survivors, educate the public and decision-makers about torture and its consequences and ensure that Britain honours its international obligations towards survivors of torture, asylum seekers and refugees.

Medical Foundation, 111 Isledon Road, Islington, London N7 7JW Tel: 020 7697 7777 *www.torturecare.org.uk*

National Children's Bureau (NCB) promotes the voices, interests and well being of all children and young people across every aspect of their lives.

National Children's Bureau, 8 Wakley Street, London EC1V 7QE Tel: 020 7843 6000 *www.ncb.orq.uk*

The Children's Society is a national charity, which runs projects all over the UK, aimed at driving public debate on issues concerning children. Their Social Policy Unit seeks to influence legislation and government policy, and currently tackles issues such as human rights submission, child poverty, health, youth justice, and refugees. The Children's Society is a member of the Refugee Children's Consortium.

The Children's Society, Edward Rudolf House, Margery Street, London WC1X 0JL Tel: 020 7841 4400 *www.the-childrens-society.orq.uk*

The Refugee Council offers support and advice for unaccompanied refugee children and employs around 30 advisers who travel all over the country to support unaccompanied asylum-seeking children. The Children's Panel of Advisers represents many different countries and languages. They also provide a drop-in advice service for unaccompanied children. Opening hours every day 9.00 a.m. to 6.00 p.m. The Refugee Council publishes a leaflet aimed at unaccompanied children which has been translated into community languages. Go to the publications website to download the leaflet.

The Refugee Council Panel of Advisers for Unaccompanied Refugee Children, 240–250 Ferndale Road, London SW9 8BB. Tel: 020 7346 1134 (open from 9.30 till 5.30).

UNHCR (United Nations High Commission for Refugees) is mandated to lead and co-ordinate international action to protect refugees and resolve refugee problems worldwide. Its primary purpose is to safeguard the rights and well being of refugees. It strives to ensure that everyone can exercise the right to seek asylum and find safe refuge in another State, with the option to return home voluntarily, integrate locally or to resettle in a third country. In more than five decades, the agency has helped an estimated 50 million people restart their lives. Today, a staff of more than 6,000 people in more than 116 countries continues to help some 17 million persons. UK office is based in Millbank, London.

United Nations High Commissioner for Refugees The Office of the Representative for the United Kingdom, 21st Floor, Millbank Tower, Millbank, London SW1P 4QP Tel: 020 7828 9191 *www.unhcr.org.uk*

Chapter 13

Areas of Difficulty
When placements break down

Wendy Gill

Introduction

Disruption (Donely, 1978) is the term used to describe a breakdown of an adoption or foster placement. When a child's move to a permanent family does not work out those involved are commonly left with a mixture of emotions – anger, sadness, guilt, despair and a puzzlement as to whether anything could have been done differently to bring about a different outcome. It is common practice for a 'disruption meeting' to be called shortly after the child has moved out for all involved in making the placement to consider the factors which led to breakdown. The primary purpose of holding a disruption meeting is to ensure that the child's future plans are informed by the best knowledge of their needs. Families who have worked to establish a parental bond with the child have valuable information to contribute.

The second purpose is for the agencies making the placement to reflect on their own practice and to adapt policies and procedures in the light of information gained. The objective is to minimise the risk of disruptions and make better placements.

Now follows a summary of practice points that have come out of one authority's disruption meetings that have a general application. They are divided into the different stages of placement.

Planning stage pre-placement

New carers and parents benefited from gaining the perception of several people who knew the child to obtain a range of impressions. In some cases the knowledge and skill of experienced short-term foster carers masked the child's true level of difficulties. The current carer described the child as they seemed to her, but this may be relative to other children she has cared for and the perspective of new carers, without extensive experience of children, may be very different.

Similarly, there was an assumption that the older the child, the greater the emotional damage. However, this does not necessarily equate. Practice shows that it is more important to consider the degree of trauma rather than the age of the child. Even very young children can have attachment difficulties due to early experiences. It is crucial that an in-depth assessment of the child's attachment capacity is carried out and this should routinely consider the child's patterns of attachment behaviour to assist in realistic recommendations regarding matching (Howe, 1999).

There is a clear link between the quality of preparation and placement outcome. As Smith (1994) comments, 'preparatory work for children involves exploring not just the facts but the feelings, answering not only what but why'. In a style fitting for the child they need to be helped to understand why they are no longer able to live with birth family members. Also, when a child faces a move of placement, a piece of work specifically about the move is required. It is of central importance that children are listened to; both to understand what they want from a new family and the fears they hold.

Does the child want to join a new family? Has the birth family given 'permission' for them to join a new family? Children need assistance to grieve for and come to terms with the loss of their birth family, in the sense that continuing to live with them as a family is not feasible, though some form of contact may be possible. Placement outcomes are poor when a child is not ready or willing to join a new family or feels an overwhelming conflict of loyalties.

To help new parents arrive at a greater understanding of the impact of life events upon a child, some family placement agencies organise Child Appreciation Days. At these people who know the child well, piece together the child's life events to see how they have shaped the child today and the impact they may have in the longer term.

Recent court cases have highlighted the duty on the local authority to share with prospective adopters and foster carers all information held on a child [A and B v Essex County Council (2002) and W v Essex County Council (1997)].

During care proceedings consideration should be given to seeking leave of the court to share reports in their entirety with prospective adopters. As part of this process it may be necessary to explain legal and technical terms.

When considering the profile of a new family for a child, it is important to look at what has worked well for them in the pattern of previous family structures. Therefore, a child who in the past has been securely cared for by a grandparent may do well if this is replicated by placing them with an older, single carer. The past is the greatest predictor of the future.

At the stage of describing a child to prospective new carers, the use of visual aids can act as another medium by which the prospective new family can learn about the child. It is important that potential carers are exposed to as many differing impressions of the child as possible. Some carers did not believe they had enough 'real' information about their child (Lowe and Murch, 1999). They commented that the reality of living with a particular child was different from that which they had anticipated. Also, assessing workers need to tease out with carers their idealised hopes and dreams of what the future might hold to ensure that this accords with reality.

Research shows that the children of foster carers spend more hours per day with the placed child than the foster carers themselves. It is therefore, centrally important to actively involve the carers own children in all stages of preparation and to hear their views and ensure that they are not silenced by their parents (Watson and Jones, 2002).

Where a child was placed without a school place secured the placement began with a built in disadvantage. School-aged children were misled to believe they may not need to go to school from this placement. Also, it singled them out as different from other children in the placement and placed pressure on the family to occupy and supervise the child seven days a week.

Introductions

Being introduced to new parents is a social event outside the experience of most children. This is an event of such significance it heightens the child's anxieties and excitement levels and can, therefore, lead to children behaving in uncharacteristic ways. Children need good preparation to talk through how they might feel and behave during introductions in order not to be overwhelmed. If the people who know the child best feel that they are behaving in an uncharacteristic fashion, thought should be given to extending introductions until every aspect of the child's behaviour is seen.

Midway through the introductions all involved in the plans should meet face to face to review the early meetings between the child and their new family. This meeting needs to consider whether or not to proceed. No assumption should be made that a placement will take place until both the child and new family have expressed their readiness for this (Fahlberg, 1994).

It is advised that placements are not made on a Friday because of the difficulty of accessing social workers and other personnel over the weekend. Beginning a placement early in the week is seen as preferable.

The placement

Whilst new families should be advised to avoid being inundated with well wishers in the early days of placement, this should not exclude those who provide the family with the support they need during a major family change. In the early stages of a placement the main aim is to establish an attachment between the child and their new parents. In some situations this may need to have precedence over education and might mean that the child has a part-time integration to school in order to have some 'quality time' with the new parents.

A precursor to disruption is commonly a reluctance or refusal to take the child on holiday. It would appear that holidays, where the props of ordinary life are removed and families spend more time together, are a barometer of family relationships. Workers need to be alert to the fragility of placements when holidays are not welcomed as an opportunity to share time together.

Just as depression can be a reaction for any new parent, those who foster and adopt should be forewarned to expect a reaction to parenthood, which might not be entirely positive.

When placing older children with histories of abuse and neglect, agencies are required to provide support packages which are detailed from the outset. The adopters or carers who live with the child know best the problems the child is presenting and the help they need if they are to cope. The benefits of short breaks (respite) were stressed in many cases. If the child can be consulted about the break and it can be designed to encourage the child in a new activity or to extend their social horizons, it need not seem like a rejection. It provides the family with a chance to recharge their batteries and it is recognised that placements are sustained when breaks are offered.

In some agencies, at the point when it is realised that the placement is in trouble, a placement support meeting takes place where all those who know the child and had a part to play in making the placement meet to consider where to go from here. This is a bit like a disruption meeting before the disruption has happened. Usually the meeting is chaired by an independent person and all are encouraged to think creatively and brainstorm ways forward to avoid the placement breaking down or, if it must, planning for this eventuality in a positive fashion.

When a foster carer changes in status for a specific child from short-term to long-term the same assessment, preparation and training should be offered as would be if the child were going to 'stranger' carers. Where carers have drifted into a different status in relation to a child without this being formally and thoroughly considered the risk of breakdown is greater.

Foster carers and adopters need to be strongly warned against threatening to end a child's placement. Children who have been looked after are often acutely sensitive to rejection from parental figures, and tend to 'get in first' by acting in a way to bring about the end of the placement. It becomes a self-fulfilling prophecy.

Ending a placement/post-placement

Endings of placements should be considered with as much care as introductions. A child's experience of rejection is heightened in situations where foster carers or adopters unilaterally decide that a placement is over and tell the child without consulting workers about who, how and when a child is told that the placement has come to an end. A team approach is vital to build in the necessary supports.

In some cases placements were allowed to get so negative that relationships became destructive and rejecting. It is important to face the fact that a placement is over if that is clearly how people are behaving even if not saying. Sometimes carers cannot bring themselves to explicitly say it is finished and the workers have to force the issue. When the negative qualities of a placement outweigh the positives the decision to terminate seems irreversible.

The child should be offered a true explanation of why they can no longer live with this family but with every effort to protect their self-esteem. This should be agreed by all involved and the child given every opportunity to express their reactions to the event. Disruptions endanger a grief reaction with all the usual associated emotions. Therapeutic work may be necessary to assist the child to reach an understanding about what took place.

After a disruption the family may require ongoing counselling and support to cope with their disappointment and loss. Attending a disruption meeting can help with this process. Some disruptions are a reality in family placement work (Fitzgerald, 1990).

The risk of disruption has to be accepted because for the majority of children their lives are transformed by the chance to belong to a new family. The duty is upon us to reduce these risks as far as possible to give the greatest number of children a successful outcome (see chapter on Mental Health and also Risk Management/Harm Minimisation).

Risk management/harm minimisation

Deborah Bone

Research with both young people in care and care leavers has highlighted their vulnerability to problematic and persistent risk-taking including substance misuse (DoH, 1997) and risky sexual behaviour (West, 1995; Corlyon and McGuire, 1997).

Adolescents are going to take risks as a normal part of their growing up as they begin to define and develop their own identities. Healthy risk-taking is a valuable experience and a positive tool for discovering, developing and consolidating who they are and how they fit in with the rest of the world. Adolescence is a time when, quite literally, young people are learning to think and how to act. Experimenting with new experiences and feelings can increase confidence and help them appreciate and understand the consequences of their behaviours. Most psychologists would agree that if there was no risk there would be no growth.

Problematic risk-taking, including heavy drinking, smoking, drug use, reckless driving, unsafe sexual activity, disordered eating, self-mutilation, gang activity, and criminal behaviours and others can prove dangerous to both the young person's physical and mental health. Young people can find it hard to imagine their lives in the future and the long-term effects of the risks they take are often of little concern. Problematic risk-taking can be motivated by poor self-esteem and lack of confidence, a common trait among many of our looked after children and care leavers. Impulsive and reckless behaviours may be seen as a way of gaining the approval of their peers. The main problem with many young people is the inability to evaluate the potential risks and the consequences of everyday behaviours. Feelings of invincibility and the desires for thrill seeking drive young people to take risks with little or no thought of the effects on their health. Any perceived risks can be quickly quashed by the partaking in risk-taking activities and not suffering the expected consequences. Young people are likely to deduce that the behaviour is not risky at all and that adult evaluations cannot be trusted. Adults are simply trying to stop them from having fun! This is often the case with drug and alcohol use. For these teenagers the risk is in social rejection or being made fun of for not doing what their friends are doing. Sometimes one poor risk choice can lead to another for example being intoxicated with drink or drugs may result in risky sexual behaviours or being involved in criminal activities.

As adolescents need to take risks as part of their normal development it is important that as carers we help our young people to manage the risks they take. We need to provide them with knowledge to make informed choices and the arena to experiment safely. We need to ensure we have the time to listen if we are going to understand why our young people make both healthy and unhealthy choices.

Identifying dangerous adolescent risk-taking is very important if we are to reduce the risk of developing mental health problems in the future. The signs can include psychological problems such as persistent depression or anxiety which goes beyond more typical adolescent 'moodiness'; problems at school; engaging in illegal activities; and clusters of unhealthy risk-taking behaviours (e.g., smoking, drinking and driving recklessly might be happening at the same time, as might disordered eating and self-mutilation, or running away and stealing).

Young people often offer us subtle clues about their negative risk-taking behaviours within their conversation; this may be by talking or almost bragging about their behaviours in order to read into our reactions. It is important to find ways to share our experiences and communicate with adolescents in order to serve as role models and to let them know that mistakes are not fatal but need to be learnt from. This will encourage a more managed form of risk-taking.

Adolescents look to their parents or carers for advice and modelling about how to assess positive and negative risks. We need to help our young people to learn how to evaluate risks and anticipate the consequences of their choices, as well as developing strategies for diverting their energy into healthier activities when necessary.

Healthy risk-taking behaviours which tend to have a positive impact on an adolescent's development can include participation in sports, the development of artistic and creative abilities, volunteer activities, travel, making new friends, constructive contributions to the community, and others. This may require a good deal of planning on our behalf if we are to make these available and encourage our young people to participate. Remember by trying out new activities with the young people we are acting as good role models and teaching how we can take evaluated risks. A good example of this can be seen on many of the outward bound style of courses where we may try a risk-taking activity such as rock climbing. Here the young people can learn what measures can be taken to minimise the risk to themselves but can still participate in something that could be seen as quite dangerous.

It is important to remember that learning how to assess risks is a process that we work on throughout our lives. Children and adolescents need support, tools, and practice in order to do this.

Helping a child or teenager understand or define their own risk-taking pattern is important. Our looked after children and care leavers are involved in numerous assessments and formal paper work generating procedures, and asking social workers or the young people themselves to do any more may seem quite daunting. However, I do feel that the process of using some sorts of formal risk management tools can be beneficial to both.

A well-designed risk assessment tool can be quick to use and will establish a level of risk both to and from the young person. It can be very useful to the young people and those working with them alike. Ideally a risk assessment should be carried out prior to the taking on of the management of care for that young person or at the first meeting. Risk management is a continuous process of evaluating immediate and future risk. It provides the opportunity to make informed decisions leading on to the planning and implementation of appropriate strategies designed to reduce these risks.

A risk assessment tool should quickly highlight the level of each risk so that all involved can be aware of the current situation and the plans to minimise the risks shared among colleagues. This should be an open procedure with the young person being aware of the decisions you may need to make on their behalf. It is not necessary for the young person to agree with your evaluation of risk but it should be clearly explained to them why you have come to that particular decision. This process will show them how they may think about managing their own risks in the future.

The risk management plan should include the date, time, nature of risk and the actions being carried out to minimise and manage these risks. It should also include any further actions required and highlight any unmet needs. The time by which any action should be carried out should be recorded along with the named person responsible for ensuring it happens. The risk assessments can be updated as the circumstances change.

In conclusion, risk-taking is a natural process for all young people as they start to head towards adolescence. In order for our looked after children and care leavers to make healthier risk-taking choices we need to provide them with the tools to develop ways in which they can assess risk and the opportunities to participate in healthier risk-taking activities (see chapter on Mental Health, and Appendix 3 on Fraser Competence in Sexual Health Chapter).

Appendix 1

Case study (please note all names and any identifying information has been removed)

A risk assessment was carried out for Carla, a care leaver aged 19. Carla's project worker felt particularly concerned for her as it had been decided by the courts that Carla's baby should be put up for adoption. Much work had been done to prepare Carla for this but Carla was finding it increasingly difficult to imagine life without her daughter. Carla has a history of self-harm and recently stated that she would end her own life after her last visitation with her daughter. Carla has a very supportive GP who manages her methadone programme. A risk assessment and management plan was completed as below. There are two risk assessment tools and plans, one for enhanced risk and one for standard risk. It was decided that Carla should be put on **Enhanced/High Risk**.

The risk assessment and plan is designed to be filled in as often as required and should not take too long to complete. More comprehensive details should be written in the young person's notes.

NCH Leaving Care Service
Risk Assessment Tool

Name of Young Person   Carla Smith

Critical Indicators (This list is not exhaustive but can be used as a guide)	**History of Risk** Outline of incidents/history (Cross-reference to file with dates)

Enhanced/High Risk **Concerns**   Please tick all that apply

Suicide attempt made in the last month		
Statement of planned suicide intent in last month	✓	Carla has talked about taking her own life. She has made a suicide plan – please see entry dated 1/05/04 in her notes for details.
Significant use of aggression in last month		
Incident of substance misuse resulting in emergency treatment in the last month	✓	Carla has a serious drug habit and is on a methadone programme – see details under medical section in her notes.
Sudden changes to circumstances which may lead to risk taking behaviour	✓	Carla's baby is being put up for adoption her last visit with her daughter is planned for 19/06/04.
Refusal to engage with services		
Pregnancy (with concerns for the unborn child)		
Unpredictable behaviour patterns		
Acute physical/mental health issues		
Other risk taking activities which are causing concern e.g. arson, exploitation, criminal damage, acute young parent (with particular concerns for the child/children) Please state:	✓	Carla has been known to have violent outbursts – please see last incident recorded in notes on 2/02/04.
Risk to: self ✓☐ others ✓☐ vulnerability ✓☐		

Refer to policy guidelines for Enhanced/High Risk

Date completed:

Signature of Person/s completing form

Signature of Manager/Deputy Manager

NCH Leaving Care Service
Risk Management Plan
Enhanced/High

Name of young person   Carla Smith

Date 1/05/04

Nature of Risk: Suicide

Possible Aggression

Risk to: self ☐✓   others ☐✓   vulnerability ☐✓

Actions taken to minimise/manage risk

- Managers and all members of the team and duty social workers informed.
- Information and risks discussed with GP – GP will see Carla daily to dispense methadone until risk reduced and advise us if further precautions are necessary.
- Carla to be accompanied by two staff members on last visit with daughter.
- Carla to stay with aunt for two weeks following last visit. Aunt aware of risk details in notes.
- Specialist nurse to visit Carla day after last visit with daughter and further regular visits arranged until risks are reduced.
- Leaving care team to make daily contact with Carla.
- Adoption team to support Carla and meeting arranged to discuss letterbox contact etc.

Please see notes for more detailed information or contact
Shirley Grove Case Co-ordinator on 01532 567439

Further Action Required: Risk to be assessed daily until reduced

Those informed of risk concerns

Duty ☐✓   Deputy Manager/Manager ☐✓   Admin ☐✓

Others *please state* GP, Specialist Nurse, Aunt, Child's Social Worker, colleagues in leaving care team, Local police liaison officer

Date of review: Daily

Signature of Person/s completing form

Signature of Manager/Deputy Manager

Health for young people leaving care and after care

Jane Scott

Whilst the health of children in the care system is of vital importance, we should always promote a growing independence in our young people in order that they develop the ability to understand their own health needs and how these needs can be met.

Children (Leaving Care) Act 2000

The main purpose of the act is to improve the life chances of young people living in and leaving local authority care. Its main aims are:

- To delay young people's discharge from care until they are prepared and ready to leave.

- To improve the assessment, preparation and planning for leaving care.

- To provide better personal support for young people after leaving care.

- To improve the financial arrangements for care leavers.

One of the key local authority aims and objectives is 'To prepare young people gradually to be ready to leave care, paying attention to practical self care needs – health, budgeting, domestic skills and personal and relationship dimensions'.

It is noted in the Act that '. . . the quality of preparation for leaving care and of the after care subsequently provided, may profoundly affect the rest of a young persons life' (see chapter on Mental Health).

It is therefore of vital importance that we in health participate in effective multi-agency partnership working and can offer a consistent high quality health service to the young people in our leaving care and after care services.

The Children (Leaving Care) Act recognises the need for interagency liaison and Section 27 gives SSD the right to request help in its discharge of these functions from any other local authority, any local education authority, any local housing authority, any health authority, special health authority, primary care trust or NHS trust. Any such request is bound to be complied with '. . . if it is compatible with (the other agencies) own statutory or other duties and delegations and does not unduly prejudice the discharge of any of their functions'. With this reservation, therefore, any such requests must be complied with as far as possible.

Each local authority (SSD) has a duty to provide help to young people it is looking after and to whom it will provide subsequent advice and assistance until a young person reaches at least the age of 21 years. (Help given to meet expenses concerned with education or training may continue until the young persons 24th birthday.)

The Act states clearly **the role of the health authority** and best practice should ensure that each trust meets the requirements stated, therefore ensuring the health needs are met for this vulnerable group of young people.

Pathway Plans (DoH, 2002)

All young people who are eligible (defined by Children (Leaving Care) Act) must have a pathway plan. Within three months of their 16th birthday the needs assessment required for the pathway plan should be completed. Health providers are amongst that group of others who will be involved in this needs assessment.

The pathway plan is intended to support seamless planning for young people up until their 18th birthday. It builds on previous plans and assessments and for this reason it includes sections on identity and emotional and behavioural development.

The pathway planning document is in two parts:

1. Records a summary of the assessment of the young person's needs and abilities.
2. Sets out the pathway plan for the young person based on this assessment.

Health providers for the young person should be consulted on part one of the pathway plan and should contribute if the plan is to have meaning for the young person.

Attached Version 1 Pathway Plan (2003)

Ideally, I feel this part of the Pathway document should be completed by a health professional with the young person.

Areas for practice development

In many parts of the country, young people's service teams are now established and this should be a multi-agency team that provides services to vulnerable groups of young people.

For young people who are looked after the pathway planning document may provide the team with some aims and objectives for services which could be developed and provided for young people e.g. in some parts of the country there are life skills courses offered to young people looked after which cover areas such as:

- **Health**
  - Sexual health services, screening etc. (see chapter on Sexual Health)
  - Importance of registration with GP
  - Dentist (using services effectively)
  - Health screening
  - Managing personal hygiene
- **Social skills**
  - Find and use of community services
  - Use of public transport
  - Access rights e.g. CAB, YPA Service, VOICE
  - Local councillors
- **Practical skills**
  - Manage and balance a budget
  - Shop for basic necessities
  - Maintain healthy diet (see chapter on Nutrition)
  - Prepare and cook a variety of meals
  - Wash clothes – undertake basic repairs

- Undertake basic household cleaning
- Awareness of basic home safety

All of these areas are covered in a young person's pathway plan. If you are an agency who wishes to commence 'life skills programme' you can adapt your course content and develop your own local needs by using the plan as a basic template.

Some areas have carried out 'focus group work' with young people ascertaining their views on how services should be developed and delivered. This is an ideal way to include and consult with young people as they have just had knowledge and experience of what a young person needs to successfully make that transition from foster care or residential care and into independence.

Following a local consultation exercise, a group of young people and carers came up with the following suggestion:

A young person be given a fixed sum of money whilst living with carers to practice budgeting for food. This would include looking at menus for the week, and balancing their diet. This could involve planning, shopping, preparation and cooking skills. Some carers are currently trying this out with young people who are 15 plus. The budget they set was £15 per week and young people were only allowed to use basic provision from carers cupboards e.g. butter, condiments, basic toiletries etc.

Young people living at home may also benefit from this exercise prior to leaving for employment, university etc. I have also been informed by some young people of a scheme supported by carers where a young person is encouraged to cook a family meal once or twice per week. This also builds skills and confidence in family eating, preparation and planning, understanding choices e.g. if a family member is vegetarian. Young people could also invite some friends to their carers' home for supper, video, chill time! The young person is then encouraged to develop social skills, assertiveness skills e.g. encouraging others to abide by house rules re noise levels, acceptable social behaviours etc. This can then be built in a safe environment with carers support and then perhaps a gradual withdrawal.

Whilst carrying out my own life skills courses the young people have said that the following issues are of greater concern for them:

- Loneliness – especially at weekends.
- Time management.
- Health – choosing appropriate GP, registration etc.
- Managing inappropriate friendships e.g. friends outstaying welcome, disorderly behaviour.
- Budgeting.

These are some of the issues our own young people have raised and we are trying as a team to address needs in innovative ways. Suggestions, so far, we are trying to develop include:

- Breakfast clubs.
- Sunday lunch provision.
- Girlie nights! – hair, nail sessions.

- Arts based activity – using a variety of arts based initiatives e.g. creative writing, painting, dance clubs, visits to theatre (not pantomime!).
- Mentoring schemes – using local university students.
- Independent visitors and advocacy, e.g. VOICE, NYAS etc.

The main message we have taken from our young people is not to start promoting independence too late! Start much earlier it will then not feel as if your carer is preparing to put you out!

Young people should be encouraged to help out – cooking, doing household chores etc. as part of daily living or as a normal part of living with a family. Our young people should be encouraged from an early age to express their ideas, views and opinions and feel they are listened to.

Listening to children and encouraging participation is vital. There are three key reasons to promote participation:

- It is a basic right to act as an agent over your environment and things that affect you.
- It is a fundamental part of healthy growth and development.
- It is an important way of improving services.

References

Corlyon, J. and McGuire, C. (1997) *Young Parents in Public Care: Pregnancy and Parenthood Among Young People Looked After by Local Authorities*. London: NCB.

DoH (1997) *Substance Misuse and Young People: The Social Services Response. A Social Services Inspectorate Study of Young Looked After by Local Authorities*. London: DoH.

DoH (2000) *The Children (Leaving Care) Act 2000*. London: HMSO.

DoH (2002) *Pathway Plans*. London: DoH.

Donely, K. (1978) The Dynamics of Disruption. *Adoption and Fostering*, 2: 2.

Fahlberg, V. (1994) *A Child's Journey through Placement*. London: BAFF.

Fitzgerald, J. (1990) (2nd Edition) *Understanding Disruption*. London: BAFF.

Howe, D. (1999) *Attachment Theory, Child Maltreatment and Family Support*. London: Palgrave Macmillan.

Lowe, N. and Murch, M. (1999) Disruptions, in *Supporting Adoption, Reframing the Approach*. London: BAAF.

Smith, S. (1994) *Learning from Disruption*. London: BAAF.

Watson, A. and Jones, D. (2002) The Impact of Fostering on Foster Carers' Own Children. *Adoption and Fostering*, 26. London: BAFF.

West, A. (1995) *You're on Your Own: Young People's Research on Leaving Care*. London: Save the Children.

Conclusion

Kathy Dunnett

Editing this book has been a challenge and an experience. The difficulties encountered when encouraging writers to come forward have been reflected in this books omissions. It is still apparent that health professionals working with looked after children are still in a minority. Whilst the education for looked after children has been highlighted and given priority within the local authority, the health of looked after children lags behind. Much of the issue is probably due to lack of robust partnerships between health and social care, or indeed all of the children's services. At last then, it appears that we all have a common aim to tie our work together, that of *Every Child Matters* (DfES, 2003) and the *National Service Framework for Children* (DoH, 2004b). All children are entitled to have their needs met, under the headings of; Safety, Health, Economic Wellbeing, Enjoying/Achieving and Positive Contribution (SHEEP) – see illustration.

In 1997, I was, as far as I am aware, the first nurse to be appointed working exclusively with looked after children on a full time basis. Coming from a school nurse background was a helpful experience, working with some difficult adolescents, but all the time trying to reflect on my experience as a professional, a nurse and a mother of three sons – was I making a difference? Many of the young people I wanted to help did not have the ability to help themselves, and sometimes no-one else to help them either, as they moved from carer to carer. I asked my son at the time (aged 14, who was a typical teenager) 'Why do you do what I want you to do?' Without any hesitation he replied, 'Because if I don't, it'll upset you . . .' and this, ultimately is the key. Many of these young people do not have that

Staying safe   **Economic wellbeing**   **Making a positive contribution**

Being healthy

Enjoying and achieving

SHEEP

key relationship that will be their guiding light. Many young people will not do something for themselves, but they may do something for someone else they want to please. Many of these young people have no-one and nothing in their lives which is meaningful enough to them to want to address the issues of education and health. They live in a constant state of bereavement due to the many losses and changes in their lives. When one considers what some of these children and young people have had to endure, I am more surprised at the ones that come through unscathed, rather than those that have problems. Some of these children and young people are so damaged by their experiences, we can not hope to make them 'better', only, hopefully to help and support them not to get 'worse', but to give them enough skills and aspirations to enable them to function in society. This is a bitter pill to swallow for many health professionals, and other helping agencies, these feelings can make us feel disempowered and floundering. This can turn to defensiveness as we struggle to find that 'big stick' or 'magic wand', and sometimes we can set young people up to fail . . .

> *. . . I know that I did a lot of bad stuff and that . . . but that was four years ago . . . I want to change, but they won't let me . . . every f***ing review they bring it up! . . . They keep reminding me I'm such a bad person! . . . I was only eleven at the time . . . why can't they drop it . . .!*

(Fifteen year old girl, prosecuted for burglary and assault at eleven, nothing since)

The chapters in the book reflect the issues in setting up health systems for looked after children. Barbara Mary eloquently describes the problems in the very early days, when the difficulties of health for looked after children was highlighted in the document, *Modernising Social Services* (DoH, 1997) and the programme *Quality Protects* gave, for the first time, local authorities targets around immunisations, registration with GPs and dentists etc. She also mentioned the need around a shared database, something that has been recognised by recent government legislation, in order that children's needs are not overlooked (HMSO, 2004). Both Callowhill and Mary highlight the problems of working in isolation, with little support, which has been acknowledged by previous writers:

> *I have to prove my worth to social services . . .*

(Hill et al., 2002)

Support to practitioners in the form of appropriate and robust supervision and governance is essential for the majority of work with looked after children (Hall and Elliman, 2003) because of the greater health needs and lack of continuity with health care.

Hughes, in the chapter on primary care trusts cites the important of the collation of information on looked after children. The importance of multi-agency working is further highlighted in the chapters on MALAPS and Healthy Care.

> *A child or young person living in a healthy care environment is entitled to:*
> 1. *Feel safe, protected and valued in a strong, sustained and committed relationship with at least one carer.*
> 2. *Live in a caring, healthy and learning environment.*
> 3. *Feel respected and supported in their cultural beliefs and personal identity.*
> 4. *Have access to effective healthcare, assessment, treatment and support.*
> 5. *Have opportunities to develop personal and social skills, talents and abilities and to spend time in freely chosen play, cultural and leisure activities.*

6. *Be prepared for leaving care by being supported to care and provide for themselves in the future.*

(see chapter on Healthy Care)

What are the essential building blocks that are needed to provide this for each and every one of our looked after children? All children that are in a care environment rather than their own home should have the opportunities as listed above – in foster care, in children's homes, in detention centres, in prisons, in therapeutic units, mental health establishments, etc. – **Every Child Matters!**

Carers need to understand the difficulties of working with needy and troubled children. They need robust training, they need round the clock support from a range of professionals, they need systems and strategies that will enable them to provide that essential sustained relationship that every child needs.

The section on 'Creative Participation' in the chapter on Healthy Care, highlights the importance of giving children and young people an opportunity to develop independence and competence when considering health issues.

John Brown's chapter acknowledges the need to recognise that looked after children do have different needs, particularly around health care. This is due to the 'fragmented' corporate parent and the transient nature of many of the professionals. This is an important admission. It is not easy to acknowledge 'difference', but in order to achieve a 'normal' standard of health care, for many children (particularly those in 'out of area' placements) an 'extra' effort has to be made.

The chapter on primary care trusts further highlights this issue. That often the most vulnerable of children end up with the worst care of all. But primary care trusts are responsible for the overall arrangements for looked after children's health care.

> *The great paradox is that these who need it most often find it hardest of all to gain access to appropriate health services.*

Hughes also highlights the importance of the *National Service Frameworks* as well as *Every Child Matters*, and also the White Paper *Choosing Health: Making Healthy Choices Easier* (DoH, 2004a).

Sharon White's chapter on the mental and emotional health needs of looked after children highlights how vitally important this issue is for all of our children and young people, not just those looked after. The section from Wendy Gill, in Chapter 13, on placements underlines the essentiality of addressing problems in relationships before they become 'destructive and rejecting'. Hopefully, with the move towards extended services around schools, the 'core offer' will address the need for a 'swift and easy referral' (DfES, 2005) to a range of supportive services to prevent care placements breaking down, or even better, to prevent care in the first instance.

The chapters on sexual health and substance misuse discuss some of the more difficult issues that carers and professionals may face when working with children and young people. Hopefully, these chapters will give pointers as to how to deal with these situations, how to talk to children and young people on these difficult topics, how to educate them, and how to use a situation that has gone wrong as a learning experience. These chapters have obvious links with the section on 'Risk and Harm Minimisation' by Deborah Bone. As

Bone says, it is essential to ascertain what risky behaviors are part of normal 'growing-up' and what behaviors are signs of something that is more worrying:

> *Identifying dangerous adolescent risk-taking is very important if we are to reduce the risk of developing mental health problems in the future.*

The chapter on the health needs of asylum seekers recognises that in recent years an increasing number of young people from all areas of the world have arrived alone in the UK and many have entered into our care system. These young people have extra needs in many ways. They have often been traumatised because of their experiences in their home country, they may have language difficulties, and their physical health may be poor due to lack of nutrition and infections. Children from other countries and cultures may be at risk from diseases not common in the UK. When these children first started to enter the care system, pediatricians were often placed in the difficult situation of having to define a young persons' age without any clear guidance, in order to ascertain whether or not they were under 18, an unaccompanied minor, and entitled to enter care and become looked after. However, because of possible poor eating and illnesses, precise age determination can be very difficult to obtain. Medical advisors and health professionals were being asked about difficult situations of which they had no training and little knowledge, such as torture and ritual abuse.

> *Children seeking asylum should have the same access to health care as national children.*
>
> (UNHCR, 1997)

But often the services that these children needed were not in existence in this country. Britain had not had to deal with these problems before in such large numbers, and not with children.

The chapter on nutrition also touches on an essential issue for all our children and young people currently, particularly with childhood obesity on the increase (NCSR, 2005). Looked after children may well have issues around food, food often being used in the western world to give reward or show rejection. As Cooper states:

> *Living in dysfunctional, uncaring or emotionally unstable families may have affected a young person's view of food. Mealtimes may be associated with chaos, neglect, frustration and anger.*

Cooper does not tackle the issues of 'a balanced diet', which can be gleaned from any good book on health, but more the specific issues as mentioned above when considering looked after children. In addition, she mentions leaving care, cooking and nutrition, as does Scott in her section on 'Leaving Care and After Care'. Scott notes that in focus group work it was the young people that identified the issue of budgeting for food, cooking and healthy eating.

I am most indebted however, to the contributions by the foster carer (AC) and the two careleavers – Ishy and Donna. The foster carer points out the difficulties with lack of information on the young people that she cared for. This is also highlighted in the conclusion in the more recent issue of *The RHP Companion to Foster Care* (Wheal, 1999). AC also mentions how difficult the situation can become if the child doesn't have a social worker:

The worst thing was that she had no allocated social worker, and so nothing was coordinated . . .

Field social workers also, are often placed in difficult situations when health professionals, through lack of understanding, can appear obstructive and unhelpful. Social workers struggle to establish a reliable immunisation record for children in their care, health workers securing the child data bases hide behind the Data Protection Act and refuse to release the information. So how can social workers ensure that the child's immunisations are up to date if a health history is refused? Some individual social workers have gone to extraordinary lengths to try and support health care, but without the necessary written protocols, partnership working relies on individuals, which fails when these individuals leave or become sick. Perhaps it is through Children's Trust arrangements (HMSO, 2004) that we will finally 'trust' each other enough to support this difficult area of working.

No-one can fail to warm to AC's article, as she describes how she has worked and supported with some of the most difficult young people that anyone is likely to come across. Having personally known AC for many years, my admiration for her skill and patience knows no bounds. I am in awe of people that can dedicate every part of their lives to caring and coping on a 24/7 rota with trauma for many years. As Wheal says:

Foster care is now a truly professional service that should be run by professionals and those involved rewarded fairly . . .

(Wheal, 1999)

I would also like to add a vote of thanks to the residential care workers in children's homes. These people work with some of the most vulnerable children in society. They deal with difficult situations relating to young people on a regular basis, and do some marvellous work. I remember working with a young girl with some personal health issues, and she spoke fondly of the manager of the children's home where she lived. She had absconded from the home, and had been missing for two days:

He didn't tell me off when he saw me, he just hugged me and told me he was glad I was safe. He took me back to the home and gave me some hot chocolate. I never knew my dad, but I reckon he was the closest thing I was ever going to get as a father . . .

(Fifteen year old girl, in and out of care since the age of six, mother had mental illness)

These people also need to have their service recognized, and yet many of the staff recruited have no relevant qualifications. Whilst it is one of the National Minimum Standards for Children's Homes that 80 per cent of care staff have NVQ3 or equivalent and is therefore a standard that homes are expected to reach, it cannot be legally enforced. When homes are short of staff, sickness rates are high, stress levels are high, training is piecemeal, poorly attended and not a priority. Even NVQ 3 I would question is probably not enough. I would like to see multi-disciplinary teams of social workers, health staff and educationalists working side by side in partnership to provide a highly supportive, therapeutic and safe environment for children's homes everywhere. I believe that without the multi-disciplinary approach, the service lacks the expertise and experience that is needed in the holistic care with such vulnerable and often disturbed children. Ishy, in her contribution, recognises the importance of training for residential care staff, particularly on issues of sexual health.

These thoughts correspond with the chapter on training and policies and the two go hand in hand to support staff with their care of children and young people.

It still saddens me, when I hear from looked after children's nurses across the country, that children with specific health care needs are put in placements where there has been no prior training and guidance. I was particularly alerted to a young diabetic boy, whom had been placed happily with foster carers since the age of two, now at twelve was having the normal adolescent difficulties and began a series of short-term placements. He was also partially sighted and deaf. The nurse was rung by a very anxious foster carer on her mobile one Sunday morning. She stated that this boy had '. . . run out of insulin . . .'. and did she need to get some more? These situations should *never* occur. They are *preventable* and should be planned for. After a few telephone calls the foster carer was able to attend casualty to collect the essential insulin. Whilst many twelve year olds can be independent in their own health care, even injecting and testing for blood sugars, this independence should not translate to the carer having no knowledge of the condition at all. Particularly in issues of emergency, such as diabetic coma, the carer must be able to cope. This is a tragedy waiting to happen if situations like this continue to occur.

There is no doubt, that across the country, there is some excellent work going on, and much of this work has been highlighted and supported tirelessly by agencies such as the National Children's Bureau, British Association for Adoption and Fostering, Fostering Network, Champions for Children and Young People in Care, Who Cares? Trust, Young Minds – and there are others. Local authorities and primary care trusts need to listen to the health care professionals working with looked after children to support them with their needs, in order to provide a robust and timely health service to these children. They need to have access to all the expertise they need, from mental health, dieticians, sexual health staff and others. They need to be supported locally by school nursing, health visiting and general practitioners; also, more strategically from immunisation coordinators, directors of nursing, chief executives in the PCT and the health authority. There needs to be negotiations over boundary issues with health care, with a resulting service that is excellent and standard across the country. It should not, and must not, be a postcode lottery for the health of our looked after children.

References

DfES (2003) *Every Child Matters*. Cm 5860. Nottingham: DfES.

DfES (2005) *Extended Schools: Access to Opportunity and Services for All*. Nottingham: DfES Publications.

DoH (1997) *Modernising Social Services*. Cm 4169. London: DoH.

DoH (2002) *Children's Homes, National Minimum Standards, Children's Homes Regulations*. London. The Stationery Office.

DoH (2004a) *Choosing Health: Making Healthy Choices Easier*. London: DoH.

DoH (2004b) *National Service Framework for Children*. London: DoH.

Hall, D. and Elliman, D. (Eds.) (2003) *Health for All Children*. 4th Edn. Oxford: Oxford University Press.

Hill, C. et al. (2002) The Emerging Role of the Specialist Nurse: Promoting the Health of Looked After Children. *Adoption and Fostering*, 26: 4.

HMSO (2004) *Children Act*. London: HMSO.

National Centre for Social Research (2005) *Obesity among Children Under 11*. London: DoH.

Royal Free and University College Medical School (2005) *Obesity in Children Under 11*. Commissioned by DoH, in collaboration with the Health and Social Care Information Centre. HMSO.

UNCHR (1997) *Guidelines on Policies and Procedures in Dealing with Unaccompanied Children Seeking Asylum*. Geneva: UNCHR.

Wheal, A. (Ed.) (1999) *The RHP Companion to Foster Care*. 2nd Edn. Lyme Regis: Russell House Publishing.